DESTINY

The War Letters of Captain Jack Oughtred M.C.
1915—1918

Edited by
Alan Wilkinson

1996

Published by
Peter and Christopher Oughtred

Distributed by
The Hutton Press Ltd.,
130 Canada Drive, Cherry Burton,
Beverley, East Yorkshire, HU17 7SB

Printed and bound by
Clifford Ward & Co. (Bridlington) Ltd.,
55a West Street, Bridlington, East Yorkshire
YO15 3DZ

ISBN 1 872167 88 8

In Flanders Field...

In Flanders fields the poppies blow
Between the crosses, row on row,
That mark our place; and in the sky
The larks, still bravely singing, fly
Scarce heard amid the guns below.

We are the dead. Short days ago
We lived, felt dawn, saw sunset glow,
Loved and were loved, and now we lie
In Flanders fields.

Take up the quarrel with the foe:
To you from failing hands we throw
The torch; be yours to hold it high
If ye break faith with us who die
We shall not sleep, though poppies
Grow in Flanders fields.

John McCrae, 1915

Captain John Alwyn Oughtred, M.C., 1894-1958.

Phyllis Bentham, Jack Oughtred's sweetheart.

CONTENTS

ABOUT THE EDITOR

Alan Wilkinson

Alan Wilkinson lives in Hornsea, East Yorkshire. He has written corporate histories for William Jackson & Son of Hull, E. Timm & Son of Goole, and is working on the story of the British Petroleum site at Saltend.

His book reviews, fiction and travel writing have appeared in publications as diverse as the *Times Literary Supplement*, *Bike Culture*, *Nebraskaland* and *Raconteur*.

His academic interests lie mainly in the American West. He has studied and written about women writers of the pioneer period, and achieved a modest celebrity in the state of Nebraska after riding a borrowed bicycle across the Great Plains.

FOREWORD
by PETER OUGHTRED

It is only since I retired from my commercial activities that I have had time to delve into the family archives and look at the historical material which has accumulated over the years. It forms a considerable collection, comprising official documents, private correspondence and a number of artefacts and other items. At first I did not appreciate the significance of a rather battered suitcase crammed with letters. Upon inspection I found that they were from my father, to my mother, and were written from the Western Front, where he served with the East Yorkshire Regiment through most of the Great War.

He wrote frequently, almost every day in the latter stages. He wrote in pencil when in action or in the front line, in ink when in reserve positions. All the letters remain clearly legible and describe vividly the trials and tribulations of trench warfare, the hardships, and the many casualties.

The postal services must have been excellent: letters were received from home almost daily, and were the life-blood of officers, NCOs and men operating in appalling conditions. A factor here must have been the static nature of the conflict — something quite dissimilar to my own generation's experience in the 1939-45 war, which was all about speed of movement and out-flanking operations. In that conflict letters from home were something of a rarity.

My mother wrote back almost every day, but my father destroyed her letters, not wishing them to fall into other hands. She also sent many food parcels, most of which arrived intact. So, throughout the war, they conducted a long-range courtship almost entirely in letter form — apart from his brief periods of leave or hospitalisation. Thus, over the period 1915-1918, one can see how their respective personal attitudes changed and how my father's view of the war became harder, more cynical and fatalistic.

My mother, in the mean time, was having a hard time as a nurse in the Naval Hospital in Hull. She worked long hours, and had to walk from Swanland to Ferriby and back each day to catch the train, which was no mean journey, especially at night. Among the papers I discovered were many letters of gratitude from her former patients, often writing from on board ship, testimonies to her ability and understanding.

Some of my father's letters were so personal and sensitive that I wondered whether they should be published or not. However, there is a tradition of historical awareness in my family. Harold Oughtred, my father's elder brother who was killed on the Somme, had obtained a double first in History at Oxford and taught the subject as a schoolmaster. Both I and my son Christopher are similarly interested. And after eighty years it seems appropriate, and incumbent upon me, to record these impressions of what were after all momentous events.

My father mentions many of his brother officers by name, most of them from Hull and the East Riding. I feel that their descendants will be interested in some of the information conveyed in these letters, and proud to see their role in the war commemorated. I further think that present and future members of my own family should be aware of these events. The sacrifice of my father's generation is epitomised in the courage, dedication, strength of will and character which they displayed as they struggled to survive those dangerous and turbulent years.

Since starting to write this foreword I have visited the battlefields of Ypres and the Somme, together with my wife, son and grandson. We went to Wancourt to see the grave of Harold Oughtred. The cemetery there is relatively small when compared with something like the vastness of Passchendaele, on the Ypres Salient. Others on the Somme are even smaller, simple collections of graves sited where soldiers actually fell. Wancourt is situated, like so many of the British cemeteries, up quite a rough farm track in the middle of peaceful French countryside. In the distance you can just see the tower of the church in the village.

The War Graves Commission do a wonderful job. All the British cemeteries we visited were quite immaculate. There was not a weed to be seen, just flowers — mostly roses — and neatly cut grass. The tranquillity of these places was almost tangible, so different from the slaughter and carnage described in the letters within this book.

Peter B. Oughtred
Captain, East Yorks Regiment, 1939-45
20 September 1996

INTRODUCTION

The Letters

There have been many collections of letters, diaries too, from, that pivotal twentieth century experience, The Great War. All are fascinating, many are moving, and a number of them are justifiably regarded as works of literature, having been penned by men of letters, artists or scholars.

Jack Oughtred's letters are worth publishing for a number of reasons. Firstly, they are extensive and comprehensive: the man survived from May 1915, when he took a commission as a second lieutenant in the Territorial battalion of the East Yorkshire regiment, right through to the Armistice three and a half years later. Phyllis Bentham, the young lady to whom he wrote so faithfully and regularly —and in the end passionately — kept every letter she received. Towards the latter stages of the conflict, after the pair had become engaged, Jack wrote almost every day. Thus we have the unbroken story of his war, a story which reaches the most satisfactory conclusion imaginable with that memorable final telegram the day before Christmas Eve 1918.

Secondly, the letters are rather out of the ordinary in being love letters. At first, they were love letters falling on deaf ears; but part of the dynamic of the collected correspondence is Jack's ardent and devoted courtship. He is a very determined young man, and has a rather winning manner, So, just as much as we hope he will survive the war we find ourselves hoping he will win the hand of the M.P.'s daughter from Swanland. Whatever the case, we are aware that we are observing in close detail the very correct conduct of a middle-class Edwardian courtship.

Thirdly, there is the local interest, the East Riding connection. There has been one lengthy history of the East Yorkshire Regiment in the Great War (Wyrall), and there has been one collection of correspondence (that of Cecil Slack) as well as a recent miscellany entitled *Empsons' War*, about the family once resident at Yokefleet Hall. Jack Oughtred's letters abound with references to local families and local events. With some material added by the editor these letters both draw on and add to the Wyrall history, as well as to the accounts of the war in the regiment's own monthly *Snapper*. The letters' very length and weight, moreover, render them one of the more detailed accounts we have of trench life as well as a valuable addition to our knowledge of the regiment — and its officers. They become flesh and blood: named, sometimes characterised, always acknowledged in their passing.

Finally, and this may be a subjective judgement, the letters stand out for being the antithesis of the celebrated *literary* writings by Sassoon, Owen, Masefield and the rest: Jack Oughtred was *not* a writer, nor was the — unlike his ill-fated brother Harold — a scholar. Indeed, an early report from his schooldays singled out his command of English as being particularly poor; and his education at a prominent Hull school was abruptly terminated when he threw an inkwell at an unpopular teacher, an act which resulted in his removal to Newton Abbot. Yet it is precisely his difficulties in articulating a response — on the one hand to the horror of war, and on the other to the wonder of love — which render the letters so vital, so real and so human. Everything he was experiencing was new to him, hence its novelty to us as we share his most private thoughts eighty years on.

The War

The western front, that great scar of earthworks, trenches, gun emplacements and ravaged earth across which the massed armies of Europe's great powers faced each other through four years of bitter hostility, stretched from the Channel coast of Belgium to the Swiss Alps. It cut Europe in two. Different armies generally occupied certain sectors of the line throughout the war. Thus it was that most soldiers within a particular army spent their time at the front in a fairly self-contained world comprising villages, farms and woods which would become quite familiar to them. In January 1916, when Jack Oughtred went out, the British section of the front stretched from the Yser, just north of Ypres, to the Somme.

Jack Oughtred's war experiences kept him frequently on the move, but generally within two particular areas. In this he was not exceptional. Plotting those moves on the map one sees that he spent the greater part of his three years at the front in two sectors: around Ypres, and in several locations further south, close to the Somme. Inasmuch as the front moved a few miles this way or that with the ebb and flow of advance and retreat, so did the battalions with which he served. Land fought over early in the war would in many instances be fought over again — and again. Places like Ypres, which never fell in to German hands, remained constants in the shifting map of frontline positions. Others, particularly further south, changed hands a number of times.

Inasmuch as the war became much more open in 1918 so Jack Oughtred's own war opened up, particularly in the later stages as the East Yorks advanced eastward along the Sambre. But as he remarks in these letters, he generally had only a vague idea of what was happening in the broader threatre of war. He had little but rumour, hearsay and the less than totally reliable news media to help him. In his first spell at the front he offers the opinion that the Germans are done for. During the first year or so he cites numerous prognostications from politicians, old soldiers, prisoners of war and even soothsayers, that the war will soon be over. But generally his ignorance of the broader shape of events is evident. Furthermore, he leaves us readers very much in the dark about what is happening, strategically, in his own purlieu. As an officer charged with checking his men's correspondence for indiscreet revelations, he plays very strictly by the rules set by the Censor and observed by those who had to inspect his own. From his letters we sometimes learn as much as a year later where he was on a particular day. More often we are completely in the dark, with only a few hints and innuendos to guide us.

Historical sources

In preparing these letters for publication, however, it has been helpful to set some of Jack Oughtred's experiences in a broader context and show how he, and the East Yorks battalions in which he served, the 4th and the 1st, were affected by the tide of warfare. The Battalion Diaries, hand-written records made at the front, provide one set of landmarks along the way to piecing together his odyssey. In those we have some record at least of his location from week to week, and of the kinds of activity in which he was engaged — wiring at night, cutting new trenches, mounting sorties into No Man's Land, drilling new recruits behind the lines. But even these accounts are less than one hundred per cent reliable. Written under conditions of privation and stress, occasionally while under fire, often at the end of a long day with sleep beckoning, the diaries contain a number of identifiable errors in dates, names of personnel, and so on. Spellings, for example, sometimes vary sufficiently to confound positive identification of an individual. The entries themselves are in some instances so abbreviated as to be almost meaningless. Terse phrases such as "quiet day"; "usual activity"; "work on Green Line" tell us little, yet in another way they tell us much: the war was often dull, routine, unspectacular. On the other hand, some accounts of actions are vivid in their detail. And most of the entries give a fair idea of where the battalion is located.

The one spell of Jack Oughtred's war during which it has proven difficult to locate him with any accuracy is the period in the summer and autumn of 1916 when he was in the Trench Mortar Brigade, mobile, sometimes free-moving, not always accounted for in the records.

A second valuable source of information is the account, written up some years after the war and serialised in the pages of *The Snapper*, of the 1st Battalion's entire war, as seen by officers who served through the various campaigns. Jack Oughtred contributed one episode to the series. This offering from himself, and others from his fellow offices, give us both a personal slant and a few illuminating anecdotes as to individual conduct. These magazines have also provided photographic and pen-portraits of several officers named in the correspondence.

A note on the editing

But the temptation to offer more than the barest details regarding the conduct of the war has been resisted. These letters reflect one man's experience, and that experience alone is epic. The war was young when he set out for the front, and so was he. By the time it ended he had clearly matured. We have only to compare the tone of his early letters — which might have been penned by a young Bertram Wooster — with the stoic, weary, clipped manner which was surfacing three years later.

And while draft after draft of men and officers are sent out, trained, despatched to the front and slaughtered, while names we have become accustomed to — and feel we know — are listed as missing, wounded or dead after this or that battle, Jack Oughtred survives. He survives by sheer chance, as when his C.O., standing beside him one morning, is blown to pieces. He survives by mathematical improbability when a bullet shatters his belt buckle, or when a piece of shrapnel knocks him down from behind. He survives by being in the right place at the right time — that is, on home leave — as the Battalion is decimated at Saulcourt in April 1918. And it is surely his instinct for self-preservation that sees him through by the time he witnesses Du Moulin, Keech and Cotton go down in the street-fighting whereby successive villages are being mopped up a mere three days before the Armistice.

Who, then, are we to argue with this pragmatic man's conviction that Fate is watching over him, that his sweetheart's lucky charm is working its magic, that his dead brother Harold has gone over the top with him and guided him to safety through the hell of Passchendaele?

The letters tell an epic tale of survival against all odds, of the triumph of hope, and of the power of love — for it is surely his love of Phyllis that brings to Jack's essential cheerfulness that steely will to live. And all of this is set against a well-drawn, if fragmented, picture of the savagery, the futility and the callousness of that awful war. Jack Oughtred's fractured narrative, his occasional inability to find the right words to convey his feelings — and his evident embarrassment when he does — convey the very essence of the experience. So where historical information has been added to the text it is mainly to identify individuals, locate the action, and add that little clarification which the shadow of the censor would not allow. Otherwise it is the editor's conviction that the letters alone tell the tale, comprehensively and with tremendous impact.

The letters as originally written run to some 200,000 words. They have been cut to around half that length for the purpose of producing this volume. With the exception of one or two sent from training camp in 1915, every letter Phyllis Bentham received from Jack Oughtred appears between these covers. What has been edited out? A few sweet nothings; an awful lot of speculation on another subject dear to every soldier's heart — that is, leave; and the usual repetitions and trivia.

Jack Oughtred's punctuation and spelling were not exactly according to the text-book. Where it makes sense to do so the text has been tidied up. Occasionally — as, for example, in the more vivid accounts of action — it has been left in its original form. His farewells at the end of letters varied, and were frequently extended by affectionate last-minute asides. To avoid tedious repetition they have been largely standardised, leaving just enough variation to reflect his growing confidence — and daring — in expressing his feelings towards Phyllis.

These are, as we have said, love letters. That is their great charm. As early as 1914 Jack was friendly enough with Phyllis to write her a handful of chatty postcards from a holiday in North Wales in that final summer of peace. It is also clear that by the time he went to France he was absolutely devoted to her. He had stolen a first kiss, to the strains of the waltz "Destiny", at a dance on 5th January 1916, a few short days before he embarked for the front. And he reminded her of the fact on the first and second anniversaries of the event.

Perhaps Phyllis felt it was only fair to surrender a kiss to a young man being sent to probable death in the trenches: her sister Doris had very likely done the same with her own suitor, Jack's brother Norman. But as far as commitment went she was — unlike her sister — having none of it. Of the tiny handful of her letters which survive, a single one in February 1916 expresses her grave reservations about allowing herself to get in too deep. In part she seemed to feel that engagement and marriage would bring to an end her very enjoyable life as an independent young woman who was free to drive a car about town, smoke cigarettes and go dancing with officers home on leave — that is, as far as her lengthy hours as a VAD nurse at the Argyle Street Naval Hospital permitted. In part, of course, she must have feared to lay herself open to the tragedy of bereavement which was the fate of so many thousands of women of her age —those, indeed, who were to become the maiden aunts of a later generation. But Jack Oughtred's determination to win the fair Phyllis was as stern as his determination to come back alive when the war was over. His constancy in love is as moving as his steadfastness in war. His cheerfulness in both is truly inspirational.

The final joy of these fascinating, moving and instructive letters is in their ending and in their post-script. They end with the clipped telegram message from King's Cross station and the final assurance of our hero's survival; and they are followed, some ten months after Jack's return to England, by his marriage to Phyllis. It is a fairy-tale ending to what was, so long as it lasted, a nightmare.

Alan Wilkinson, Editor,
July 1996.

[In 1915 Jack Oughtred, aged 20, was working for the London Joint Stock Bank in Hull. His father worked for the same company in Stockton-on-Tees. Like most young men of the time, he was only too anxious to get into uniform – but firstly he had to seek the permission of his employers, as he explains to Phyllis in this opening letter.]

The London Joint Stock Bank Limited.
Formerly the York City & County Banking Co. Limited

Feb 9th 1915

Dear Phyllis,

Many thanks for your letter. I am glad to hear that you are enjoying yourself and also that the air of Harrogate has acted on you in such a beneficial manner. You will return no doubt in the pink. I managed to get my "boss" to write up to Head Office for permission to apply for a commission for foreign service.* I expect to hear their decision on Wednesday morning and am anxiously awaiting it. I hear that girls are going to be installed in the Bank to fill up the vacant places until the end of the war. Some rather curious times in store for those remaining, don't you think.

Don't you think you are running a grave risk in immersing yourself in water at such a late hour. You should really take more care of yourself. It's not safe. I am informed that all the nurses are requested to prepare their bandages and knowledge for the 18th inst as a "raid" is expected and they may be required. However we shall see.

Yours ever, Jack.

P.S. Please excuse paper. Economising in war time you know.

*[It appears that Jack never did gain his employers' permission. Either they were too dilatory or he was too impulsive, perhaps both. He was gazetted as a 2nd Lieutenant as of 11 May 1915, and a few days later travelled north to training camp at Benton, outside Newcastle-upon-Tyne. He had joined the II/4th Battalion of the East Yorkshire Regiment.

In February 1915 the 4th East Yorks, a Territorial Battalion, had itself formed three separate battalions. The I/4th was at Newcastle-upon-Tyne, preparing to join the BEF. The II/4th, formerly the reserve Battalion, was at Darlington. By the time Jack joined, it too had moved up to Newcastle, preparing for the front. The III/4th was at South Dalton, near Beverley; it comprised men ready to sail for France. It was from Newcastle – or, more precisely, Benton – that Jack wrote his first letters to Phyllis Bentham as a serving officer. She was training as a V.A.D. nurse, preparatory to starting work at the Naval Hospital in Argyle Street, Hull.]

4th East Yorks, Benton Camp, 20.5.15

Dear Phyllis,

I have arrived here alright without a mishap. Just preparing for my first night under canvas. I am sharing a tent with Gillett.

Tomorrow, I understand, we are to be received by the King and Lord Kitchener at Newcastle. As I rise at 5.30 tomorrow morning I must draw this brief note to a close.

Yours ever, Jack.

Benton Camp, undated

Dear Phyllis,

I am getting on moderately well here.

I took part in the review as I told you I might. A Platoon was assigned to me and in the march past the King and Kitchener had to give the salute. It was rather a trying ordeal for my first day, but with the assistance of your charm, which never leaves me, all went well.

Every morning the reveille sounds at 5.30. We parade for Physical Drill at 6.30, which lasts for about 45 minutes. We then dismiss, breakfast being at 8. One has a lot to do throughout the day, but nevertheless it seems a long time. I suppose it is because we rise so early.

My heels have caused rather a lot of trouble, but I have hopes that they will soon right themselves.

How is your nursing getting on? I hope that you wear my little souvenir sometimes, you know my luck goes with it.

It feels very strange not being able to see you or even ring you up, but I suppose I must make the best of things possible and write to you. But for that I like this kind of life very much, being in the fresh air all day amongst other things is tophole. There are three Batts on the camp, and altogether quite a decent lot of Officers. Well, I must turn in now. So au revoir.

Yours ever, Jack.

N. Moor, Camp, Cramlington, Nr Newcastle, June 3 1915

Dear Phyllis,

Thank you very much for your letter and Photo which I am sure are quite good. What has happened to the one in which you are reclining on that classic chair, while I was standing behind. Not lost in the wash I hope.

I see from your letter that you have commenced at the hospital. I am sure that you will do well there and wish you the best of luck in this career.

I am given to understand that we shall go out to the Front as a Batt. and not in drafts. How far off this is or how near I cannot say. But without doubt it will not be many months before we shall test our luck in this direction.

One hears very little news here at all and therefore one does not see the list of casualties which is a good job in some ways.*

If we are not rushed away to some unearthly place I hope to get back to Hessle in about a fortnight's time. For the last few days amongst other things I have been learning Bayonet fighting. It is indeed an art, although the graphic description of the instructor is rather gruesome.

This open air life is a splendid thing. I have never been so well before and am as fit as a flea. Talking of insects I discovered a man today who had not taken off his shirt for 10 weeks. He was absolutely alive with them.

Well the hour is late and I must be turning in. Please continue writing to me a few lines now and then. You could not imagine how eagerly one awaits these epistles.

Yours ever, Jack.

*[**The Snapper** reported in June that "Hull has responded well to the call for recruits to swell our ranks after the losses sustained in April and May in the Ypres salient".]

N. Moor Camp. Cramlington, 9 June 1915

Dear Phyllis,

I was very much relieved to receive your telegram and later your letter, for which many thanks. You have without doubt been in the thick of it. I hope that Hull will not be chosen again as the object of another raid. I trust that in these stormy times you wear that little charm for good luck, as now of all times it is not to be overlooked.

One of our Officers was in Hull at the time of the Raid and gives me a most vivid description of the same. It must have been a terrible experience for all and I am glad, perhaps more than my words can express, that you have emerged scatheless.*

I had from the Brigade Sgt Mjr today that we should in all probability go out to India shortly to relieve troops there, for the front.

How much truth is contained in this it is impossible to say. On Monday I had the honour of being Capt. of the Day and Brigade Orderly Officer. The most amusing thing about this is that at the 6.30 Parade over which you preside, all the subs have to salute and report to you. I had Harold as my supernumery officer and had to instruct him in his duties.**

I have just been with the 4th three weeks today. It seems years ago since I joined. Please excuse my writing, which is not good, but considering that it is written on an old *London Opinion* as a pad and resting on a rickety table in a windy tent it might be worse. Well, keep your pecker up you know won't you.

Yours ever, Jack.

*[*Hull suffered its first Zeppelin raid on the night of 6 June 1915. Bombs fell on several parts of the city. One killed several people in Waller Street, Holderness Road. The raid resulted in a total of 25 dead and 100 injured.*
***Harold was one of three Oughtred brothers serving in the Army, the other being Norman, who was courting Phyllis' sister, Doris – see following letter.*]

Benton, July 9 1915

Dear Phyllis,

Many thanks for your letter which I received yesterday.

I am glad to hear that things are going well with you just now and that the Zeps have not paid another visit.

We are just about getting settled down here after our move from Cramlington.

The draft of Officers have not gone yet, but as a great many have been sent home it looks like business. The Brigadier asked my O.C. Coy if I was fit for the front today. I can't get out of him what he said. But I expect that they are so hard up for officers that they will take practically anybody.

I hear that Norman has had the pleasure of seeing you. He has almost I believe got his Commission in the R.F.A.

Tonight a great number of our officers are holding a "Wake" in Newcastle to celebrate their departure to foreign lands. They will without exception arrive back some time before 5.30 a.m. more or less blind to the world. The tastes of some people are most extraordinary.

How do you think the war is getting on? Just heard today from an old schoolpal just home wounded from the front. He says it looks hopeless out there and is absolutely "Hell on earth". I often wonder whether one will come through this business. Shall I ever have a dance or see anything of you again, beyond a merely passing visit. God only knows and so I must leave it like a lot of other things to fate.

Yours ever, Jack.

15

Aug. 6 1915
Dear Phyllis,

Many thanks for your letter. I am glad to hear that you are having a good time just now and enjoying life. I have been doing quite a lot this week so far in the way of theatres. I wish that you were here to come with me if you would.

We had a busy day here on Bank Holiday and it just struck me what I did last year. If I remember rightly I celebrated that occasion by cutting your tennis lawn.

I celebrated my birthday in a very quiet manner as I was unfortunately on Duty and therefore C.B. [*confined to barracks*] for the Day. It cost me quite a lot in standing drinks all round, but I think that on the whole I made a slight profit. The new C.O. Lt. Col. Springhall has arrived and has made everyone without exception dash about as if pursued by wild horses.

He has insisted on etiquette at Mess and all that pertains to it. If you remember that little book I once brought over on that subject some time ago you will know fully what I mean. The waiters to be dressed in white suits, wines served round every night and toasts drunk etc. One cannot rise from the table until he gives the sign or until the coffee has arrived. Rather like being at school again. When he speaks to you, one feels queer inside I guess you will comprenez what I mean. To quote someone else the C.O. is "it".

Hoping that you are well and that you will not forget me, ma cherie. I will draw this letter to a close.

Yours ever, Jack.

Aug. 11th 1915
Dear Phyllis,

I have just heard that you have been subjected to another air raid.

I hope that *you* are safe and sound and everything alright. Please excuse envelope. In haste.

Yours ever, Jack.

Castle Crag, Grange-in-Borrowdale, Keswick, Aug. 15th 1915
Dear Phyllis,

Many thanks for your letter and I am glad to hear that you were untouched by the last air Raid.

Harold has passed his Strensall course with a 1st Class Distinction which is quite useful. He is now quite a "nut". I must see if I can scratch through mine somehow or other. I feel somewhat nervous about what I have to go through, but to apply that well worn expression to myself instead of to yourself namely "Keep your pecker up". I am afraid that I have not much more to discourse to you as news is scarce and so wishing you what I always do I will conclude.

Yours ever, Jack.

Lyddon Hall, Leeds, Aug 26 1915
Dear Phyllis,

Many thanks for your letter.

I have applied for leave for the coming weekend, but should I get it, which is rather doubtful, it will be very brief. I should not arrive until getting on to 4 o.c. so that Brid. would hardly be possible.

However at the conclusion of this present course I hope to get 4 or 5 days before I rejoin the Batt. in which to recuperate. If this comes off I hope that we may have a bit of a flutter somewhere or other. What do you say?

With the exception of two nights in the week everyone has to be in by 10 o.c. Many come in at 10 but speedily go out again to return by climbing through windows at a much later hour.

Yours ever, Jack.

Benton Camp, Newcastle. Sep 15 1915

Dear Phyllis,

I arrived back here without any incident of note.

It felt rather strange to be sleeping under canvas again and rather cold. I found a thin coating of ice on my bath in the morning which needless to say I did not have.

I hope you had a good time at the theatre, although I hear from an indirect source that were was a Zep alarm.* I must thank you for your society during my brief visit. I had quite a good time, which I hope you enjoyed as much as I did myself. I will not go into the question of my feelings towards yourself. For though perhaps I may not have told you them directly in words. You must know them as well as I do myself. I wonder what you think of me.

There has been a great addition here in the number of Officers since I left. We have 44 in all, thus 14 above strength. The words *Draft for France* therefore become very prominent. I can see myself treading the soil of France at a very early date. However we all have our jobs to do. In your own job of patching up people you have already done splendidly; it is time I got actually to work in my own direction. Please remember that toujours vous etes l'object de mon adoration.

Yours ever, Jack.

*[*There were as many as 50 'Zep' alarms in Hull during the war, often caused by sightings of aircraft which were heading up the Humber towards other targets such as Goole, hit on 9 August, or Scunthorpe, hit 31 January 1916.*]

24.9.15

Dear Phyllis,

Many thanks for your letter. I am sorry to hear that your night at the theatre was interrupted. Terrible bother these Zeps aren't they?

Last Friday night the Brigade spent in the Trenches here. I was put, strangely enough, in charge of the bomb throwers. We were attacked several times during the night but about 4 a.m. they came to really close quarters. With my bomb party, armed with tin cans filled with earth in place of bombs, at 15 paces, we did great execution, which episode was most amusing to everyone except the attacking party who did not apparently enjoy the same.

Yours ever, Jack.

Oct 5 1915

Dear Phyllis,

Many thanks for your letter. I am glad to hear that you are having a fairly good time.

There has been a great change here lately. Harold and I with some others are training 4th Yorks recruits and have not much to do with the E. Yorks at all. The C.O. told Harold and myself last Saturday that we should not be very much longer with the 2/4th E. Yorks and in the course of the next month or a trifle longer we should depart for France [*where the 1/4th are already posted*]. It will be rather good going together won't it. I must say that when one knows for a certainty that one is going the Outlook of everything broadens quite a lot. On account of this I have rather lost interest in my present Regt.

It seems that we shall have the pleasure of a winter in the trenches, rather cold, what! I don't know quite how I shall manage to tell Father and Mother, but it will have to be done, sometime or other. It will cut me up terrible leaving you. You know the reason why I have no doubt. After all I shall not be very much farther away, and if fate is kind I will return. I hope that in the past I have not worried you. If I have pass it over. I cared for you more than you can imagine and *do still*. And must say thank God for it. So cheerio...

Yours ever, Jack.

[*The Battalion now took up winter quarters in Newcastle.*]

Northern Conservative and Unionist Club, Newcastle-upon-Tyne
October 13 1915
My dear Phyllis,

Many thanks for your letter. I have really some important news at last. Twenty Officers are being sent next Thursday from the 2/4 to the 3/4 at S. Dalton. I and Harold are included among the same. It will be I suppose to train recruits. The rest of the Batt will be going to Gainsboro or Retford, but that has now ceased to interest me.

I am not very sorry on the whole. Fortune smiles for *once* upon me in sending me so near to you. I trust in fact I am sure that we shall have a good time together. I promise not to kidnap you, although I often feel like doing so.

With love, yours ever, Jack.

2/4th Battalion, East Yorkshire Regiment, John Knox Hall, Newcastle.
Oct 31 1915
My Dear Phyllis,

I had rather a rotten journey up here due of course to the fog — the train being quite an hour late into Newcastle.

I feel very glad that I have told you that I love you Phyllis. I have had it on my mind for months and have never actually told you till now. Have not had the courage to I suppose. So much hangs in the balance. I do hope Phyllis that you will care for me some day as I do for you.

Do have a shot won't you. You must have thought me rather undemonstrative during my last visit, but I might not have seen so much of you had I been otherwise. I started to write you quite an ordinary letter but I could not keep it up. I have burnt two attempts already. I could go on for an indefinite length writing to you in this strain, but it would simply be repeating "I love you" in one form or other. I should never have thought it possible that I could ever write to anyone like this at one time, but now I know very different.

It is very strange to see some of my feelings that I hold most dear down in black and white. You are the only girl in the world who could make me burst forth like this. With perfect seriousness I thank God for the day I met you. Hoping to hear from you soon I will conclude.

Yours ever, Jack.

John Knox Hall, Nov 7th 1915

My? dear Phyllis,

I have just returned from the station after seeing off three Officers to the Front.* Everybody turned out including the C.O. Everyone felt a bit cut up after it, which is after all not at all surprising. Seven more men were detailed for the Front — these were the first three. The remaining four are still waiting to be called. I have the honour to be one of this four I believe.

So I may be coming home almost any time. However things change so rapidly in the army that one really never knows when one is going until you are on the way.

We move to Gainsborough or Retford on the 20th of this month. The C.O. says this is a cert. Rather an awful place to go to Gainsboro from all accounts isn't it?**

Signing myself as usual but not without significance,

Yours ever, Jack.

*[*Drafts of men were by this time regularly leaving the base for France: on 25 October 2 Lts Spragg, Vivian and Duncan, along with 22 other ranks left. Jack and Harold Oughtred were noted as being assigned to 'C' company.*
**Phyllis probably knew Gainsborough well enough: her father was the Liberal M.P. for the town.]*

The Camp, Dalton Holme, near Beverley. Dec 25 1915

(Ready now to leave for France, Jack was at South Dalton.]

My dear Phyllis,

I wish to thank you very much for your s'nice present which has considerably brightened this festive season for me. You have indeed divined my desires correctly by sending me cigarettes. I will really try and not inhale them as you have said on many occasions that it's bad for me. Thus for once I will follow your advice.

I was awakened early this morning by the Band playing carols outside our lines. Rather nice don't you think. It certainly brought home that it was Christmas Day.

I hope that when next Christmas arrives, the war being over, I will not be so isolated from you.

It is one week today since I last saw you. It is really awful. However my week is now rapidly drawing to a close. Thank Heaven.

So hoping that you will have a good time now and always I remain

Yours ever, Jack.

1916: (1) YPRES

[*Early in the New Year Jack embarked for France to join the 4th East Yorks in the northern sector of the line near Ypres. During much of the year that followed the battalion was engaged in static trench warfare, a period synopsised by the regiment's historian Wyrall in the following manner: "Shelling, trench mortaring, machine gun fire and sniping occurred at all hours of the day and night: no part of the line was ever free from one or the other; patrol work was assiduous; casualties were sometimes heavy and at others extremely light, but speaking generally (and comparatively) ... those months spent in the Ypres trenches and at Kemmel may be written down as 'quiet'."*]

4th E. Yorks Reg., Base Camp No. 17, Havre, France, Jan 9 1916
My dear Phyll,

We crossed over this morning leaving Southampton at 7.30 a.m. Sunday morning. The water was quite smooth. We then proceeded up to the Base Camp at which address you will be able to find me. If I move which I may do any time I will let you know of the change in address.

Everything seems very strange, but my little knowledge of French has already come in useful. Havre looks rather like Scarbro I think when approaching it from the sea.

The uniforms of the French soldiers are very bright and gaudy when compared with ours. They must be rather unserviceable I should think. I saw quite a number in light violet.

One finds that there is indeed a war on here. No doubt about it. A lot of Officers are going up the line tomorrow. I don't think I shall be amongst them. But [*Lt*] Slack and [*Lt*] Robson might do.

As the saying goes here they are going up the line to Hell. I say quite frankly the longer I stay here the better I shall be pleased.

I shall await a letter from you Dear Phyll with great eagerness. I think that the nearer I get to the front the more I care for you.

I hope Phyll that when you say your prayers at night you will not forget me as I will need them all.

It seems rather strange that but a week ago from the time I write I was at Swanland with you. Believe me in those few days you made me quite happy although to leave you was awful. I will continue to write you frequently while I can, so expect shoals of letters.

With love, yours ever, Jack.

4th E. Yorks Reg, 50th Brigade, 50 Division, B.E.F., Jan 10 1916
Dearest Phyll,

You will see from the above address that I have got my final marching orders. Tomorrow night Tuesday I proceed to Ypres via Rouen. I shall not reach the front until Thursday night at the earliest. This is rather swift but Slack and Robson have both gone tonight. [*2 Lt*] Rollitt and I will soon follow them. Those long months of training spoken of are all a wash out. It seems rather strange that a few days ago I was in England and in 48 hours from now I shall be under the German fire and in one of the hottest places of the line. However, I am quite cheerful and I promise you I will take care of myself. It is all a matter of fate. You ought to see me in my gas helmet: it's rather an amusing sight I assure you.

I have not yet been into Havre but shall go to complete my kit tomorrow. I wonder whether I shall ever see you again Phyll. Somehow I think I shall. Anyway if the worst comes (which won't) I will be game as long as I draw breath. I will never forget a certain girl — (the sweetest and dearest in the world to me) who lives at a little village called Swanland in E. Yorks, England.

I could tell you a lot of interesting things but I am my own censor and therefore in a way upon my honour. I often wonder what you are doing and I hope you will not worry.

I have been getting my hand in with bombing today. It seems most destructive.

With love, yours ever, Jack.

Jan 12 1916 Wednesday
My dear Phyll,

We left Havre at 1 am and arrived here [*Rouen*] at 6.30 am Wednesday morning. We go on to Hazebrouck at 5 pm today arriving there sometime tomorrow morning I suppose. I spent the night in the train using my pack as a pillow. As there were only three in our compartment we had a fairly comfortable time and managed to get a little broken sleep in.

The trains here travel as fast as one can walk. If you are left behind by any chance it is quite an easy matter to catch up again.

You ought to hear me speaking French. Makes me nearly die with laughter. At this hotel however they can speak moderate English, so all is well. I nearly fell out of a taxi yesterday. I was sitting with my back against the door, when it suddenly opened. But I just saved myself in time. A good omen don't you think.

We have 15 miles to go from Railhead to the trenches. From Railhead you can hear the guns and as you get further up spent bullets and shells come screeching by. I expect it will be rather a shock but I am quite cheerful just having had breakfast.

We had breakfast at the Y.M.C.A. on the platform. They are open Day and Night. One cannot praise them enough. Needless to say I am wearing your charm and I think it has already brought me luck.

I often think of you. Do you think you will be able to care for me enough when I return for me to put that ring on your finger. Don't worry anyhow. Lots of love,

Yours ever, Jack.

Jan 14 1916
My Dear Phyll,

I have arrived at the front and am now situated in a farm house about 5 miles behind the firing line. I have spent a very comfortable night and after our long journey in the train from Havre lasting 48 hours, have at last had a good meal.

As I write to you now I can hear the English and Bosche guns plugging away at one another.

The Battalion are in the trenches and we shall go up on Sunday morning.

As we came up last night we could see the star lights sent up by the Bosche continuously.

From all accounts we are indeed on top of them here and our artillery can blow them to Hell any time they choose. This is rather a change to what it used to be. There are four of us in the farm house. Capt. N. Ingleby, Lt Ferraby, Rollitt and myself. The natives still live here and work their farms. It is very strange to see them at it amongst the shells. I feel quite cheerful and quite bucked. I must close now.

   With love. Yours always, Jack.

Jan 15 1916

My Dear Phyll,

   I go up to the firing line tomorrow morning (Sunday Jan 16) and have to be there by 8.30 a.m. So that I shall have to start about 6 a.m. There is nothing very much doing here now, although you can hear the rumble of the guns all day and night.

   When you get this letter I shall be quite a hardened soldier as it takes 3 days to England from here. I cannot tell you where I am. All that I can say is somewhere in France. A lot of aeroplanes have been over here today (English) and have seen them shelled by the Bosche guns. None of them I am glad to say were hit. The mud round here is truly awful; some feet deep in many places without me pulling your leg at all.

   A village about 300 yards from the farm I am at now was shelled today. It is very much blown about as they have shelled it a good many times. It does not however interfere with my sleep I assure you.

   The nearer I get to the Bosche the stronger and more steady becomes, Phyll, my love for you. It means more here than *ever* I imagined it would and that is saying rather a lot.

   Any parcels of food or anything to eat would be accepted by me now with a great welcome. I have got plenty of soap, you will be pleased to hear.

   With love. Yours ever, Jack.

      xxxxx ad infinitum.

P.S. Hope you do not mind the crosses. J.

Jan 17 1916

Very many thanks for your present and letter, both of which I was delighted to receive. The Photo of you and the neat portable case in which it is enclosed will be greatly valued by me. It is really s'nice of you to send it.

   I have just returned from the trenches to some Dug outs [*Railway Dug-Outs*], behind the firing line to which we return in a few days.

   A bullet went between Slack and myself yesterday (Sunday) as we were taking observations with the compass. About two feet between us at the time. Another just cut my pack later on in the day. However this is really nothing.

   Yesterday I spent the most peculiar Sunday I have ever known. Our artillery strafed the Germans for a long time. It was a fine sight to see great trees, boulders and large masses of earth being thrown about as if they were nothing.

   Last night in the Dug-out it was awfully cold as I only had my British warm and trench coat. However tonight I have got hold of some blankets so that I shall be much warmer I hope.

   The general feeling out here is that the war will not last much longer. Because without any doubt we have the Bosche beaten. They hardly reply at all to our artillery and beyond the snipers, which are very active, there is not much doing.

   You ask me if I have forgotten last Wednesday night [*January 5*]. That could not be done. When I return we must have a repetition of the same. Don't you agree.

Somehow or other I like to write to you very much. I hope that, if it is not troubling you, you will write as much as you can. Letters mean an awful lot here, yours more than any. The warmer the better. No more now. *With Love.*

Yours ever, Jack.

Jan 18 1916

Dearest Phyll,

I received your letter late last night when I came in from duty and have taken this, my first opportunity to thank you for it.

I promise you Phyllis that I will take care of myself as much as possible, for the one thing I most desire is to come back again to you. But in all things there is a good deal of fate and in war I think fate plays a more prominent part still.

Last night (Monday) I went out at 5.30 pm with a working party of 100 men. We went up to about 200 yds from the Bosche in the open country and started to fill sandbags and make bomb proof shelters. We were in a wood in which there has been much fighting and many men buried there. The place stank of dead men. Awful isn't it.

We remained there with a few trees between us and the Germans for 5 hours. Bullets humming by every minute. However no-one was hurt at all. When we went back by road the devils turned a Machine Gun onto us but we doubled into shelters and escaped that also. Altogether rather an exciting evening do you not think Ma Cherie.

I hear from Norman that you are looking fairly well. Please Dear do not worry about me. I took your Photo in its case up to the woods last night and looked at it frequently. It is top hole.

The Photo has found its home in my breast pocket and as I have not got undressed in the slightest (not even taken my boots off) for at least 8 days now, it is never away from me either day or night.

Remember that the cloud has a silver lining and that we must keep the home fires burning.

With love and ? Yours ever, Jack.

Jan 21 1916

Dearest Phyll,

I have just taken this opportunity to drop you another line or two.

We went back into the trenches tonight [*relieving the 5th Yorkshire Reg't*] and shall remain here until Monday night.

I am writing this letter in a little Dug out in which it is impossible to stand up. One has to crawl into it like a rabbit into its hole. I have got the walls and floor covered up with sand bags so that it is not so bad. I am getting quite accustomed to living in all my clothes on the ground. It really saves a lot of time in the morning not having to get dressed. Simply put on your hat and equipment and all is completed.

I am going on Duty tonight at 1030 pm until 2 am so I shall not get much sleep as it is 10 o'clock now. I wonder what you are doing now, My Darling Phyll. It seems years since I last saw you and yet it is only about a fortnight I suppose. The number of risks one has to take every day are sometimes rather startling. But I won't tell you about them because they are past and done with. And if I did you might worry a little more. So I won't. I often think that I am a Lucky dog to have such a *girl as you* to write to me and who I believe cares for me just a little?

Do not think that the front has made me sentimental, but being face to face with Death every day one realises what is most vital to one's entire being. I have found that first above all, not that I was ever in any doubt, is my love for you, the Dearest and sweetest Little Girl on earth. Upon this point I will not be contradicted.

It is really a sight around here to see the ruins of villages and houses. Large forests of trees which look as if a tornado has just passed through them.

A large number of rats inhabit the trenches and they are of a very large species. These, so far, have been the only target for my revolver.

I hear the footsteps of the orderly coming up the trench to drag me out so that I must hurriedly conclude. I hope that you can read this scrawl.

Do write please Phyll as often as you can as letters here are like bread to the starving. With love.

Yours ever, Jack.

Saturday Jan 22

My Dear Phil,

I was very pleased to receive your letter yesterday and to hear what you have been doing. Everything is going quite smoothly out here. The only thing that really gets at you is the lack of sleep. In the last three nights I have only had six hours.

I saw rather a fine sight last night at 3 am. We blew up one of our mines. I was not far away but it nearly shook me off my feet. The earth and other things blown up went at least 60 ft in the air.

I have only two officers left for the moment in my Company. Capt Barkworth and myself. The others have either gone off on courses or have broken up. Three nights ago one of them went off his head for about ¾ of an hour. We all tried to calm him and at last succeeded. An 8in shell burst 15 yards from him during the day and I suppose gave him rather a shock.

The way we feed here is most remarkable. Everything we get is in tins and they all are stood in rows about the table. Our servants cook for us and very well they do at times. Every now and then the transport cannot get through. On such occasions we subsist on bread and Perrier water.

There is a big bombardment on as I write. I must say however that I would not have missed this experience for a good deal.

Your charm is still hung around my neck safe and sound. I am generally on duty from 1030 pm till 3 am and as I wander about I often think of you, sleeping cosily in your bed. With Love.

Yours ever, Jack.

Jan 23 1915

My Dear Phil,

I do not know quite what to say to thank you for all the s'nice things you have sent me. I was positively overwhelmed when they arrived in a body, not least the writing case. All these things and the letters you have written seem to bring you "Miss Phyllis" very close to me, yet as I write in my Dug Out I can hear the boom of the Artillery and the rattle of the Machine Gun.

You remember my British Warm perhaps and its most delicate colour. Well, just before I came in tonight I was repairing some trenches blown down by the Bosche, when they turned a Machine Gun on us. I immediately dropped down on the ground and in doing so had to land flat in a pool of slimy mud and water. Goodbye to my B. Warm.

There is a story here that we may go in the near future to Salonika. I do not know how much there is in it.

Today in the ordinary state of things is Sunday, but here there is no difference of course, except a little activity on the part of the Germans.

In peace time this place would not be half bad but now at times it's Hell. Some day I hope to show you over the places where I have been fighting. In a way I like war a bit (I do not mean the killing) especially as one regards it as a big kind of game and instead of chessmen one uses men and lives. One gets plenty of thrills, perhaps too many.

I miss you an awful lot you know, gives me quite a pain; do you miss me at all. In spite of this however I am glad that I have come out. Here one can learn and soon become a good soldier because when one's life depends on one's quickness to pick up things, you very soon do it.

With love, Yours ever, Jack.

P.S.   I was just on the point of posting this letter when I heard a bit of news. Quibell has just been shot through the chest but it has not touched any vital spot so he will probably recover. Rotten luck isn't it. JAO*

*[Battalion Diary: "Maj. Quibell severely wounded in the chest. Condition critical until the evening when a more favourable report was received."]

Jan 26 1916
My dear dear Phyllis,

I wish to thank you very much for your parcels and letters all of which are ever welcome. The food one gets in the trenches is good but very plain and the parcels one receives make all the difference in the world. Your letters brighten life considerably you know.

I have replied to Mrs. Bentham [Phyllis' mother] in response to the parcel of socks. The men I gave them to are very bucked. One needs a lot as the trenches are so very wet and muddy.

We have returned to a place some miles behind the firing line for a 4 days rest [relieved by the 5th Yorks]. The relief to get out of the range of shells and bullets is tremendous. To be able to walk across the road or go in a field without having to take cover from the German's fire is greater than anyone can imagine.

I had to do rather a risky bit of work the other night. I was ordered to put up a barbed wire entanglement in front of our trench. This I did at night and there were no casualties at all. But to be over the parapet with nothing but air between my party and the Germans was a little bit of a strain. However all is well and suppose I shall soon be more hardened to these risks.

Quibell is pulling round slowly I believe and there is some chance of his recovering.

We have a gramophone here amongst other things they played that Waltz "Destiny" which brought back many pleasant memories of both old and recent date.

The sight of a Battalion leaving the trenches after 4 days and nights for the first time is a thing I will never forget. They are not neat and tidy, spick and span as they are in England. To see them with all kinds of hats, some carrying sacks, others having sacks torn up and wound round their legs for warmth over their puttees. And all marching in single file on these awful roads with the tall avenues of trees on either side of the road and picking their way as they go between the shell holes on the road, mile after mile they go on until they at last stagger not walk into the rest Camp. The pace at the end does not exceed 1½ miles per hour. I leave the rest to your imagination. War is a terrible thing. The attitude between the Officers and men and vice versa is very different. The men still keep their absolute obedience to orders, but there is more of an entente cordial between them. This is after all only natural between men who live and die together.

Well it grows late and I must close. But before I do I wish to tell you that you are indeed a "Dear" etc to write to me as often as you do. These letters mean more perhaps than you know. Well Good night Dearest. With Love (etc).

Yours ever, Jack.

Jan 29 1916
My dear Phyllis,

Many thanks for your letter which I received yesterday as I was on the point of leaving for the Trenches. I must thank you very much for the fruit, which arrived perfectly alright and in excellent condition.

I note that in your letter you refer to some of my former letters as a little wicked in parts. Don't you rather like them like that. I hope that *when I do* return home on leave you won't lecture me very seriously on that subject.

Everything in this world I have come to believe is a mere matter of fate. Some rather extraordinary things always happen to the particular trench I have left (when leaving trenches for Dug Out). In one the Germans blew in the parapet and in the other the snipers got to work. Your charm hung around my neck is doing its work well.

I am now in the trenches in a fresh part, which is rather hot stuff, as we can be fired upon from three sides. The sooner we get out the better.

Our *own* artillery (Bless them) put eight 8in shells into our trenches yesterday in mistake for the Germans I suppose. There was much strafing done on the Phone to Headquarters.*

The shells in bursting disclosed 3 Frenchmen, who had been buried about 9 months and were in a rather advanced stage of decay. I was sick on the spot. The men removed the buttons from their tunic and then mixing the Mess with Lime put it into sand bags, and used it to build up the parapet.

You will observe that I am not using your notepaper. I have not finished it but it being so easy to carry about I am keeping it in reserve. Hoping to hear from you again shortly. With Love.

Yours ever, Jack.

*[*The bombardment by their own guns was not all that extraordinary: only six days earlier the Battalion Diary recorded that "a 25-yard section of trench was blown in at this time when our 8" howitzers shelled our own trenches". However, "most of the shells were 'blind' and there were fortunately no casualties." It has been reckoned that early in the war as many as one-third of British howitzer shells turned out to be dud.*]

Sunday [*probably January 30*]
My dear Phyllis,

Shortly after I had dispatched my letter to you yesterday we had a most thrilling experience.

The Germans attacked not far away with gas, followed up of course with infantry.

We could see the gas coming from the Bosch trenches towards our own.

The Artillery of both sides went at it in such a manner as I have never seen before. When the Germans left their trench, they were treated to shrapnel, but no rifle or Machine Gun fire.

We waited until the Germans got to our own barbed wire and then they got Rapid rifle fire and Machine Gun. A perfect hail of bullets went at them and none of them got beyond our wire and very few ever returned to their trench Thank Heaven they appear from all accounts to have lost heavily. A lot of the men engaged on our side went west also I am sorry to say.

Today again they are bombarding, whether they intend to attack I do not know, but any how, I thought I would just get this letter off as repulsing a German attack is rather a dangerous business for all concerned.

It is very hard to realise that today is Sunday. At Swanland and Hessle all will be quiet and peaceful, while here it is hardly that. My God no.

Your photograph is on occasions like this a great assistance to me, and quite sort of pulls you together. Don't think I am depressed, I was never more cheerful in my life than today.

War is very interesting without any doubt, though of course it is very terrible.

Well, no more now, and cheero, With love, Yours ever, Jack.

Jan 31

My dear Phyllis,

Very many thanks for your letter.

We move out of this trench today for another rest. [*Relieved by 7th & 5th Northumberland Fusiliers, the East Yorks decamped to Railway Dug-Outs, thence to Dickebusch Huts*]. We have had a fairly hot time just where I am. Last night we lost 2 killed 4 wounded. Two of the wounded are now dead.* This morning about 11 o'clock we were bombarded by the German guns. They made a horrible mess of the trench, blowing down the parapet in several places but no one was hit.

Well I must close now but before I do I'll give you a *kiss* (Photograph deputy) and then say Goodnight. With love

Yours ever, Jack.

P.S.   Since writing the above I have received your parcel of cigarettes. It is really very s'nice of you. You know better than anyone how I like the brand of cigarettes you have sent. It is very sweet of you Ma cherie. J.A.O.

*[*There is no mention of the casualties in Bn Diary, which generally notes officer casualties by name, men as so many "O.R." or "other ranks".*]

Feb 2 1916

My dear dear Phyllis,

We are now back at rest again for another 6 days, but unfortunately we have gone to a new camp. The huts in which we sleep are good, but there is no Officers Mess, and so we have to feed in our huts, sitting on the floor with our Knees taking the place of tables. We do better than this in the trenches.

I often wonder what things taste like out of china plates and cups. Ours are all that enamelled tin ware, very serviceable and unbreakable.

Today I went down to a certain place called P---- [*probably Poperinghe*] and had a BATH! I feel very cold now but very strange to be at all clean. Some times for days together I never wash or shave at all. No time and no water.

Everything round here, even the water smells of dead men. Most objectionable, I assure you My dear. And if one digs at all the discoveries underneath are not at all agreeable. If I could only tell you where I am you would quite understand.

Hal Seed has left for the Hospital en route I believe for England. The trenches have broken him up. Hall too, that Officer I was with once in King Edward Street, when I was meeting you one day, has cracked up also.

Today I have been able to speak for the first time for many days. At one time I was practically dumb, my throat being in a terrible state. I cannot now get at you about *wet feet* because my own are never dry although I change my socks every 2 hours when in the trenches. The cold at night is simply Hell (pardon this). No fires or anything.

I lost 2 men killed (2 of the wounded dead now) 4 wounded the other night. Very glad to get out of that trench, very unhealthy. I was nearly sniped at 4.30 pm Sunday night missed by 2 ins. I got a rifle however and got my own back.

Will you have a kiss for me when I return. I have thousands for you.

With Love, Yours ever, Jack.

Feb 4 1916

My dear Phyllis,

Many thanks for your letter, written on the 1st which I received today. I am sorry to hear that you have not heard from me for some days. My letters must have been lost or delayed in the post. This is a pity as some of them were wonderful concoctions for me.

I am afraid that I wander a little bit sometimes in my epistles and keep constantly telling you in one way or another how much *I love Miss Phyllis*. I hope you don't mind, I can't help it now. I think somehow that you are well on the road for caring a little for me too. Please tell me?

I often think of the good times we have had together also of Jan 5th 1916.

With Love heaps of it. Yours ever, Jack.

Feb 7 1916

My dear Phyllis,

We are now back in the trenches, where we shall remain for 12 days before we are relieved.

I am fortunately in a fairly quiet trench at least as trenches go out here.

With Love, Yours ever, Jack.

Feb 9th

My dear Phyllis,

Many thanks for your letter and parcel containing cakes. A portion of the contents I have already enjoyed.

I was most surprised to hear that Norman has left for the front. I had heard nothing about it until you told me. I shall no doubt see something of him as I believe we are both in the same Division.

I am of course still in the trenches. We shall remain here for about another 8 days. We work all night and try and get a little sleep during the day. I am so sorry to tell you that Quibell has not been able to survive his wound. He died about 4 days ago. It is rather sad is it not.

I am glad that the men I gave the socks etc to have written. I remember now censoring some of them. I feel quite bucked to hear that you do *miss* me a bit. Here with the war on every side both day and night one finds out here what one really feels for different people. You seem so cut off from the old world you have known and put into a new, where you either kill or are killed. It is under these conditions that I find my feeling for you more strong than ever. You won't think *that wicked* will you.

My nerves were rather turned up yesterday. The Germans fired 150 shells in ½ an hour into our trench. NCO's and men went down like ninepins. By the way I always burn your letters as you wish.

With Love. Yours ever, Jack.

Feb 11 1916

My dear Phyllis,

I am just taking the opportunity to drop you a few lines before the post goes. Everything here today is terribly wet as it has not ceased raining since 2 am this morning. The trenches are not exactly a health resort in the finest of weather but on a wet and snowy day they are simply b----. (Excuse unwritten expression)

Yesterday the Artillery on both sides had a day out so to speak and strafed each other in quite the best style. As long as they do not treat us to a prolonged dose, all is well.

Unfortunately we had three men sniped during the day. All three will never see England again. I had a working party close to them; only 3 or 4 yds away. Very unpleasant believe me. But it is a most remarkable thing how soon one forgets. Very callous I suppose but without any doubt it is just as well.

During the day we do nothing except *sleep* eat or play Auction Bridge. Playing Bridge with the Bosche shelling you is distinctly thrilling.

By the way I was talking to an Artillery Officer yesterday and I think that Norman will be quite close here. [*Norman is a 2nd lieutenant in the Field Artillery.*]

So sending you my *love* and --- (what?)

Good night. I remain Yours ever, Jack.

Feb 13 1916

My dear Phyllis.

I was very pleased to receive your letter last night, written I believe on the 8th inst.

My Dug Out let in a terrible lot of water last night, but fortunately today I am moving into another part of the line, where I hope it will be a little drier. On Friday [*18th*] we go for 6 days rest.

This morning I washed myself, the first time for three days. I really look an awful sight. I am sure if you met me you would pass me by mistaking me for a man who goes down the drains or something of that sort. We still keep up some small pretence at civilisation. For instance we dine at 7 pm every night. Why we call it Dinner I really do not know, for it is not the kind of meal that you or I would class under that heading. The water here of course cannot be used for drinking purposes until it is boiled, and even then without exaggeration it stinks fearfully. The smell however I have found can be successfully drowned by cocoa. Tea will not do it. But to change the subject, you mention in your letter that I ought to *forget* an episode that happened on a certain night in January 1916. You can't see me doing it can you. No fear. It was quite the s'nicest thing that I have ever done and the one thing that I long to do is to *repeat* it. You know it was really top hole. What do you think about it?

Yours ever, Jack.

Feb 14 1916 Monday
My dear Phyllis,

Many thanks for your letter which I received yesterday written on the 10th inst.

In my letter yesterday I mentioned that a German attack was in the air. Well I need not have worried you with the idea as it failed to come off for which I am very thankful.

I am now separated from the rest of the Company and have a trench on my own. It is like a headland jutting out of our line. I have the Germans on three sides of me at one place. Every day they blow in my parapet which has of course to be rebuilt at all costs.

It is *very sweet* of you to drop me a line whenever you can. They are much appreciated. Your last letter went through some of the most dangerous places of the line to reach me. It was brought to me by the bombers while I was on Duty.

Well I must close now and do not forget that there is some one who never forgets Miss Phyllis.

With Love. No more now. Yours ever, Jack.

Feb 15 1916 Tuesday
My dear Phyllis,

We have just had a most stirring night last night. Shortly after I had finished and sealed up my letter to you, about 4 pm Monday afternoon, the show began.

A tremendous artillery bombardment took place, both sides taking part. I was in a support having some tea and had of course to get immediately to my post. This I managed to do without being hit. In the point which I hold it was almost impossible to make the men hear anything on account of the noise. I put them all under cover of course except the sentries.

The Germans put over all kinds of things into our trench, no one however was hit. The Germans attacked on our Right flank. Imagine if you can hundreds of guns going at it "Hell for leather" and in addition Rapid and Machine G. fire. I cannot adequately describe it I am afraid. At this moment the Bosche fired off 4 mines underneath our trenches. One was only 20-30 yards away from our parapet. The earth seemed to heave up and down and the Dug Outs and parapets rocked. I have never yet been thoroughly shattered, or as they say in the line "got the wind up" until those mines went up yesterday. Men were buried in their Dug Outs some of them alive.

I was then reinforced by bombers. After this things quietened down and I was relieved by Rollitt at 9 pm. I turned in at 11 pm but was awakened by the guns at 12 midnight. We all "stood to" and prepared to repel an attack. The other strafe earlier on was child's play to this one. The whole place rocked with the reports. The men stuck it fairly well although they were in a bit of a panic.

We attacked the Bosche on the Right and he returned the compliment. The Division engaged lost some trenches I believe although I cannot get to know for a certainty.

Things then quietened down, we remained ready however to repel an attack. At

4.30 am it began to snow hard and soon everything was covered with white.

It was rather rotten, especially the cold. I did not lose a single man in my platoon and you must I think lay the credit down to the charm you gave me. It was marvellous. [*Total casualties for the Battalion were 2 killed, 14 wounded.*] When I came down to the support this morning for breakfast the first words my O.C. Coy said were, "By God, Oughtred, I never expected to hear your voice again. I thought you and your platoon had gone west."

I thought I should never be able to see Miss Phyllis again last night you know. But fortunately I came through. I think that I must thank you in a way; something indeed took care of me in the last 48 hours. By the way the General commanding the Division thanked the 4th East Yorks for their splendid behaviour during the night. Rather s'nice what. Well I must close now for the present.

    With Love. Yours ever, Jack.

Feb 18 1916
My dear Phyllis,

I have received your parcel containing cakes, sent off on the 11 inst for which many thanks.

We have been having a very hot time here the last six days, as you may perhaps be able to see from the papers although the official news is always rather brief.

Yesterday or it may have been the day before that I was hit by a piece of shrapnel. The buckle of my web equipment however stopped it so that it did not do any damage to me at all. Nevertheless it was rather lucky

We have lost well over 50 men during the last 3 days. Captain Dibb was hit this morning in the leg in 2 places by rifle bullets. As yet there are no other Officer casualties. A large number have been taken to the hospital sick.

We go out of the trenches tonight [*relieved by 6th Durham Light Infantry*], which I hope we shall do without having many casualties. I hope Phyllis you did not think my last letter to you rather brief, but I was absolutely beat to the world. Lack of sleep soon tells on one. We did not succeed in getting back all the trenches we lost the other night.

The Division engaged lost a large number of men from all accounts. We shall want some more officers out here soon if this business goes on like this. The strain is very great on everyone. The Battalion as a whole are just about done.

    Much Love. Yours ever, Jack.
P.S.   Please excuse writing, conditions rather bad. JAO.

Sunday 20th Feb 1916
My dear Phyllis,

I was very glad to receive your letter yesterday written on the 15th inst.

We are now back at rest [*Dickebusch 'A' Huts*] where we shall remain for 6 days before returning again to Hell or perhaps better known as the trenches. We now do 12 days in and 6 days out. I think that the period in the trenches is rather too long. Everybody is absolutely finished at the end of it.

The crater left by the mine in front of our trench was 80ft long by 60 broad and 30ft deep. You may gather from this that it was some explosion. This is just one mine. There were quite a number of the same. Lumps of earth as big as a man flying about in the air.

All the trenches the Germans gained on our Right have not yet been recovered.

It is rather hard to believe but had it not been for the buckle on my web equipment, my last letter would have been written some days ago. At the time I hardly noticed it but now I realise I have had quite a narrow squeak.

It is very nice of you to say that you think I have stood everything fairly well so far. But when I am by myself up at the line I am an awful coward. Thank Heaven that when I am with men leading or directing them I am as right as rain. I cannot account for it, I suppose it's because one cannot be anything else but calm when you feel the men are watching you.

I thought of you quite a lot last Monday night and early Tuesday morning in fact throughout all the bombardment. Such an experience I have never had before. It has altered me considerably. I shall never be the same as when I left England.

My leave might come off in about a month or perhaps a little longer, If a big show is coming off however, all leave will be stopped.

I am sorry to hear that my letters have become wicked again. It would not be me if they weren't would it. I don't like to ask you, but do you think you care for me a little more than you did? Please Phyllis let me know if you do.

The slightest step in the *right* direction would buck me up awfully. Well cherrio. Much Love.

Yours ever, Jack.

P.S.   Perhaps the above question is rather unsporting, but I'll leave it.*

*[*In a letter written by Phyllis to Jack she refers to his question thus:*
"*As to the very wicked question in your last two letters, what can I say? The truth is, Jack, I simply **daren't** promise. I'm afraid I'm a little funk, but it's rather a big thing you'll agree? However, I do like you very much really, so cheer up and don't be vexed with me, will you?*"
She adds a P.S:
"*You say the question was unsporting. I think it would be if you didn't burn the reply at once, don't you?*"
Unsportingly, he did not do as she requested. It is, as far as is known, the only letter Jack received from Phyllis while in the trenches which he did not destroy. The only others which have survived are ones received when he was in hospital – some in France, most in England.]

Feb 22nd 1916

My dear Phyllis,

I was very pleased to receive your letter today. As you say it was rather a bad time for us. I am sure I feel years older and in a way I suppose I am. Our losses were not more than 60 or so. No so bad when everything is considered.

I am afraid that we are going to make a big push here soon. If that is so we shall be in it. But I will not worry you before I need. We are now behind the line at Rest Camp. We call it a Rest Camp but as I write through the window I can see German shells bursting 600 yds away.

Today we have had a heavy snowfall and everyone is profoundly thankful that we are not in the trenches.

Two Russians came into trenches close to us having escaped from the Germans. They rushed across No man's land to our lines and they cried out to our sentry "Comarade Russki". One was slightly wounded but both got into our trench. Then they both embraced each other, kissed and wept etc.

Talking of the duration of the war, two men were heard to say the following when on a working party.

Fedup No. 1   "D'yer know mate wot I thinks going to stop this war?"

No. 2   "Wot?"

No. 1   "There won't be no more earth to fill sand bags."

A lot of truth in this.

The Battalion have been up here 10 weeks or so and have lost 10 officers one way or another. Rather heavy is it not. I will do my best ma chere to take care of myself, though there is really very little that I can do.

The end of my last letter was perhaps rather wild and I asked you a little question. Don't let it worry you if you can help it will you. But I think such a lot on that subject that I can't help mentioning it now and then. I *am* sure you will understand won't you. I am afraid that I am an awful worry.

We were not in the second attack Thank God. They were nearly wiped out poor devils.

I shall never forget the first two men I saw killed. Two of them close to my side. Made me quite sick. But I am quite hardened now. When you see a man go west, you simply say Poor Devil and then go on and forget him almost at once. If we did not do this life here would be awful. We don't have really a bad time. The cold is the worst really. I have just been playing bridge with two chaplains. I still keep in fairly good society you see.

By the way if you have any more socks in hand some out here would be greatly appreciated.

Good night Phyllis. With Love. As ever, Jack.

Feb 24th 1916

My dear Phyllis,

I was very pleased to receive your letter of the 20th this afternoon.

Norman came over today to our camp. He looked very well and seemed in good spirits. He told me all the latest news from England also all he could remember connected with yourself specially for my benefit. It was most interesting.

By the way has that miniature of me reached you from Turners. I forget whether you said it had or not.

We are now in reserve just behind the line, rather a rotten place for shells and that kind of thing.

Norman tells me he has a fire in his room etc. Lucky dog. He is well behind the easy range of fire so that one of us will be alright anyhow. Now Phyllis I don't want to worry you, but in the next few days a *very big* push is coming off just where we are. We shall not be in the attacking party but we may be called to back them up.

The other affair I was in will be a fleabite to this one. I cannot of course tell you where it will be, but if you look at the papers you will soon find out I fancy.

I expect that I shall come through alright. I ask you Phyllis to remember me in your prayers the night you receive this and the night after. I shall need them My dear if I ever did.

Don't think that I am depressed. I was never more cheerful or better in health.

It really means an awful lot to me to be able to write to you expressing my feelings quite freely as I do. I do not know what I should have done out here if it had not been for you. The thought of you has saved me from many temptations and sort of pulls you together when bullets and shells are coming fast and men are being knocked out beside you.

I think you will understand what I mean. It would have been better perhaps had I not told you of this engagement until all was finished. But I did not like the thought of going into a big scrap without dropping you a line first you know.

Yours ever, Jack.

Sunday Feb [27th] 1916

My dear Phyllis,

I was very pleased to receive your letter and also the parcel of socks etc for which the men are very thankful. I have written a brief note to Mrs. Bentham on the subject.

The last two nights I have taken a party out at 7 pm and worked till 2 am digging, snowing like the D--- all the time. It gets feet deep in places.

Every now and then a man gets hit and I have him carried away but the work still goes on. I find my flask coming in most useful for the wounded just now. I had a man hit in the leg last night the bullet having previously gone through a tree. The bullet remained in his leg however. He seemed quite cheerful about it.

On the way up to our job we lost 4 killed 5 wounded, nevertheless we got there alright, which is what I set out to do. We are quite in the open one can hear the bullets whistling by and hitting the trees as they go. This kind of thing makes you rather callous. It is far worse than the trenches themselves.

I often wonder how it is I never get hit as I am naturally the most exposed as I have to stand and walk about on the top of the parapet to direct them.

I think Phyllis that indeed some great Power is watching over me.

I always wear your charm and am beginning to put a great deal of faith in its power. However I will not boast about my immunity from the German lead as I may get one "Touch Wood".

Everybody is getting rather knocked up both Officers and Men. Standing in icy water up to your knees for hours and then going and sleeping in the same things is after all hardly conducive to health n'est pas.

In spite of this I feel more or less fit.

I often think of you when I am out on those parties, on which I go every night.

I never know when I leave my Dug Out in the reserves whether I shall ever see it again.

Tut-tut — I am getting very serious and you must think I am depressed, but it is not so believe me, all is well.

I must bid you au revoir now or in Anglais Goodnight.

With Love. Yours ever, Jack.

Feb 28th 1916

My dear Phyllis,

I am very pleased to be able to tell you that show which we were going to take part in here has for a few days been postponed. Had it taken place our casualties would have undoubtedly been large.

We are still hard at work with spades every night. The wood in which we work has seen some of the most intense and bloody fighting of the war. [*The Bn were preparing new positions in Maple Copse prior to moving there next day.*] The whole place is like one big cemetery and you will easily see that it is not a pleasant job

34

digging there. A man with me last night lost his nerve when they started shelling us a bit on the way up. We had hardly started out before he was shaking like a leaf and after a 100 yds or so he fell down and grovelled at the bottom of the trench. I of course sent him back with another man to look after him. Not his fault really I suppose, but a thing like that takes away the spirit of the men very quickly and also has a little effect on yourself.

There are no girls up here in fact I have not seen one since I landed that was at all thrilling not that it would make any difference if I did. For is there not Miss Phyllis in England. I do not forget easily in fact to strictly adhere to the truth I never forget you.

By the way would you like the nose cap of a German shell or any souvenirs. I can get any amount of them. You must let me know if you would care for anything of the sort.

Would you like some of those silk postcards? I see from what the men send that "forget me nots" are very popular. Would you care for one?

With Love etc. Yours ever, Jack.

Feb 29 1916
My dear Phyllis,

I must thank you very much for your parcel containing cake and *Punch* which arrived today. It is really very s'nice of you to send me these things. The cake is really excellent and some of the stories and articles in *Punch* are priceless absolutely.

We are still having quite a hot time here. Last night when returning to these Dug Outs I was shelled the whole way with shrapnel and High Explosive. One burst in the parapet close to us but no one was hit. We were crossing a bridge about 20 yds long when they put over 4 salvos of shrapnel.

I do not think I ever did a quicker sprint in my life than across that bridge. There were no men lagging behind either. This nightly trip of dodging shells is really most exciting.

Tonight we leave these dug outs and go nearer the line to the places where we have been working. Before this letter reaches you the show I mentioned will be finished one way or another I expect.

Yours ever, Jack.

March 3
My dear Phyllis,

Many thanks for your letter received last night. We just arrived back at the reserve line last night after being up for the "Push". I am pleased to say that I have survived it in spite of many very narrow squeaks.

The show was a success and a good amount of Bosche trench was captured. About 400 or 600 prisoners were taken. They all looked quite young and almost pleased that they were captured.

On Thursday night we bombarded the Bosche at 5 pm till 6 pm and with short breaks throughout the night.

At 4.29 am on Friday morning [2.3.16] (Our artillery having stopped for some time) our infantry went over the parapet without having given the Bosche any warning.

At 4.31 we were in the trench. Our artillery fire was so accurate that the Bosche communication trenches were blocked; thus the number of prisoners taken.

Later in the day they made a few counter-attacks which were repulsed with heavy loss. Since when they have bombarded us day and night causing heavy casualties.

The bombardment of this trench, the number of flares and rockets all colours was almost like a Guy Fawkes display. But personally I was rather fed up with it.

For 3 days and nights I have only had 6 hours sleep and that was on Bully Beef tins.

The men are finished. I do not think the sight of a Bosche to stick with a Bayonet would revive them.

My nerves are very ragged just now.

By the way all leave is stopped for 2 months.

We shall have to take part in a counter-attack if the Germans take the trenches back. But I do not think they will. Things out here look quite cheery on the whole. I think the Bosche is just about done.

The effect of our 15in guns on the Germans was excellent. each shell (shrapnel) contains from these guns 40,000 bullets. Some Gun what?

I hope that you do not think me bloodthirsty do you?

I am afraid that I am becoming rather cold-blooded.

With Love, Yours, Jack.

March 7th 1916

My dear Phyllis,

I was very pleased to receive your letter last night and also very many thanks for the cigarettes.

Almost immediately after I wrote my last letter to you we were unexpectedly sent up to the trenches again. Everybody was very depressed because we all thought we should get back into rest without any more. This is the 15th day in and I do not think we shall be relieved for a day or two. The trench is most unpleasant as you are shot at from four sides.

They put over all kinds of shells at us, Krumps, Whizz Bangs etc. They blow our parapet in every day and we mend it at night although a Machine Gun is constantly playing upon our working party.

The other night I went out over the parapet on patrol in No Man's land.

On those chores one only carries bombs. I got out and fairly near the Bosche and then returned not having seen or met one. It is rather a strange sensation to march about in the open and to hear the bullets whistling about. Every time a Very light goes up you fling yourself on the ground and lie as still as a log.

It does nothing but snow here and freeze. Truly awful weather. A friend of mine called [2nd Lt] Hewatt was hit in 3 places by a 'sausage'. Very serious but I think he will survive. I have had no men hit today yet although one has broken his ankle. I intended writing you some days ago but I have had no time. I went to sleep this morning while standing up against the parapet. With Love.

Yours ever, Jack.

P.S.   I burn your letters as you wish me to.

March 9/16

My dear Phyllis,

Thanks very much for your last letter, which I was very pleased to receive.

We have had a very hot time but last night we arrived back at our rest camp ['*D*' *Camp, Ouderdom*] after doing 17 days in the trenches.

We marched back through Ypres. It was a sight that I shall never forget. We passed through about 2 am with the moon on it. It looked very weird to say the least. Not a soul about and everything so quiet.

I think that we had at least a foot of snow. I do not think that I have ever seen the men more done. When we had a brief halt several lay down in the road and went to sleep.

We are out for eleven days at least, quite a long time. I hunted out Norman today. He is only about 600 yds down the road. He looked very well indeed I shall see a lot of him I hope.

I will send you some cards but I fear that the other souvenirs would be too difficult to send. I could send you a *ring* if you would like one. Would you do you think.

I heard that there has been a Zepp Raid on Hull. I trust that you are alright. We both are under the Bosche fire so to speak.

Tonight I shall turn in and get a good 12 hours sleep. The prospect fills me with joy. For once I shall be really warm and not have cold feet. Well I must close now.

Much Love. Yours ever, Jack.

March 10th 1916

My dear Phyllis,

I was very pleased to receive your letter today and to hear that you are quite safe and sound after your trying experience of the Bosche bombs.

I am very pleased to hear that the miniature has turned up at last.

I am writing this letter from Norman's hut as it is quite close to our camp. And it is much warmer and more comfortable than mine. Tonight we are going out to have a little dinner at an estaminet close by called 'Aux Trois Amis'. I feel quite thrilled at the prospect of eating off China plate and having a proper glass to drink out of.

Norman informs me from Doris' letter that someone has been talking again. Congratulating Mr. Bentham* on both his daughters being engaged. Just a little bit previous perhaps is it not. Still the thought is very pleasant to me and I hope it is to you. [*Doris has become engaged to Norman.*]

Today I went down to a place not far from here and had a *Bath*. I really feel quite chilly now. I am sure I must get in a most disgusting condition.,

A Bosche shouted across at us the other day that Verdun was taken. One of our men stood up on the parapet and shouted at him "Go and bump yer (h)ead." Most expressive what.**

I saw rather a plucky thing done the other day. A man called Veary (Rollitt's servant) was the main feature in it. A Bosche shell blew in our trench and blew a man through the parados*** and a yard or two beyond. He was then fired at by a Machine Gun. Veary dashed out and dragged him in. In doing so his equipment was so riddled by bullets that it caught fire although he was untouched. Some pluck that you know.

He is or perhaps was a member of Fred Till's class. Even Mission halls it seems can turn out the right stuff. It is most remarkable how you run across people.****

I told you in my last letter about a certain place I passed through [*Ypres*]. You will now know whereabouts I am.

37

I have been given the job of Company Wiring Officer. The work entails putting up wire in front of our parapets. Rather a risky occupation, and one which you may be sure I did not apply for. However I shall be alright. I have been in perhaps the hottest part of the line during my time out here and so far I have come through. I shall be able to tell you all about it when I come home. I've got an awful lot to jaw about — war and *many other things besides.* Can you guess one of them. How are you getting on after your fall down the steps. Better I hope.

I do not quite know when we are going back into the trenches. I rather think from rumours that I hear, that we are having a little longer out this time. The longer the better say I.

I wish we could get out to Egypt or better still England. I would give anything to get out of this "muddy bloody salient". A positive death trap absolutely.

    With best Love. Yours ever, Jack.

    *[*Mr. Bentham was Phyllis' father, Chairman of Wm. Jackson & Son, also Liberal M.P. for Gainsborough.*

    **Verdun *was not captured, of course; it remained inviolate throughout the war. 650,000 men died there.*

    ***The parados *was a bank of earth thrown up behind a trench to protect men from being seen against the skyline as they put their heads above the parapet.*

    ****Fred Till, *a Hull solicitor, married Jack's sister Ethelwyn. He later became Lord Mayor of Hull.*]

March 13th 1916
My dear Phyllis,

We are not going to be left as long at rest here as we had imagined, as we go up for a further 12 days in on Tuesday next [*14.3.16*]. We certainly do get pushed about all over the place.

This time we are going to hold the trenches recently captured from the Germans. I expect that we shall all have a fairly warm time of it, although not so hot as our last trench. I did not tell you very much about it as it was the limit. We were right in the point of the salient. When we marched back through Ypres, we could see the Bosche Very Lights on our Right and Left and in our rear.

Ypres has been an old walled city. The walls in places still remain as they are 30 to 40 feet thick in places. We marched into the place over a drawbridge, which still runs over the moat and between the walls, towering above you. It quite made you think you lived in the Olden times. With the moon shining on it and the quietness of the place, it was most weird. But it was indeed a city of the dead. Some of the stones blown from the Cloth hall and Cathedral are tremendous in size. The Germans must have put in some big shells to shift them at all, of course they still shell the place frequently, habit I suppose, because there is nothing much left to knock down. It does seem a shame really, because once it must have been quite a picturesque sort of place you know.

It is the intention of the Batt. to avenge in a small way the recent air Raid on Hull. I must see what I can do in that direction.

I was very pleased to hear that Jim [*Carmichael*] is coming home again. I am sure he has done his bit for the time anyway.* I wonder if there will be any developments in the Smith Direction. What do you think. By the way after careful calculation I find I am only 7 turns off leave.

I hope that you have recovered from your fall down the step. You might let me know if you are still black and blue or not. Keep merry and bright and don't get depressed will you. Will you.

  With Best love, yours ever, Jack.

*[*Jim Carmichael was a member of the Hull family engaged in the jewellery business.*]

March 14 1916
My dear Phyllis,

  Very many thanks for your letter and parcel which I received today.

  We are just off again to the trenches in a few hours. I expect we shall have a rough time in the next few days. To begin with there are no dug outs at all. So that it means sleeping out in the open. Rather chilly at this time of year don't you think. I must say I hope the Bosche do not try and get the trenches back while we are there, though of course we should give a good account of ourselves. The 4th E. Yorks has a reputation to keep up out here, though it is a territorial regiment. The nine months it has been out it has lost 30 or so officers and 800 men. Pretty fair isn't it.

  With Love. Yours ever, Jack.

March 18 1916
My dear Phyllis,

  I was very pleased to receive your letter yesterday and to hear that everything is alright with you.

  Nothing stirring has happened here at all the last two days. It has been very quiet indeed. everyone's trenches have been so knocked about that both us and the Bosche spend our time putting them right again.

  We are on the top of a hill and can see for miles round as the country generally speaking is very flat.

  I was asked by the Adjutant the other day if I was willing to become the Trench Mortar Officer. I said I was so I expect to go away on a course very shortly. I don't know what kind of a job it will be, but at any rate it will be a change.

  That man called Veary I mentioned in my last letter has got the D.C.M. Had it been any other war but this I am sure he would have got the V.C. There is a rumour about that leave is starting again soon. If this is so I shall no doubt manage to get home in April sometime. We must have a bit of a fling together. What do you say.

  One of our Officers, Ferraby, [*Battalion Transport Officer*] was hit in the thigh yesterday. A sure "blightie". We no sooner get reinforced than we lose some men.

  What a grand afternoon this would be for Golf or even tennis — as warm as summer. Swanland and Hessle would look very fine today.

  On our right we have the 1st Gordon Highlanders. They look very amusing in their kilts especially when they get in the mud. They are a fine lot though and nearly all scotch too.

  Well I must close for the present so Goodnight.

  With Love. Yours ever, Jack.

March 19 1916
My dear Phyllis,

  Thank you very much for your letter of the 14th.

  This morning (Sunday) I went along our trenches until I came to the trenches just recently taken from the Bosche. They are up to your knees in mud and the signs of the fight are very evident as the dead have not yet been removed. Some of the sights there are rather awful, although I am quite accustomed to that kind of thing now. You find yourself walking on bodies at times. But I will not tell you any more about it as these things must be unpleasant to you.

I have got a few Bosche souvenirs, a couple of bombs and some ammunition, but I can't post them so I shall have to wait until I come home on leave.

Leave was started again yesterday but today it has been stopped again for the infantry of the Division. What this means I do not know.

It is very hard to realise that it is Sunday today. It took us all some time this morning to find out what day it was. I saw a British aeroplane brought down by a Bosche. It fell behind our lines. The airman was shot through both hands but still brought his machine to the ground in safety. Rather plucky don't you think.

With Love. Yours ever, Jack.

March 26 1916

My dear Phyllis,

I am back at rest again now from the line. We are shortly moving away from the salient. It cannot possibly be worse than there.

I am sending you a few souvenirs in the shape of a Bosche Bomb and ammunition. I picked them up in a German trench. I have personally removed the explosive from them so that they will be no danger to you.

I went down to Poperinghe last night and after having fed went to a small Music Hall show run by some Officers and men who are permanently billeted in that place. I heard "Friend o' Mine" and "Red Devon by the Sea". Many is the time you have played those tunes pour moi.

I hear that you have had another air raid scare in Hull, but the Bosche did not come it appears. I don't think that all those measures that people have in case of a raid are much good. Best thing is to stop in bed. If the bomb drops on you it does.

You will not have any time for Golf now I suppose. It's a pity because you ought to keep it up. I suppose tennis will be starting shortly; you ought to be able to get some, don't you think. Be able to rake some men up from somewhere or other.

With Best Love, Yours ever, Jack.

March 28th 1916

My dear Phyllis,

We crossed the frontier yesterday and left Belgium behind and are now in France.* I am living at a farm house some miles behind the line so far indeed that you can only just hear the rumble of the guns in the distance. The country here is splendid, far better than Belgium which shows in such a marked degree the signs of war.

The feeling of being inside a house again is very strange, actually having a roof that will keep the rain out.

We had great difficulty in establishing ourselves at this farmhouse although we had a perfect right to be here. We were ejected on the first attempt but after about two hours of waiting for the interpreter we took possession in spite of the Lady of the house. She is I believe not quite right in her head as she has lost three sons in the war. The people here though on the whole are much better than the Belgians who are rather a sour lot.

Tomorrow morning (Thursday) we move off again to the line for a few weeks. No rest for the infantry.

I am going into a small town not far from here this afternoon which is I believe famed for the lace that comes from it. I wonder if I shall see anything there that I think Miss Phyllis might like. Quite a chance I should say. Wouldn't you.

 With Love. Yours ever, Jack.

[The Bn has arrived at a rest area south-west of Schaexken, having marched via Reninghelst, Westoutre, Mont Vidaigne, Mont Noir.]

March 30
My dear Phyllis,

Many thanks for your letter which I received yesterday.

We have marched a long way today and have now halted for the night [*at Locre*]. Tomorrow we shall go into the trenches. We are billeted in a Convent here and very nice it is too. They welcomed us positively with open arms (the nuns I mean). I have a beautiful clean bed to sleep in with clean white sheets also, an absolute paradise. Everything is so spick and span that you feel horribly afraid lest you dirty everything up.

I was indeed very much struck with that Boudoir cap (is that right) I got for you the other day. Quite the nicest thing I have seen in that way out here. Hope you will like it.

You must accept my congrats on getting your Red Cross Badge. Quite one of the "Nuts" now, what?

You ask me if I think the war will be over soon. I don't know really because I only know about the particular bit of Bosche trench that happens to be opposite me from time to time.

The German infantry are done and not so many in numbers. Were it not for their artillery, which is damn good, we could wash 'em out any day.

I should give this war another six months or so. I don't think it will last another winter campaign.

 With Love. Yours ever, Jack.

Apl 3 1916
My dear Phyllis,

I was very pleased to receive your letter yesterday.

I hear a rumour today that Hull & District has been the object of another air raid. I hope that you are alright. I become quite anxious about these raids until I hear from you. We indeed live in stirring if not altogether pleasant times don't we. I am glad to hear that you are getting on so well at the Hospital.

The last few days we have been rather busy round about here. Quite a big strafe was going on on our left. I have not the faintest idea what has happened there though.

I saw some top hole aeroplane fights yesterday, the Bosche properly "got the wind up" and made as quick as they could for their own lines.

I am glad that you have not forgotten that famous valse "Destiny". We had quite a good time at the Dance you mention. A most important event second to none took place in me during that valse with you.

I must thank you for writing me as much as you do. I love to hear all you have

41

been doing, especially the small things you tell me. I think the little things matter most. They are the more intimate. Is it not so?

I fear that my letters contain nothing much except war news or something as you would say rather wicked. Well I must close now. Best Love.

Yours ever, Jack.

Apl 5th 1916

My dear Phyllis,

Since I last wrote you we have been subjected to quite a severe bombardment for two days. I have spent most of my time lying on the trench boards to dodge the shells.

Two of our guns' shells burst in our trench, quite close to where we were having lunch. We all thought we had gone west for the moment. Dishes, cups etc were all knocked on the floor by it, most alarming I assure you.

We have had about 50 casualties so far. [*The Bn Diary laconically sums up this action: "Enemy artillery v. active."*]

2nd Liet. Burton was killed by a bullet at 2 this morning. Fine chap only just come out from Dalton [*arrived 11.3.16*]. Tomorrow I go for 6 days on a Trench mortar course for which I am very thankful as it will get me out of the trenches for a short space.

I went out on patrol the night before last and got quite close to the Bosche trenches. Nothing really thrilling happened though except falling into shell holes and getting out again.

With Best Love. Yours ever, Jack.

Apl 7 1916

My dear Phyllis,

Many thanks for the parcels and letters that arrived today from you. Please thank Mrs. Bentham for the socks won't you. They will be very useful indeed.

I was very relieved to get your letter saying that you were alright after the Air Raid. I am sure I don't know what I should do if anything happened to you. It would indeed be too awful.

I am very glad you received the Munitions of war in safety and also that the boudoir cap turned up. I am very pleased you like it.

The bombs etc I sent you I picked up in a German trench known out here as the "Bluff". They have been fighing over that particular set of trenches for days now. I can hear the guns as I write. [*The 4th East Yorks were not involved in this counter-attack.*]

I am now undergoing a course on the Stokes Gun (Trench Mortar Quick Firing). I came down from the line yesterday morning with 10 men detached to be trained with me, we left the batt. still in the trenches. There is only another Officer and myself on the course. We live and feed at a farm with the instructor. A first Lt in the N.Fs [*Northumberland Fusiliers*]. Only three of us all told.

I am more comfortable here than I have been since I came out and the food, after what I have been having, is tophole. I am afraid you will think I am becoming rather a glutton. But food and warmth are the two most important things of life out here.

I shall have two guns under me and be under the O.C. Battery. We shall move about all over our Brigade front not merely confined to our own Batt. I shall cease to be a common infantryman and turn into something of a specialist.

The gun can fire 45 shots in a minute. Some gun what. We had a very hot time in the trenches. 50 casualties in 4 days at least. My nerve is not what it was I'm afraid. Feel just a bit shaky at times. What a fearful lot of shop I have written to you. Hope it won't bore you.

 With Best Love. Yours ever, Jack.

Apl 8th 1916

My dear Phyllis,

Many thanks for your letter which I received this afternoon.

What a terrible bother these Zepps must be, keeping you up every night. I hope that they will not do you any harm, the "Dirty Dogs" (very mild that, not what I should really say about them). I am still going on with my course and find it most interesting and quite a pleasant change.

I shall be under the Brigade direct and not under any Battalion Commander. More or less able to wander about in the Brigade trenches as I please. rather s'nice I think. I am quite eager to try it on the Bosche. It will be most successful I think in destroying things generally. Don't think me too bloodthirsty will you. I naturally wish to put out as many Bosche as possible.

On coming down from the trenches a few days ago I ran into a lot of "Tear Gas". I had to put on my goggles to save my eyes. It is quite sweet and not unpleasant. Although it makes you weep and makes it impossible for you to see for a few moments, it is not really dangerous.

I saw a few days ago my first aerial torpedo. It has a cone shaped body sharp at both ends with fins about 3ft long. It struck the ground and then went in before it exploded.

The crater it made was 40ft wide 30ft deep. It was like a small mine going up. Trench boards, Sandbags and pieces of Dug Outs all going up in the air together. Quite a sight although unpleasantly near.

There is a big strafe tonight. All the windows rattle and shake as I write to you. I have just been out to look at it. Quite a fine sight when viewed from a safe distance.

 With Best Love. Yours ever, Jack.

Apl 12 1916

My dear Phyllis,

Many thanks for your letter of the 7th received this morning.

You have indeed been having a lively time with the Zepps haven't you. Must be a terrible bother having the buzzers going every night. Though I agree with you it does much for everyone's feelings, when our guns do a little firing at them. It must have been rotten before when you had to sit still and let the Zepps bombard you with impunity.

The bursting of shells at night is rather a fine sight isn't it. I hope they won't come again. These expeditions of the Bosche to Hull make me feel quite anxious about you.

I am leaving here tomorrow and going back to the Batt. Not for long, but until the guns arrive. I am only about 4 men off leave now. I am looking forward to it very much. I want to see you very much. It seems such a long time since I left England, Home and Beauty.

There has been in fact still is quite a big battle going on near me. I can view it though in perfect safety.

 Yours ever, Jack.

Apl 14th 1916

My dear Phyllis,

I have got back to Battalion again from my Course of Instruction.

We start for the trenches again tomorrow, but our Company is to be in reserve, although it will mean I suppose working parties every night.

We have just been re-inforced by some further drafts of Officers. One of them a Capt. from the third line (South Dalton) will have to remove two of his spots and so revert to a 2nd Liet. Strange are the ways of the army aren't they.

All leave I much regret to say has been stopped. Most annoying when I was getting so near isn't it. I think — just between you and me — there is going to be a *big* do here shortly. I do not think that we shall go over the parapet, the men are not anything like fit for it.

I hope that you won't be worried anymore than you can help. I have really had some truly extraordinary escapes since I have been out here. Some men get out almost at once. It's luck or fate I suppose.

No more now. With Love. Yours ever, Jack.

Apl 16 1916

My dear Phyllis,

Many thanks for your letter received yesterday.

We are up in the trenches again, a long way from the firing line you will be pleased to hear. The men have Dug Outs but we live in a farm house still used by its original inhabitants. It is quite a quaint old place. We have a room with a huge fireplace in it in which we burn immense logs. Quite the old-fashioned style you see. I sleep on a bed made up of trusses of straw. Much better than sleeping on the stone floor believe me.

I am writing this epistle to you sitting underneath a big tree so you can tell the weather is pretty good.

You appear to have been doing great things at the Hospital. I always said you would be a success in that way didn't I.

I fear there is no prospect of leave starting for some time. One chap when he heard it was stopped smashed all the furniture in his billet. I only cursed profusely.

Well I must close now so I will wish you Goodnight. With Love.

Yours ever, Jack.

Apl 23 1916

My dearest Phyl,

Very many thanks for your letters and parcel which I received this morning after we had got back from the trenches [*to Kemmel Shelters*]. The tinned fruit and cream I am sure will prove most excellent. The cake I have already devoured as owing to circumstance I had had no food for 20 hours at least.

I think that without exaggeration I have had quite the worst time I have ever experienced, although we only had 3 days and 2 nights in the front line.

To begin with our artillery smashed up some gas cylinders in the German trenches and the gas came over to us. About 16 men got gassed not badly. It also went down the Bosche trench and did a lot of them in. We could see them being carried away.

We have been strafed by a Bosche gun called a Minenwerfer [*literally, "mine-thrower"*] which throws a shell weighing 250lbs 3ft long 8ins in Diameter. You can

Jack and Phyllis at the tennis courts.

Jack and Phyllis at Swanland.
Jack is sporting the ribbon of his Military Cross, awarded November 1917.

Phyllis Bentham, in V.A.D. nurse's uniform, wearing her engagement ring.

Inside a ward at the Naval Hospital, Argyle Street, Hull.
Phyllis Bentham is seated, on the left.

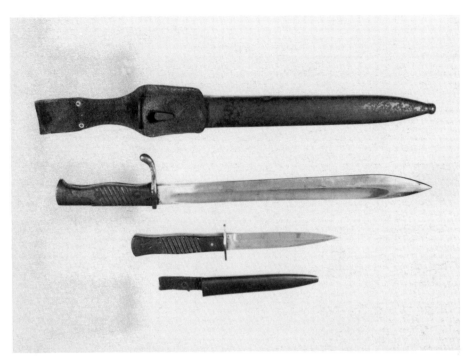

*An assortment of weapons sent home by Jack. (**See letter of 4 September 1918**).*

*Cigarette case sent by Phyllis, Christmas 1917. (**See letter of 27 December 1917**).*

47

*The pair of "tophole" prismatic field glasses which Jack picked up towards the end of the war. (**See letter of 21 September 1918**).*

Decorative item made from a German 'whizz-bang' shell case.
*(**See letter of 16 July 1917**).*

*Pewter mug of the sort Jack sent home from Walincourt. (**See letter of 20 October 1918**).*

*Various items of hardware sent home by Jack. In his letter of 26 March 1916
Jack assures Phyllis that he has rendered such items safe by
removing the explosive.*

see them coming through the air and are then able to dodge them. Yesterday they hit our trench in several places, making huge craters. They are the most frightful things I have ever struck. One of them alone killed 4 and wounded 10 men of our Company. I had only just moved from the place and was blown along the trench by the wind of it.

I unfastened the coat of one of the wounded. He said he was dying but I told him not to be such a damned fool. Almost before I got his coat undone he gave a sigh and his head went back. His wound was in his leg. He must have died through shock I imagine. I suppose that this is possible. Two men also were struck deaf and dumb. Another lost control of himself and climbed over the parados and hared off across country. He was killed up at the support line. One of my men when he saw the wounded and dead lying as they were all over the place ran down the communication trench and has not been seen since.

You may gather from this that we have been going through the mill a bit recently. Thank Heaven that we are out again now and that we are going out to rest at last. I do not think that I shall ever forget Easter Saturday afternoon in 1916.

It has rained here for days on end. Coming down from the trenches last night I was waist deep in places. I wonder what kind of Easter you are having.

There is a very pleasant story about now that leave is about to start again. I hope so for it is all you live for out here.

I went to a Wesleyan Service here today and quite enjoyed it. Just fancy me becoming religious. Not so bad as that believe me.

It is a strange business about the Russians landing in France isn't it. I wonder if it will make any difference to us.

That charm you gave me is still hung round my neck with a piece of dirty string. I am sure that it has done its work very well so far.

Your photo reposes in one of the breast pockets of my tunic and is still in excellent condition. I would not be without it for worlds.

With Best Love. Yours ever, Jack.

26 Apl 1916

My dear Phyllis,

Many thanks for your letter which I received yesterday. We move away from here I believe in a couple of days time.

I had a hot bath here today at a Convent and was ministered unto by a cool nun. They seem to be quite a decent lot. Leave starts again tomorrow so that there is hope of me getting home.

Our artillery smashed some more of the Bosche gas cylinders and from the O.P. it is reported that a Company of them were carried away. The wind of course being the wrong way for them — blowing the gas back on themselves. Splendid isn't it to do the Bosche over with their own gas.

With Best Love. Yours ever, Jack.

Apl 27 1916

My dear Phyllis,

We are actually going out to rest tomorrow [*between Fletres and Caestre, some way west of the line*] and shall march off from here early in the morning.

Everyone is naturally very pleased at the prospect of one month away from the sound of the guns. I find that one's nerves get worse week by week. I went to the hospital today to see some of my men who have been struck deaf and dumb. Rather a rotten kind of thing. I hope they will recover.

Something quite exciting has just happened since I started this letter to you. The Adjutant has just come in and told us that two Germans have just given themselves up, informing us that the Bosche intend to let their gas off at the first opportunity. Pray heaven that they do not do it tonight. Because if they do we shall have to go up to reinforce the firing line. This would be a most expensive expedition as they always shell lines of communications very heavily. We shall have to sleep in our boots and clothes though which is rather a bore.

Well I must close now so Phyl Goodnight.

With Best Love. Yours ever, Jack.

P.S.   Since I wrote the above I hear (rumour only) that a Company of Bosche have given themselves up to a Batt. in our Brigade. I hope it's true.

Apl 29 1916

My dear Phyllis,

We were not called out on account of the gas. The Germans made an attack with it on our right. But as we had been warned they were not caught napping.

Yesterday we had a long march, each step taking us further away from the firing line. The country is very fine. I am billeted at a farm house but only have my meals there. I sleep and spend most of my time in a tent. We can just hear the guns faintly in the distance.

We crossed the frontier into France yesterday. You can notice the difference in the people and the style of the houses almost immediately.

Well no more now. Yours ever, Jack.

May 1st 1916

My dear Phyllis,

Many thanks for your letter of the 26th which I received this morning. I do not understand how it is you have not received any letters from me for a long time. After working it out, a letter appears to take nine days to get to England while a letter takes only 4 days to get out here. It's beyond me completely.

I was sleeping peacefully in my tent this morning, when suddenly my servant rushed in at 3 am and bawled those mystic words "Stand to" at me. I at once rushed into some things, put on my equipment and ran to parade. All the men were out too in fighting order. You cannot imagine how strange we look in our steel helmets (I wear one too).

It appears that the Bosche had made a gas attack on the trenches we last occupied. We were called up to make the Counter attack across the open and take them back.

From the first alarm we had to be on the road in an hour. The word to move however did not come and so we stood on ready to go at once. The waiting was rather boring especially as we knew what a stiff job we had to do if we were ordered to advance. The Battalion would be very small when we came out of it. Strange feeling to know that before sunset half or more of us would be wiped out.

However at 10 am we received a wire which greatly to our relief told us to resume our normal duties. [*According to the Diary the orders had been cancelled at Battalion level at 4.00 am.*] The most pleasing bit of news I have ever received. I don't think there is much danger of us having to go up now Thank Heaven.

These riots in Dublin [*The Easter Rising*] are absolutely ----- (I'll refrain from using bad language here). They are a lot of Dirty Dogs. I wish we could go there for a week or so we would give them Hell and no mistake about it. What they want is bombarding with a 12″ or 15″ gun that would soon bring 'em to their senses. Blow the whole place to bits and them with it. I don't suppose they know what war is. You don't play the game of war with velvet gloves on. People at home I fear are too much afraid of killing people, even the enemies of their own country. Don't you agree. Perhaps you will think me bloodthirsty and rather horrid, but I've seen a good deal during my visit to this benighted country.

But to change to a more cheerful subject, Phyllis, I expect to get leave soon. Unfortunately however I shall only get 6 days instead of 10. Four clear days at home. This new order has just been issued. Rotten I call it. But it would be worth coming all the way home even for 24 hours to see you and the people again.

Well Goodbye for the present "Old Girl".

With Best Love. Yours ever, Jack.

May 2 1916

My dear Phyllis,

I was very pleased to receive your letter this morning.

I have just finished a course of bombing since until I take over the Stokes gun I am to be Company Bomb Officer. We had a sweep on a bomb throwing contest today, which I am pleased to say I won. Leave is still carrying on alright, so that mine may come before long.

I am afraid I shall look a very tramp-like looking person when I come back. I must buy some more things in town when I come through.

I see by today's paper that the Rebels at Dublin have surrendered. I hope they all get what they deserve. Don't you agree with me?

We play a good lot of footer every afternoon as there are no parades at all. I visited all the neighbouring towns round here in search of amusement. As yet I have not found any. In times of peace it must be a very dull kind of life in these market towns. All the best people I suppose must have cleared off long ago. I don't blame them with the Germans so near.

The room I am writing this letter in was once occupied by a German Officer. The inhabitants speak quite well of them although they are French. They do [*not*] seem to have committed any brutalities. I think that nearly all the horrible things they did may be put down almost to one Corps. Don't think though that I have any love for them. They are all a lot of Devils but some have at any rate a slight idea of playing the game. I am glad to hear that you have not been visited by Zepps for a bit. These raids so frequently on Hull and District made me most uneasy.

With Love. Yours ever, Jack.

May 7th 1916

My dear Phyllis,

Many thanks for your letter which I received yesterday. We are still in rest and I don't think that there is much chance of us being taken out of it now until our allotted time has expired.

I set out from here this morning (Sunday) at 7.40 am with a party of 100 men. We were met by motor buses and taken to our destination. The work proved to be laying a Railway Line, which we carried out with some success.

It is astonishing what different kinds of jobs you have to do one time and other. I am fast becoming a "Jack of all trades".*

I go off tomorrow to undergo another Course of the Stokes Gun. The School is not far away so that I shall be able to get back to my present billet every night. My Battery will be eventually the 150/2 Trench Mortar Battery.

There are always a great many rumours about you know. The two most prevailing at the moment are that we are going to East Africa — the other is that we are to be put on to build a new Railway line "somewhere in France". We shall end I have not the slightest doubt back in the trenches again as usual.

That last gas attack did not do any harm to those holding the line; but the civilians and cattle got it hot. You can see cows and other beasts dead all over. The crops and trees have suffered also; some of them look absolutely bleached and colourless. The Germans do use some "Devilish" things to attain their ends. This time however they only wasted gas at least as far as we are concerned.

I am very pleased to see from the papers that the Irish Rebels are getting treated as they deserve. I was rather anxious lest they should let them off lightly. In olden days they would not have tried them at all simply shot them first and then found out if they were guilty afterwards. This method certainly has its advantages.

There is another story about that leave is going to be stopped again on the 29th of this month. I expect to get away on the morning of the 21st though at 3.30 am arriving in Hull at 10 pm in the same day. Whether I shall get away on the day I have mentioned I cannot say of course for a certainty, but I think there is quite a chance of my so doing.

Well no more now Phyl, hoping to see you soon I bid you Goodnight.

With Best Love. Yours ever, Jack.

*[*According to the diary of the Divisional Mortar Battalion, the mortar crews at the time were engaged in training in a variety of skills including Gun Drill, Telephony, Signalling, Erecting Mortar Positions, Squad Drill, Musketry – hence the remark about being a Jack-of-all-trades.*]

May 11th 1916
My dear Phyllis,

Many thanks for your letter I received two days ago. I have been quite busy recently, what with Courses and one thing and another.

I went and saw Norman again the other day. He was over here to lunch today and as I am Mess President I gave him a good spread and sent him away full.

I celebrate today my first year's Commissioned Rank. I was gazetted last year on the 11th May. On conclusion after the war I get 183 days pay and allowances for it and every succeeding year 83 days.

It seems rather extraordinary that I may be home and see *you* in about 11 days time. My life at home before I came out seems to have been lived in a previous existence.

Well no more now.

With Love. Yours ever, Jack.

May 17 1916
My dear Phyllis,

Many thanks for your letter and also the parcel containing cakes which arrived safely.

I have been on a gas course today. After having put on my helmet I was put in a Dug Out and the gas turned on. You felt a curious sensation, in the nose and mouth, but nothing else unpleasant. The gas was very thick. Three or four breaths would be sufficient to put you beyond all earthly troubles. All your buttons become entirely black. I have of course had gas in the trenches, but this was very much stronger.

Three Bosche aeroplanes were brought down here the other day. Quite a good piece of work don't you think.

We must have a good time together when I come and do *everything*.

Best Love. Yours ever, Jack.

OFFICERS CLUB, BOULOGNE-SUR-MERE May 29th 1916
[*Jack's home leave is now over; he is on his way back to the front.*]
My dear Phyllis,

I have arrived here safe and sound after crossing the Channel. It was very calm and quite a pleasant trip. We all wore life belts though in case we were sunk by the Germans.

I go on up the line at 7 pm tonight, which means I shall arrive at some frightful hour, about 1 am. I am not looking forward with any pleasure I assure you to another night in the train. They are very feeding [*sic*].

The French time is still the same as before. All our watches had to be put back 1 hour. I have lost two hours of leave that way.

I have tried to alter the tone of this letter but I can't do it. I cannot forget that when I am writing to you it is to the girl I love.

I thought when I was at home it would be hard to write to you in a cold although friendly way; but now I am out here again I find that it is impossible. I shall be just the same whatever happens.

No more now. With Best Love. Yours ever, Jack.

150/1 Trench Mortar Btty. 2nd Army. BEF. May 30 1916
My dear Phyllis,

I have at last arrived at my destination [*near Locre*].

We left the port where we landed at 7 pm and were thrown out at Railhead at 3 am. It was raining in torrents when we arrived. I went into the town and tried to get put up for the night at an Hotel. I made many attempts to waken them but was not successful.

I then went and climbed into a Motor lorry where I tried to make myself comfortable on the floor. I used my pack as a pillow. The floor being made of iron I found it somewhat hard, but soon dropped off to sleep. When you are really tired you can sleep anywhere.

I was awakened again by the rain and had to depart to the Hotel, which was now open. I had breakfast there and afterwards caught a Motor Ambulance which dropped me at the desired spot. It was quite an eventful night.

I am going up to the trenches tonight. I shall be up there [*at Lindenhoek Dug-Outs*] for about 5 weeks on end. So *please* write as much as you can won't you.

With Love. Yours ever, Jack.

May 31st 1916
My dear Phyllis,

I have settled down quite well again and feel as if I had been back for ages.

54

My new job is a most pleasant change; as you are your own boss in nearly everything.

I am sharing a Dug Out with a man called Palethorpe [*an R.F.A. Lieutenant, Officer Commanding the Trench Mortar Battery*], who is quite a decent sort. As I shall be here for a long time it will pay me to make myself really comfortable. I have brought my flea bag (sleeping bag) up to the trenches with me for the first time and am thus able to sleep in comfort.

I cannot end my letters to you with yours very sincerely and affectionately or something of that kind. It is too strange and foreign to me altogether.

Don't whatever you do doubt my feelings for you will you. They are at any rate an established fact and will remain so. Well no more now.

    With Best Love. Yours ever, Jack.

3/6/16

My dear Phyllis,

I was very pleased to receive your letter of the 29th this afternoon.

You will be on your way or perhaps may have arrived at Ilkley as I write this. You see Phyllis I *constantly think about you* and wonder what you are doing and where you are. I really think that if I had not someone at home for whom I cared for very much I'd go off my head. I have so much time out here to think and when I come home so little time to do anything at all. You know I would do anything in this world for you. That's what I feel like. Perhaps I am too keen, but that cannot be undone it simply is so. I leave it with you.

To return to the war. I strafed the Bosche this afternoon and fired 60 shells at him. I got some glorious shots and blew his trench and Dug Outs about toppingly.

There is going to be a strafe tonight on our Right, but I shall not be in it, at least I don't think so.

    With Best Love. Yours ever, Jack.

June 6 1916

My dear Phyllis,

Many thanks for your post card which I received today.

We had a big strafe on here the other night but I came through it without any mishap. I don't think that there is anything of note that has happened here. Just the general routine of war.

I should be very glad to know what you feel about me and things generally. Don't think that I wish to rush you into anything. I have your friendship I know, but have I anything else? Sometimes I rather think so, but I really don't know either. Uncertainty is terrible as you naturally enough realise. It is awfully worrying for both of us. I wish we could get it settled, don't you?

    With Best Love. Yours ever, Jack.

8/6/16

My dear Phyllis,

I was very pleased to receive your delightfully lengthy letter. I do not think that you have ever before been so fluent in your letters as now. Please continue as they are very nice. The parcel you sent me I shall no doubt receive in a few days, although as you so truly remark the contents may be somewhat stale. Nevertheless they will be much enjoyed.

I am very interested about Norman and Doris also about the ring which I am glad to hear is a nice one. What kind do you prefer? You must really let me know.

I still wear your charm on which I put a great deal of faith. It has at any rate served me in good stead so far.

I hope it will bring me good fortune in more ways *than one*. What I mean here you will easily guess.

I will not ask you the same old question in this letter as I have done so very fully in the preceding ones. You will I feel confident let me know the moment you arrive at any definite conclusion, whatever it may be. You may think to yourself "How impatient he is" or "What a worry". But I guess you will understand all right. I quite realise what Mr. Bentham said about waiting, and think it is a very sound idea.

But supposing you don't care for me now when I am in danger of my life every day and night when will you. Don't think that I am taking a mean advantage on account of the war; nothing is farther from my thoughts. I am trying to be perfectly frank with you.

You know Phyllis I care for you enough to wish you to be happy above all things though it may mean the reverse of happiness for me; which I *trust it won't*. As I am only human just as you are.

Well no more for the present, Yours ever, Jack.

10/6/16

My dear Phyllis,

Many thanks for your last letter which I received this afternoon.

The Palethorpe I mentioned to you comes I believe from Newcastle. He is about 27 years old. I wonder if he is the same. He has been relieved by another Officer called Price.

The Bosche had a little evening hate a few moments ago and put some big shells quite close to our Dug Out. It takes it all its time to stop a bullet let alone anything else. They seem to think that the Dug Outs round here are just the place to hurl scrap iron about.

I had a bath yesterday not in the usual civilised manner but in a big shell hole. It is very strange what circumstance one can get accustomed to.

The rats here are very bold. Last night as I was on the point of dropping off to sleep one of them ran right across my face. I don't mind them running over my legs but when it comes to your face it's too much. There are limits. There is man outside now with his shirt off picking "chats" off from the same. He appears to be having good sport. I expect you will be at home when you receive this.

I wonder when I shall get out of these trenches. I shall shortly have been longer in them than ever before. I must try and establish a record. Time hangs very heavy on your hands, as we are not always strafing. If you have any Magazines lying about that you have done with I wish you would send them to me.

With Best Love. Yours ever, Jack.

12 June 1916

My dear Phyllis,

Many thanks for your long letter which I received today. I notice from the date on it that it has taken 5 days to cross.

Everybody as you say seems very anxious to get you engaged don't they. It is really rather amusing. I hope that you will follow their wishes in the matter as soon as you can. Incidentally mine too.

The battle you talk of is still going on and we naturally feel the effects of it. There is a big strafe going on now on our left.* If it spreads we shall be in for a hot time I have not the slightest doubt.

I had some very narrow escapes the other day from the Bosche Minenwerfer shells (Trench Mortars shell weight 200 lbs). I gave them H-ll for it with my guns afterwards though which was rather pleasing.

My nerves I fear are not quite so strong as they once were. But I can go on for many many months yet.

I am still in the trenches of course and see different battalions of infantry come in and go out again.

I burn your letters as you wish. I must close now for the present hoping to hear from you as frequently as possible. (Long one if you can).

With Best Love. Yours ever, Jack.

*[*The "big strafe" was probably the massive German attack – largely unsuccessful –on the Ypres salient, launched on 2 June.*]

16 June 1916
My dear Phyllis,

Many thanks for your letters and parcel which I received today. The toffee you sent is delightful and the magazine just the thing I required. I am afraid that I have not written you for a few days but I have not been feeling very fit recently; although I am much better now. My prolonged stay in the trenches is without doubt the cause.

A fairly large piece of shell hit me in the back the other day and gave me quite a rotten bruise. But it was not coming fast enough to go in far.

My luck you see is still very good but nevertheless I'll touch wood as I write this. Luck is everything out here as it is also of course at home.

I am afraid that there is not much news in this letter but there is not any to give you.

Well I must close now ending as usual but not without significance.

With Best Love. Yours ever, Jack.

17/6/16
My dear Phyllis,

I am just dropping you a line to tell you that I am still in the land of the living.

Last night we retired to rest about 1130 pm. We were awakened at 1230 am by a tremendous Bosche bombardment. I must say I was absolutely taken off my guard. The whole place was alive with shells. A big shell (an 8″) fell near my dug out so I doubled across to the mess and sat with them. Two Whizzbangs hit the top of the Dug Out and two 8″ burst 5 yards away. The Dug Out I was in is on the slope of a hill well down behind the crest. You could hear the shells come over the crest, skim the top of the Dug Out and burst beyond. It is marvellous that we were not killed a hundred times over.

The Bosche also let loose the gas (Chlorine) which came over into the front line in a very few seconds giving our men very little time to put their helmets on. Many I regret to say were not able to do so in time.*

I personally was not up in the front line but quite a fair way back. The German barrage came right through our Dug Outs, so we had a very hot time although not very much trouble with gas. Our Battalion has lost at least 70 to 80 casualties, among whom 2 Lt Carlton killed 2 Lt Gresham wounded 2 Lt Sutton wounded Liet R.R. Brown (second day in trenches) shell shock and many others slightly gassed.

About 4 am the wounded began to arrive and also the dead and dying. To see men dying of gas poisoning is most horrible thing I have ever seen. Some men were blown in two and had to be brought down in sand bags, only bits left.

The dead are still lying outside the Dressing station in rows waiting for burial. A very gruesome sight believe me.

The trenches too are much knocked about and all over drops and splashes and pints of blood can be seen. War is indeed a horrible thing. I tried to get up to the firing line during the strafe but the shelling was too hot and life too sweet to throw it away without cause.

One can still detect the gas; not at all bad in small doses.

The Germans also got something to go on with.

I am very glad that I am able to write you this letter. Last night I never thought I should be able to write you another.

With Best Love. Yours ever, Jack.

*[The Bn. Diary states: "Gas cloud very thick and lasted about 20 minutes. Few casualties were caused at first but the after-effects proved fatal in several cases." Total casualties amount to 89, plus 6 others killed by shell-fire.]

20/6/16

My dear Phyllis,

Many thanks for your parcel containing the books and socks. It is very good of you to send so much in the reading line. I have given the socks to the men and they seem very pleased with them. I am out of the line now and doing a course of Instruction. I should not be in this but the Officer detailed has become a casualty, so I had to go. Rather a bore really but it can't be helped. I gave you a little description of the show the other day in my previous letter, but I see that there are a few lines in the paper about it today.

My nerves were very much shaken by the last show. Quite the closest thing to death I have had yet I think. Nights like those leave their traces on you in a most marked manner which after all is not very extraordinary.

I hope that you will stop worrying yourself now. You will drive yourself into an early grave if you are not careful.

Can't you talk over your troubles with someone. Always a great relief to share them with somebody else.

With Love. Yours ever, Jack.

27/6/16

My dear Phyllis,

I received your letters of the 18th and 20th this morning. Very many thanks for the cigarettes, they are the kind I like best.

The Officer of another Battalion who took over from me when I left the line has been blown to pieces with 4 of his men in my old position. Nothing left of them at all.

During the time I was there nothing the Bosche fired ever came very close. I am very lucky I think.

I am still on the Course and when you get accustomed to it it is not so bad. Safe enough anyway, which is no small consideration in these times.

The most trying thing though is getting up for Physical jerks before breakfast, always a most depressing moment. I am afraid that I have not a great deal to say this time but there is not much doing.

    With Love. Yours ever, Jack.

1/7/96
My dear Phyllis,

Many thanks for your letter of the 27th received this morning.

I was indeed surprised to hear of Harold coming out. I am very pleased in one way that he is coming but rather sorry that he is in another. I know what a rotten job the infantry is out here.

I have not seen Norman since last Sunday but will go over and see him tomorrow.

I am still on the course. I shall be going back to the trenches next week; which is rather unfortunate but can't be helped. I am glad to hear that you are feeling more cheerful. It is no use getting depressed you know it does no good at all. I have given it up long ago.

I am going to have dinner tonight in a little town about 3 miles away from here with a chap called Spooner. It is strange how far one will walk for a good feed.

    With Best Love. Yours ever, Jack.

July 5th 1916
My dear Phyllis,

I have your letter of the 30th this morning in which I was very interested.

Often I could write you pages of stuff which I am sure would interest you but caution and the censor forbid it. This makes my letters dull I fear as there is little else in the way of news to write about.

At one time I used to write and tell you every day how much I cared for you. You will have noticed that since I have returned from leave I have not been so warm in my letters to you except perhaps at the end of them. Do not think for a moment that I have altered in my feelings for you. But I have made up my mind not to write those kind of letters to you in any way at all until you give me the *right* to do so; feeling then that the love I send to you will be returned.

I hope Phyl that you do not misunderstand me. I have I think all at once become very much older. I shall still of course write to you in the ordinary way as often as usual and although you only have my word for it I shall not change.

I am going into the trenches on Thursday and will write you again from there.

Please let me know that you do not misunderstand what I have written above.

    Yours ever, Jack.

7/7/16
My dear Phyllis,

Very many thanks for your letter today.

I am afraid that you may think the letter I wrote to you before this somewhat strange; in fact I myself don't know quite how I managed to write it.

But please Phyllis do not mis-understand me. I don't wish you to be worried as you are. Life is too short to be worried like that. When I come home on leave I must talk things over with you.

Don't think I want to rush you into anything that you are not quite sure about, nothing is farther from my thoughts.

I have been up the line today and have never seen such rotten trenches in my life before.

There is a raid coming up shortly in which I shall be up to support. Not altogether a pleasant prospect.

I am at present 2nd in Command of the 150th T.M.Btty and if I keep it I can see another star coming along; which will be very pleasant.

I have not seen Harold yet he is still down at the base.*

Yours ever, Jack.

*[Harold arrived at the front 11.7.16 and was assigned to 'D' Company]

15/7/16
My dear Phyllis,

Thanks ever so much for your letter of the 9th received yesterday.

I had quite a big strafe on yesterday and fired a large number of shells. The Bosche nearly found me out quite a number of times and put his bombs and fishtails too close for comfort.

Harold was up in the line and had his first experience of a Bosche afternoon hate. He has quite enjoyed himself so far, but when the freshness has worn off he will feel very different.

There are very few of the original Officers who were with the Battalion when I came out first. It makes one feel quite veteran. I hope to be relieved today and get out of the line.

I must also get a bath as I have found several creatures on me. Most unpleasant really.

Yours ever, Jack.

I am very glad that you do *not* misunderstand me and think I am cooling off or something of that kind, because it is not so by any means. It is no use getting agitated about it.

July 19th 1916
My dear Phyllis,

Many thanks for your letter of the 14th received today.

I heartily agree with you about wishing I could come home and instruct others in Trench Warfare. But I fear there is not the slightest prospect of it. What a good time I should have if I did.

You say that I am becoming quite a Knut; what about yourself. You are doing very well at the hospital aren't you. I always said that you would be a great success there now didn't I?

By the way I got hit by a bit of shell in the left hand the other day. Quite slight though as I never bothered to go to the M.O. Never felt it until after everything had finished. I put some Iodine on. It doesn't half smart then.

Yours ever, Jack.

20 JY FIELD SERVICE POST CARD
I am quite well
Letter follows at first opportunity.

22/7/16

My dear Phyllis,

I have unfortunately had to come up to the line again before it was my turn to do so, owing to the Officer being killed and seven men wounded. This was all done by one shell. Rather a bad business altogether.

Things are quite lively just now, too much so for my liking.

The East Yorks [appear] to have been having quite a rough time losing Ashby* killed Vivian and Webster wounded.

Harold I am very glad to say has been sent on a Course. So he will be all right for the time being.

I wonder how much longer this war is going to last. A large number of people out here give it a very short time now. I hope that they are right.

These trenches are full of all kind of creatures. One gets bitten very badly at times. The other Officer of our lot who is working with me at present is very sensitive in regard to them. He takes his shirt off about once every hour and has a most glorious hunt, which I must confess generally ends in a kill.

No more now. Yours ever, Jack.

*[Ashby was out on a night patrol and failed to respond to a challenge from one of his own listening posts, whereupon they threw a bomb, killing him.]

25/7/16

My dear Phyllis,

I was indeed pleasantly surprised to receive two letters from you together the other day. You may think that I have been rather a long time in answering them, but we have been rather badly strafed the last few days and consequently I have not felt like writing.

I am glad that you are still senior pro at the Hospital. I hope that you will not descend again when the other nurse returns. It must be much more interesting.

All being well I hope to get out of the trenches on Thursday next, as we have managed to get another officer to join the Suicide Club.

We are always getting fresh men from the Battalions now to join us; as our own become casualties so quickly. [4 new second lieutenants had arrived on the 22nd, making 5 in the space of three days].

I hope that you are not working yourself to death you must not really.

No more now. Yours ever, Jack.

B.E.F. July 29th 1916

My dear Phyllis,

Very many thanks for your good wishes and also for the cigarettes cakes and magazine. I received them yesterday by the same post. What an age it appears to be since my last birthday. I hope that I may celebrate my next one at home in "blighty".

Elsie Smith and Jim [Carmichael] have soon fixed it up haven't they. I must say I was greatly surprised to hear that they had been married at such short notice.

I saw Harold yesterday and he seemed very pleased that they had brought it off. So everything is alright in that direction.

I am out of the trenches now. The other Officer who shares my tent was taken away this morning, having German measles. I rather think I have got them too. It will be a blessing in disguise.

61

Things up at the line are very active nowadays. A German 5.9 shell burst within 10 yds of us the other day in the open. It gave me rather a shock. But I was too near to get damaged in any way,

I have become a great fatalist. Things rather tend to make me so.

No more now. Yours ever, Jack.

1/8/16

My dear Phyllis,

Many thanks for your letter of 27th received yesterday.

I have really extremely little news of any sort. I have a canvas hut now which is fastened together entirely with straps and buckles. So that when it gets really hot —you simply undo all the straps and the sides simply swing open. A most effective method and saves you from getting stuffy.

I am glad to say that I have not as yet caught measles. A large number of spots have made an appearance on my face and arms but they are all bites from various kinds of creatures.

All this sun is making me look like a Red Indian.

Cheers. Yours ever, Jack.

B.E.F. 9/8/16

My dear Phyllis,

Very many thanks for your two letters of the 2nd and 8th and also for the parcel of cakes which arrived safe and sound.

I am very sorry to hear that Mr. Bentham is still ill. I hope that he will soon be well again. I am out of the trenches now and billeted in a farm house many miles from the line, in fact almost out of the sound of the guns. [*Probably at Thieushoek, to which the 4th EYR marched on 7.8.16.*] I have a great big room on the ground floor with a tremendous fire place. Six people can stand in it with ease. Must be rather a job to get fuel for it I should say.

I marched the men here yesterday and a very hot one it was. All the men push handcarts with our guns in tow. Most exhausting work at 12 Noon in this weather. I should never have got them here at all if it had not been for beer, which I gave them in large quantities. Wonderful how it brings them along.

Yours ever, Jack Oughtred.

1916: (2) THE SOMME

[The 4th East Yorks now marched south. After a week of preliminary bombardment of German positions the long awaited Somme offensive had started on 1 July. This was the infamous occasion on which 20,000 British lives were lost in a single day. The battle was to last into November, and the movement of the East Yorks to the battle area represented one of many drafts of reinforcements as the losses mounted.]

12/8/16

My dear Phyllis,

I have great pleasure in telling you that I have got my second "Pip" and am now a 1st Lieut. This of course is only while I am attached to the Trench Mortar Battery. But nevertheless it is quite pleasing in many ways. We are not in the same place as we were when I wrote to you before. But we are having a very quiet time in the heart of the country. There is a most picturesque chateau here although it is going to rack and ruin — Ghost and everything complete. The greater portion of it does not appear to have been lived in for many years.

Harold is not far away but I do not quite know where Norman is at the moment, but I expect we shall all meet before long. The weather is still frightfully hot and the roads are inches thick with dust.

Hoping you are keeping well.

Yours ever, Jack.

[This letter is probably written at Vacquerie, just outside Bernaville, where the Bn marched 10.8.16 on its way down to the Somme; Jack refers to this journey, which was by train as far as Doullens, in a letter dated 11.4.17.]

17/8/16

My dear Phyllis,

I was very pleased and much relieved to hear from you yesterday.

I saw from the papers that there had been an extensive air Raid [*resulting in nine deaths*] and was thus naturally rather anxious to know how you had got on.

It is rotten of them dropping bombs in Swanland and neighbourhood. You must have had quite an anxious time. It is rather strange that you who live so far away from the fire of shells should have explosive hurled at you from the clouds. The Bosche does not in any respect fight like a gentleman does he?

Guess who I saw today "Jim" Batey [?]; the former Hessle Wesleyan pastor. Hal Seed, Harold and I are going to dine with him. I am staying just now in an estaminet; which is most convenient, in many respects. I am attaining great fame as a Mess President and turn out some excellent dinners in spite of at times rather adverse conditions. Norman I might add shines conspicuously in that post also.

I am glad to hear that Mr. Bentham has been able to get up again. I hope he will soon be well.

Yours ever, Jack.

17/8/16

My dear Phyllis,

I am having quite a good time now. Just at present I am staying in a chateau [*at Millencourt, near Albert*] which is in fairly good condition since the family to which it belongs still live in it. Madame la Marquise apologised most profusely because she could not give us all beds.

The General's quarters in the place are splendid. All the walls covered with tapestry and with marble pillars statues etc. All the rooms have that old fashioned French furniture in, covered with brocade. I occupy a kind of superior box room. I have quite made up my mind to be a Brigadier in the next war.

I saw Norman this morning on his horse controlling his mules wagons etc. I passed him in our motor and felt a tremendous nut.

Yours ever, Jack.

23/8/16

My dear Phyllis,

Many thanks for your letter of the 26th received yesterday.

I must thank you for your congratulations although I don't know about deserving it. I told my O.C. that as I was the only remaining member of the Battery it was about time I got something. Two days later the "Star" arrived.

I have just seen a Bosche prisoner. He was quite young about 18 I should say. He seemed to be very pleased with himself as of course he has good cause to be. His troubles for this war are over at any rate.

The King was not far away from me but I did not see him although Norman only missed him by a few minutes.

Well no more now. Yours ever, Jack.

28/8/16

My dear Phyllis,

Many thanks for your two letterrs which I received yesterday and today respectively.

I have just heard a minute ago that Roumania has declared war on Austria. I wonder if this is true. We might get home by Christmas yet with any luck.

The great trouble here just now are the great number of flies. You wake up about 4 am to see half a dozen sitting on your nose. Most aggravating I assure you.

You appear to be having a large number of air Raids lately. I hope that none of them have been near you at all. They must be rather unpleasant. Shelling of any kind is always worse by night I think.

I am afraid that I have no news much that I can tell you. We are not in the trenches in fact we are many miles behind the line. The longer we stay here the better I shall be pleased.

No more now. Yours Jack Oughtred.

3/9/16

My dear Phyllis,

Many thanks for your letter of 28th received this morning.

By the way Basil Hallam was in the same balloon with my cousin when he was killed. Both jumped off from the car in parachutes but Hallam's did not work.* I agree with you Phyl that the news in regard to Roumania ois the best we have had for many a long day.

The question often comes into my mind what on earth shall I do when the war is *finished*. Peace of course and all the pleasures thereof will be delightful and perhaps it would be wise to leave the question of the future to look after itself until it more immediately concerns one.

Anyway I look forward to giving you a good time too and having one myself apre le guerre finis — in spite of Miss Grundy.

No more now. Yours, Jack

*[*There is no information available to shed light on the ballooning incident.*]*

FIELD SERVICE POST CARD dated 1/9/16, post marked 4/9/16
    I am quite well.
Letter follows at first opportunity.

FIELD SERVICE POST CARD dated 10/9/16, post marked 12/9/16
    I am quite well.
Letter follows at first opportunity.

12/9/16
My dear Phyllis,
    Many thanks for your letters and parcel.
I have been in the line again since I last wrote to you and had quite a rotten time.
I am sorry to hear that you have had another Zepp Raid. Anyway you will be out of their area at Buxton I should think. I hope that you are having a good time there. We are very busy indeed here.

The cakes you sent were very nice and as I had been round the front line this morning and arrived back too late for lunch I made it on them.

I shall not for the next few days be able to send you anything but Field Postcards. Don't worry will you I still have your charm. It will pull me through.

    Yours Jack

FIELD SERVICE POST CARD, dated 13/9/16 post marked 14/9/16
    I am quite well.
Letter follows at first opportunity.

FIELD SERVICE POST CARD, dated 14/9/16, post marked 15/9/16
    I am quite well.
Letter follows at first opportunity.

FIELD SERVICE POST CARD dated 16/9/16, post marked 18/9/16
    I am quite well.
Letter follows at first opportunity.

19/9/16
My dear Phyllis,
    Many thanks for your two letters I have received in the course of the last few days. I am very pleased that I am able to say that I am still in the land of the living and out of the line for a few days.

I can't tell you what I have been in; but I will tell you all about it sometime. I was

65

buried by a shell amongst other things and had quite an unpleasant time.* My O.C. and I were both complimented by the General for the work we had done. So that you may see me with a decoration yet. I don't think.

Glad to hear you are having a good time. Wish I was with you.

No more news. Yours Jack.

*[*The action referred to here was the Battle of Shelter Wood. The 4th had marched to Shelter Wood, then to Mametz Wood, which had been captured early in July. There followed a three-day artillery barrage, after which the battle began in earnest on 14 September. High Wood was a notable gain, as was the village of Martinpuich. Total of casualties for the 4th Bn East Yorks, alongside whom Jack's T.M.B. fought, was 32 dead, 218 missing or wounded. Rollitt, with whom Jack had travelled from England, was among the wounded.*]

21/9/16

My dear Phyllis,

I am pleased to say that all goes well with me just now. You will have seen from the papers that we have been "over the bags". It was very exciting at the commencement but very rotten afterwards.

You will be able to see from the local papers the officers and men who have been wounded etc. Rollitt was hit do you know him. Harold is alright although he had a near shave.

It is rather a wonderful thing that I have come through so far. Lost a lot of men. Our T.M. did very well indeed. Every one seems to be very bucked.

Hope you are well. I suppose you will be back at Swanland now.

Yours, Jack

P.S.   The Bosche did not half run. [*They withdrew to Eaucourt l'Abbaye*]

Tommy Atkins   1.

Oh Antoinette,
I don't know yet
The way to "parley vous"
I say "bon jour"
And "Mon Amour"
But thats all I can do

Antoinette   2.

Mon brave soldat
Je suis tout ca
It is so difficile
Mais promenade
Is got so hard
I sink it tres facile

Tom A.   3.

Oh Antoinette
I'm glad I met
A girl with hairs like you
If you just walk
And do not talk
I need not parley vous

Antoinette   4.

Mon cher soldat
You "juste la"
You compris me the best
You squeeze my 'and
You understand
Ze eyes will do ze rest

22/9/16

My dear Phyllis,

All is going very well here. In fact this morning the news of the situation round here seemed too good to be true.

It is rather depressing when you go round the Battalion. There are so few of one's

66

old friends left. In our little lot we lost three Officers (gassed) and a lot of the men killed and wounded. However it makes me feel very thankful of having come through so far.

Harold was the only Officer left in his company. That tells its own tale does it not. A bullet hit his revolver and smashed it up on his belt, but saved his life undoubtedly.

I have been reported wounded many times, but so far I am not much the worse.

The men were splendid and did not half give the Bosche Hell.

Quite a number of prisoners were taken however. It was grand to see the Bosche run. I would not have missed it for worlds but do not want to do anything of that kind again. I may very shortly be able to give you some very good news in regard to myself as I believe I am in for something or other. Don't breathe a word about it though as it may not come off.

Yours Jack.

25/9/16

My dear Phyllis,

Many thanks for your letter and P.C. of the 18th received yesterday. I as you say we have had quite a bad time. I am out of the trenches now for 24 hours and then we go in again for 24 hours.

I told you about Harold's revolver saving his life didn't I. Well it now appears that a splinter of his revolver has entered his side. So he has been sent down to the Battalion transport lines.

I hear from other sources that Norman is alright. By the way don't let my people know that Harold has been hit will you.

I see that you have had another Zepp Raid last night. Got the news by wireless.

No more now. Yours Jack.

27/9/16

My dear Phyllis,

I am out of the trenches again for a brief space but shall be going back again almost immediately. We are going quite well here and succeed in driving the Bosche back frequently.

I was in a show again last night but not a very big one.

It seems years since we came here. I feel just about done up myself and I think everyone is about the same. Lack of sleep, and constant shelling can knock people up.

I have not seen or heard from Harold or Norman lately but I believe that both are safe and sound.

Yours, Jack.

28/9/16

My dear Phyllis,

I am very pleased to be able to tell you that we are out of the line for a bit now [*His Trench Mortar Battery has retired to the old German front line.*] I don't know how long for but some days at any rate. It was a very good job that we have got out as we were all on our beam ends. If we are having a bad time what kind of time is the Bosche having — a damned awful one I should say. In fact the prisoners admit they have been in Hell. They are absolutely done and have not much fight left in them. In these last few weeks I've seen enough fighting to last me the rest of my life any way. Some things I have seen I could not even tell you about. Our lot have done simply splendidly, but they have paid the price. Harold is O.C. Company again and back at duty. His wound is better although it is still bound up. How he and I have managed to come through God only knows. It is nothing short of marvellous.

I hear from Sanderson of our Battalion that Norman is alright. I am going to try and see him today.

No more now. Yours, Jack.

30/9/16
My dear Phyllis,

I was very pleased to get your letter of the 23rd today. I also received today a wire from Mother at home saying that they had had an official telegram about Harold being wounded. What a pity I did not tell them about it as he is quite fit now. And it would have saved them a bit of worry. I think I told you all about it. Do you think that you could let them know the particulars I gave you about Harold. It would ease them a lot.

Very pleased and interested to hear about the boudoir cap. I thought when I saw it for the first time that it was a good thing, but I am not a judge of lace at all.

Yours, Jack.

Oct 3. 1916
My dear Phyllis,

Many thanks for your letter of the 26th and also the parcel containing cakes etc which both arrived yesterday. It was believe me most acceptable and arrived at a most opportune moment.

I am glad that you have kept to yourself what I told you about me getting something or other. Not that I had any doubt that you would breathe a word about it if I asked you not to.

We are still out of the line [*in the vicinity of Mametz Wood*] although of course not very far away. But we are in no danger to speak of.

I was sorry to hear that the Zepps had paid you another visit. It must be a horrible bore waiting for the relief buzzer to go. [*The main alarm in Hull was a buzzer sounded at Blundell Spence's factory in Beverley Road*].

The Bosche are having a rough time now aren't they. I guess they are taking in a small way what we had early on in this war. I haven't any friendly feeling for them at all, but the reverse. But some of the poor wounded devils one feels rather sorry for in a way. After all they are only doing their duty. I bandaged one or two of them up strange to say. There were some pitiable sights. But I won't bother you with details as I wish to forget them.

It is pouring with rain here today. It's a terrible war when it's wet. I think all the strafing must cause rain as it seems to come after we have been at it a day or two.

I am living in a most palatial dug out which needless to say was not built by the British. It has a perfect kitchen range on which we have prepared many excellent meals.

All the walls are covered up with that rush matting. There is accommodation for about 10 persons to sleep and also up above a mess room with a round table; including one plush arm-chair for which there is always a lot of competition. I don't think I have any more news at the moment.

Yours, Jack.

9/10/16

My dear Phyllis,

Many thanks for your two letters of the 29th and 2nd which I received today.

I saw Harold's name in the paper. He is however quite well. He is now entitled to wear his bit of gold braid as having been once wounded.

I went to a town not very far away from here a few days ago and had a bit of a fling. It was quite pleasant to see civilisation again. I don't like these continental towns much though. I think at times I get a bit homesick. Rather foolish isn't it.

I have seen the "tanks" you mention in your letter. When we advanced [*on 15 September at Shelter Wood*] they went with us. They were really very funny, lurching over trenches. The Germans fired all kinds of things at them but did not appear to do them much harm. I have as a matter of fact been inside one. Not much room.*

They look rather like large snails with a guiding wheel behind and 4 or 5 black things sticking out of portholes in her sides. These on close examination turn out to be guns of various sorts.

Whatever they did or did not do they certainly put the wind up the Bosche.

I am very sorry to hear that those beastly Zepps are causing you so much trouble. You never seem to get "peeps" or have a little game at "shut eye" do you.

Hosts of new Officers have come out and joined us [*3 on the 4th October, 6 on the 11th, 3 more on the 13th-15th*]. We have got 3 more in our little show. All the Officers of the Brigade were gathered together for a lecture by the Brigadier today and one thing I noticed particularly was how few of them I knew.

All one's friends have gone. Some of them to Blighty others of course have not been so fortunate and will remain here always. However it's all in the days.

I don't know if I told you that the war is said to come to an end by Oct 31st. That is what an astrologer said anyway.

Yours, Jack.

*[*Jack had witnessed a historical event at Shelter Wood: tanks were used in battle for the first time on September 15, being involved in the capture of High Wood. The Diary notes that it was at 6.03 a.m. that "the first 'tank' crossed our line and proceeded northwards".*]

15/10/16

My dear Phyllis,

I have been detailed to go tomorrow the 16th to the sea side for a rest cure. I believe it will be rather cold there just now but if it keeps fine I ought to have a good time.

It is exactly a month today since we went over the bags. Time passes very quickly does it not.

There is a Church parade this morning, which we have to attend. The first one for two months I should think. I am really getting quite a heathen in my old age.

I hear from various sources that the 2/4 E. Yorks has departed to Bermuda on garrison work [*to remain there for the duration of the war*]. Rather a bon job that. Some people have all the luck. Jack Ferens had gone with them too.

Well! I don't think I have any more to say at the moment so will close.

Yours Jack.

19/10/16

My dear Phyllis,

Many thanks for your letter of the 8th received two days ago.

I have arrived at the seaside and am having quite a good time. I must see if I cannot send you some postcards. I do not think the usual restriction will apply here. We travelled down here in open cattle trucks which was not at all pleasant. At one period of the journey the train took 16 hours to do 12 miles.

There are some fairly large towns near here, one of which I have already visited. By the way the cheese was *very good*. I am not merely polite believe me.

I regret that I have no Bosche buttons; but I may be able to lay my hands on some, if not when we go up again I will get you some.

Another week I fear may see me in the trenches again. But never mind I shall have a good time here and let the future take care of itself. I will write again soon.
Yours, Jack.

Grand Court Hotel, Dieppe, 20/10/16
My dear Phyllis,

I am stopping here for a day or so having quite a good time. Nearly everything of course is shut, but it is a very pleasant change.

It seems to be very strange to be so close to England, only 3 hours journey and yet unable to go there.

It is a great change to have a decent place to live in. I have the most palatial bedroom I have ever seen. It is on the first storey and looks right onto the sea. Bathrooms, and every luxury opening off it. A great change after les trenches is it not.

I have found one or two people who can talk English thank Heaven.
Yours, Jack.

FIELD SERVICE POST CARD, dated 27/10/16, post marked 29/19/16
I am quite well.
Letter follows at first opportunity.

FIELD SERVICE POST CARD dated 31/10/16, post marked 4/11/16
I am quite well.
Letter follows at first opportunity.

B.E.F. 4/11/16
My dear Phyllis,

Many thanks for your letter of the 29th received yesterday.

I am afraid that recently I have been replying very badly to your letters. I went up the line and stopped there for 10 consecutive days and so was unable to send you more than Field P.C. unsatisfactory as they are. [*On 24.10.16 the Bn. moved up to High Wood again and were subjected to a heavy enemy bombardment*].

I am out again now thank Heaven and can once more make an attempt at getting clean again. I was indeed in a most disgusting state. I am glad to say that this time the Battery did not lose any men killed only a dozen or so wounded.

Hope you are keeping fit and not working yourself to a shadow.
Yours, Jack.

5/11/16
My dear Phyllis,

Many thanks for your letter of the 25th received safely today.

I trudged over through a sea of mud to see Norman today and had tea with him. He is in the same old place and as usual is very comfortable.

The war in the mud is a most terrible business.*

I live in a tent now. My bed is composed of a sheet of corrugated iron balanced on two biscuit tins. It is most remarkable the amount of spring it has in it.

Outside 30 yds away is a 12″ gun which when it fires blows all the pots etc. off the table. Fortunately for us it does not do a great deal of firing.

I should like very much to send you some Bosche souvenirs, but when I am up in the trenches I never bother with them although every time I get down into safety again I wish I had done.

I don't think I have any more to say so au revoir.

Yours, Jack.

*[Bn. Diary: "Trenches in deplorable condition owing to heavy rain and lack of revetting material....Experiencing great difficulty in keeping men's feet in order."]

12/11/16

My dear Phyllis,

Many thanks for your two letters of the 31st and 3rd which I have received. I do not understand how it is that you have not received any letter from me. I can only write to you when I get out of the trenches.

They are the most awful trenches I was ever in, not a single Dug Out and the water and mud up to one's waist. Of course you cannot stand that for any length of time and scores are taken away every day with Trench fever and trench feet.

We are out of there now and I hope shall be for a bit. One of the Officers in our Battery was wounded through the arm. A really beautiful blighty. [2Lt Hollis, "slightly wounded by shellfire"].

Harold has gone to Hospital. I have just heard that he is going to Blighty. I thought he was pretty bad when I saw him off on the ambulance. I am very pleased. I only wish I could get there too, but I always am so disgustingly well.*

No more now. Yours, Jack.

*[Shortly after the Battle of Shelter Wood Jack confided to Harold that he had nearly reported to the First Aid Dressing Station with shell-shock, but felt that he had shaken it off. A letter from Harold to Jack early in 1917 alludes to the incident.]

14/11/15

My dear Phyllis,

Many thanks for your letter and for the parcels of cakes and magazine for which the other chaps in the Mess wish me to send you their thanks.

You are quite right when you say that the trenches are terrible. It is due to a great extent to the awful weather.

But I hope that now we shall get out of it a bit. Even here we get shelled a bit with his long range guns. This is most annoying when you are out of the line and don't expect it. By the way I have great hopes of getting home on leave soon great isn't it.

Do you think that you could get some time off from the Hospital when I do. We must have a bit of a fling together you know must we not? As you say I am long overdue with it.

Yours, Jack.

18/11/16

My dear Phyllis,

Many thanks indeed for the cigarettes and also for the socks which arrived today. The men will be very pleased to have them as it is d--- cold.

I have not moved very far from the line since I last wrote to you but hope to make a move in that direction tomorrow. I am living in a tent at present in which it is possible to exist by having a fire. As there is no outlet for the smoke the air inside gets a bit close.

I still have hopes about leave and all being well shall see you shortly.

    Yours Jack.

18/11/16

My dear Phyllis,

I have at last reached a decent place where we can keep warm and what is more are farther from the line [*at Becourt*].*

Do you know if Harold has reached home yet? The E. Yorks have had a rough time the last few days. I saw them coming in today.

I was gazetted a full Lieut. the other day and was dated back to July 12. Rather good as they will have to make up my extra pay from that date. I always like to get cash out of the government.

    Yours, Jack.

*[*On 16.11.16, after a heavy artillery barrage, the enemy attacked and drove the 4th EYR out with heavy casualties to 'A' and 'B' Coys. The Bn. then withdrew to Becourt.*]

21/11/16

My dear Phyllis,

Many thanks for your letter of the 12th received today.

I think there is quite a prospect of me getting home about Xmas this time. My O.C. Capt Wilkinson goes on leave in two days time. He will not be back much before the 8th December. So that I shall probably come any time after the 9th. I shall take the first chance I get whether I get Xmas in it or not. Leave is so often stopped. Will *you* be *off* from the *Hospital* at Xmas do you think?

I have nothing of interest to tell you at present. We simply eat sleep and get warm by the fire and have occasional parades. Not a very thrilling programme perhaps; but believe me a very pleasant change to les trenches. Sorry I could not get any German buttons for you; but the ones I saw were not worth bothering with.

    No more now. Yours, Jack.

23/11/16

My dear Phyllis,

It is really *very sweet* of you to bother to write to me when you are feeling so groggy. But you *always* were a "*dear*" you know weren't you. I must come home and buck you up although I'm afraid it won't be for a week or so. There are many men who have not had leave for 15 months or more. You must give them a chance although in regard to leave I am a very selfish person I'm afraid.

I found a place near here where one can buy food. This is simply great; as for some time we have been existing entirely on army rations; which though good enough in their way are not exactly luxurious.

Hoping to *see you soon* I will close.

Yours, Jack.

28/11/16

My dear Phyllis,

Many thanks for the parcel which arrived today. It was most excellent and I was in some need of a magazine to read.

Have you recovered from the attack of flu you had. I hope so I'm sure.

Now that we have got fires to sit by in our huts we are all getting colds too. Funny isn't it as we never get them in the trenches no matter how wet we get. I suppose we are getting too civilised again.

Well no more now. Yours, Jack.

3/12/16

My dear Phyllis,

Many thanks for your letter of 24th which arrived yesterday.

I am now living in a real house and out of the range of the Bosche biggest guns [*probably at Contay where the Bn. is billeted in barns and houses*]. We have quite a good room for a Mess. It has one of those big fireplaces which takes up one side of the room entirely. You can sit right inside it too.

Nearly all the Officers in our show are on leave at present. There are only two of us left. I am putting mine off a bit in order to try and get Xmas in.

I am glad to hear that Harold is getting on nicely. He has had a rough time.

I think I shall leave here for England at 2 am on the morning of the 21st Dec. I shall get to Hessle sometime on the 23rd. Of course all this is liable to alteration.

Yours, Jack.

4/12/16

My dear Phyllis,

Many thanks for your letter of the 27th received yesterday.

I am sorry to hear that the Zepps have been paying you another visit. It must be rotten sitting up nearly all the night for them.

By the way I put my name in this morning for the job of Divisional Trench Mortar Officer. I wonder if I shall get it as it is one of the softest jobs I know. You will see me with Red tabs yet I don't think.

Well I must close now. Cheers, Jack.

9/12/16

My dear Phyllis,

Very many thanks for your letter and also for the parcel of socks. Please thank Mrs. Bentham for the cuffs or mittens they are very s'nice indeed. I have them on as I write.

It is very pleasing to hear that you have been complimented on looking so *fat* and well. I can quite imagine how horrified you were. I could not help laughing when I read that part of your letter.

I have great hopes of getting away myself on the 20th. I really intend to kidnap you this time and no doubt about it. You will want an armed guard to march about with you. I don't think.

73

I was very bucked to hear that the Zepps had been strafed again. It must be a topping sight to see one coming down in flames.*

I have not much news here as everything is much the same as usual.** We parade in the morning and do what we like in the afternoon. I personally never hardly parade at all as I am acting O.C. Lieut. with the powers of a Lt. Col. A very agreeable change I assure you, bossing other people about and doing no work oneself.

Yours, Jack.

*[Early in 1916, in response to the raids, a huge anti-aircraft gun had been sited on the roof of Rose, Downs & Thompson's foundry near Cannon Street station. When in subsequent raids it was observed to be silent, it was explained that it was a dummy, made of wood, and placed there to deter the Zepps. There was a huge outcry and Hull was swiftly granted four separate anti-aircraft guns around the city, each aided by a searchlight.
**For most of December the 4th EYR would remain at Contay re-fitting and re-organising, moving up to Becourt and High Wood again on 30th & 31st.]

11/12/16
My dear Phyllis,

Many thanks for your letter of the 3rd received yesterday. I think that I shall get home for Xmas. I shall leave here on the 21st and ought to manage it.

I have had rotten toothache of late and my face has swollen up disgustingly. The M.D. put on a lot of bandages today, and damn hot they were too at first. I am going to have the offending tooth or teeth removed.

Nearly 7 months isn't it. I wonder if I shall be at home for Jan *5th*. I have very pleasant rcollections of the last one. Haven't you. Well no more now.

Yours, Jack.

15/12/16
My dear Phyllis,

Thanks very much for your letter of the 10th received yesterday. It came very quickly didn't it, only 4 days this time.

We are quite comfortable here, just a bit bored.

My teeth you will be pleased to hear have almost come right again. Having had one strafed the others have taken the tip and ceased their activities almost — about time too as I was getting desperate and was contemplating a big counter-attack. What a lot of rot I'm writing.

We have been playing a lot of cards lately. Poker — Vingt et un and so on. Rather an expensive hobby, for they never play for love you know out here.

Talking of Australians the words they address to their mules and horses when they get stuck in the mud are most astonishing. They startled even me, and I've heard a few. But yet on the other hand when their respective mules or whatever it is get hit or killed they weep like kids. Strange isn't it but rather fine.

It is strange what a lot of swearing there is out here. I suppose it is nearly always so when you get a large number of men herded together for months on end. In England of course it can never be so bad really; because there are quite a lot of the opposite sex. Most startling the difference they make on mankind. They stand for an awful lot. One anyway, whose name begins with P- and ends with s- has made a lot of difference in things to me — putting it mildly. Can you guess who it is.

Yours Jack.

P.S. I cannot get on leave for Xmas. Rotten isn't it. Shall be home some time about New Year. Jack.

16/12/16

My dear Phyllis.

Many thanks for your letter of the 5th which I received a day or two ago. I would have replied sooner only with the rotten toothache I've been on the sick list for a bit. One looks awfully stange with one cheek three times the size of the other. However all is well now as the offending tooth was removed yesterday.

Well in case I don't see you before Christmas I want to send you the very best of greetings and hope you will have s'nice time. I only hope that I may be able to be there too.

No more now. Yours, Jack.

1917

[There are no letters for January or most of February; Jack got his leave in time for Christmas after all, but then fell sick with trench fever which rendered him unfit to return to France. Still only able to undertake light duties, he was then posted to Scotton Camp near Catterick, where he would remain until the middle of April. The 4th Battalion meanwhile had been having a relatively quiet spell prior to the Battle of Arras, which began early in April. South of Arras the Germans had withdrawn some way, behind the new and immensely strong fortifications of the Hindenburg Line.]

4th E. Yorks Regt., Scotton Camp, Catterick Bridge, Yorks., Feb 27th 1917
My dear Phyllis,

I have managed to get here alright; although it took a terrible long time to do it.

Before I left home I received a letter also Railway warrant from the Batt. telling me to report on the 26th. So that you see everything was in order and I was not strafed at all at least not so far.

I do not know what is going to happen to me exactly. The Adjutant says the War Office have been enquiring about me in reference to Trench Mortars. So that this spot may be only a termporary resting place.

I shall have to watch things rather closely; otherwise I may find myself out again before I know where I am. The Camp here is quite decent and the huts are very warm. But it is a terrible long way from anywhere.

I have had to remove my grenade for the time being I regret to say. Very distressing isn't it.

It was a terrible rend parting from you; but of course it had to be. I am never satisfied am I. Anyway I have had the best and happiest time that I ever have had so far in my life and look forward for ever better times yet to come.

With Best Love. Yours ever, Jack.

March 2 1917
My dear Phyllis,

Very many thanks for your letter of the 28th received last night. I have not heard anything further yet from the War Office about myself. I am having quite a harmless sort of time here; not having done much yet. I am Orderly Officer today and had to be up by 6 am and inspect some men at 6.15 am. It is a terrible business getting up in the middle of the night like that. This place anyway is safe — no horrid old shells dashing about or anything of that kind.

I was very pleased to hear that the Butte de Warlincourt* had fallen at last into our hands. But that place has not half cost a lot of lives one time or another.

I shall not forget to burn your letters as I promised. You can trust me about that you know completely.

It really seems a terrible long time since I saw you — you know. Time hangs rather heavy here. You really are a "darling" you know — this world would be a rotten old place without you.

With Very Best Love, Yours ever, Jack.

*[*The Butte de Warlincourt was a strategically valuable eminence on the Somme, south-west of Bapaume. When it was taken, by the Durham Light Infantry, a wooden cross was erected on it; the cross is now in a D.L.I. chapel within Durham cathedral.*]

6/3/17
My dear Phyllis,
  Many thanks for your letter of the 4th. I am glad to hear that you enjoyed David Garrick last Saturday. Darlington of course is the only place near here that runs to a Theatre and that's not much I believe.
  How are things going on at the Hospital. I suppose that they have not put you on night duty yet. I see that *married* Officers of Rank below Major are going to have £104 per annum extra given them. Hope yet isn't there. Well Goodnight Darling.
    With Love, Yours ever, Jack.

14/3/17
My dear Phyllis,
  Many thanks for your letter of the 11th received this morning.
  I act as O.C. Company and 2nd in Command respectively — as the OC Coy has a bad throat and can not give any words of command. There is as a matter of fact absolutely nothing to do — as the N.C.O. instructors do it all. We simply stand about and gape. One gets simply bored stiff with this after a time.
  They are building — in fact have almost completed — a big Bosche internment camp here. With huts, everything just the same as ours. Far too good for them I think. Round it there is a thick entanglement of barbed wire. Rather unnecessary I think — as they will be too comfortable to want to escape. When you think how the Germans treat our prisoners — we seem to be rather balmy. But perhaps I am rather hard-hearted in regard to them.
    Goodbye for the present "Darling", With Love, Jack.

26/3/17
My dear Phyllis,
  I have managed to get back here quite safely.
  By the way there is quite a good account of the attack of Sept 15th 1916 in the *Strand* Magazine for April — written from the German point of view — all about the tanks and that kind of thing — it's only short but I'm sure that it would interest you.
  I must thank you for the topping week end that I have had — I was awfully bucked at seeing you again and enjoyed it ever so much.
  I hope that you will not be angry with me for mentioning the subject — "Darling" but I am getting most frightfully anxious about you. You may call me balmy and strafe me about it but it is so. Oh — Phyl I'd give anything to see you really — really well. I am nearly always so disgustingly well — so much energy and blood that I don't know what to do with it. I only wish that I could give some of it to you — I'd part with it for you willingly. God knows I would do anything.
  I don't think that your people at home realise how you are getting on as they see you from day to day. But with me it's very different I only see you after lapses of some weeks and because I care for you a lot I see the difference in you (Please don't breathe a word of the above to anyone will you). You could have knocked me down with a feather on Sunday afternoon. Please do take care of yourself for your

77

own sake let alone mine. I used to be the same as you once but they gave me blood to drink. Horrid is it not; but it has done me good.

But there is one thing that would soon put you right and that is a *wine* called Tintara. You ask Nurse about it and you will find I am not pulling your leg. I am quite serious about that wine: I remember Father and Gladys took it when they were so groggy. Its just about the only non-acid wine there is.

Well I must close now as it is past 11.30 pm and I must hie me to my couch.

Goodnight Phyl Dear

With much love, Yours always, Jack.

27/3/17

My dear Phyl,

You must think my letter of yesterday — when you read it rather a strange one. I am not often taken like that I assure you — But I have been thinking an awful lot about you for a long time now. I have intended to say what I have done for quite a while but always kind of put it off until last night, when I felt I could not sleep until I had got it off my chest so to speak.

I have just seen the Battalion Orders for tomorrow and find that I am due for a Medical Board at the Hospital here at 3 pm. I have been expecting it for a long time now so that it is not exactly a shock. I do hope that they don't pass me as fit for General Service as when one gets that — continental travel commences almost at once.

Laverack the Adjutant is going on Draft Leave I believe prior to going out again and will revert to Lieutenant on doing so. I guess he will lose about £300 per annum by it.

With Love, Yours always, Jack.

29/3/17

My dear Phyl,

Many thanks for your delightfully long letter of the 28th received this morning.

I only wish you were as you say right as rain. However I am glad that you took my advice about the Brandy and Soda. If I had my way you would have a lot of that sort of thing. I don't mean Brandy but other kinds.

I had my Medical Board here at the Hospital yesterday. I am afraid I looked too well. The President of the Board a Major was very nice. He beamed at me and asked me how I was. I told him fairly fit. And then he asked if I felt like going and chasing Bosche. I said I was not keen about it and liked England quite well — but if I was sent I suppose I should have to go. So I think I shall be passed General Service. If that is so I am entitled to 4 days Draft Leave. This does not mean that one goes out forthwith. But generally nowadays you only get 24 hours leave before having to report at the port of embarkation.

By the way Harold has managed to get back to the 4th East. He is very bucked about it although he will lose a Captaincy by it. The Colonel of the 11th had already given him a Company and promised him 3 stars at an early date. However I have no doubt that congenial society matters more than promotion with him.

I was surprised to see Mess Bill larger than usual when I returned — so I have made up my mind to stop having any drinks for one month. Two days have already passed and I don't find it at all difficult to refrain.

With Love, Yours always, Jack.

2/4/17

My dear Phyllis,

A lot more Officers have received their orders to proceed overseas tonight. Laverack the late Adjutant of the Battalion amongst them .

I do not wish to depress you but I think it extremely likely that I shall get mine soon also. Sometime next week I expect. I am on the list for Draft and with my experience of active service they will soon push me back there I'm afraid. In fact there are very few Officers left here except those who are unfit and therefore marked as Permanent Home Service. One has to accept the inevitable I suppose — still it is rather rotten.

How are you. You never tell me about yourself do you.

With love, Yours always, Jack.

6/4/17

My dear Phyllis,

I heard yesterday from Mother and she seems to be quite happy about my G.S. business.

I am still on the Course of Physical Drill. I have to qualify to become a certificated instructor next Friday; although if I do succeed I do not suppose that I shall ever be given an opportunity to use the knowledge I have gained. The army is like that you know — one gets sent away to various places and specialises in different things. Then when you return to your unit — you carry on just the same until you have forgotten all about the things you have learnt. The best thing about this Course is that you are excused all parades with your Battalion. Thus you escape that horrible business, early morning parade at 5.30 am. I often think of you, when I do get up to attend it, tucked away under heaps of clothes, and all the windows open to their fullest extent. Don't you find it a bit cold in this weather? I have mine open too; but not so much as yours I warrant.

Exactly a year ago today I was in the trenches and encountered the first Bosche Minerwerfer shells or Trench Mortar Bombs that the Battalion had ever seen. I will never forget that ever I don't think.

I hear that there is going to be a push there at Kemmel and in that neighbourhood in order to get Lille. It will be a hard nut to crack.

With Love, Yours Jack.

8/4/17

My dear Phyllis,

Many thanks for your letter of the 6th received this morning.

I was on the C of E Parade this morning again. The parson held forth on the War and the connection of the Scriptures with it. It says somewhere that there will be a big dust-up near Jersulam and that the Turks will get the push. Still we shall see how far this comes true.

I must get that book of Bairnsfather, *Bullets and Billets*; from what you say it looks most interesting. Ypres was pretty rotten but not half so bad as the Somme in my opinion. But of course advancing is always more expensive although much more interesting.

Did you read the bit in the papers about the Germans when they evacuated Noyon taking 50 girls with them to act as "Orderlies". They always seem to excel in doing some dirty trick like that don't they.

I often wonder what our men would be like if they ever got into Germany. They would be pretty hot stuff I should think. But of course it largely depends on those who command them really.

You know you really are an absolute "Darling". I only wish that we could get engaged straight away; it would be tres bon. You may not of course agree. But looking at the situation from the practical and finanaicl point of view there does not seem much prospect for some time to come. This is very sad you know really because I do love you so much. It really gets worse and worse you know. Well I suppose that things will pan out alright sometime. The sooner the better as far as I am concerned. Fortune, Fortune turn thy wheel. Well Goodbye for the present Phyllis Dear

With Love, Jack.

11/4/17

My dear Phyllis,

Many thanks for your letter of the 8th received this morning.

I hear that the 50th Division is again on the move up north I believe. There is a story about that they have been in this last push — rushed up at the last moment. Perhaps you had better keep that bit to yourself. A short time ago anyway they were at Doullens. The place where we detrained before our route march down to the Somme last July 1916 [*actually August: see letter of 12.8.16*]

I am quite keen to arrange my leave so that I could join you for a few days when you go away. That is of course if you would have me. But May is a long way ahead and I very much doubt if I shall be in this country by then. So I think I shall apply for it next week — from Wednesday to Monday — 6 days. I might miss it altogether if I wait.

Of course I might manage some other leave on "Urgent Business".

This Daylight Saving — will make it mugh lighter for you walking up the hill [*from North Ferriby station to Swanland*]. I notice that it's fairly light up to 8 pm. It's a rotten road for you to walk up by yourself in the dark. Nearly everyone forgot to put their watches right — I did for one. Church parade was at 8.30 am. I just managed it but had to omit breakfast altogether.

With Love, Yours Jack.

POST OFFICE TELGRAM post-marked 12 APR, Darlington

To: Bentham, Swanland, North Ferriby.

Ordered France depart Folkestone Monday coming Hull today Jack Oughtred.

Grosvenor Hotel London S W, 15/4/17

My Darling,

I have arrived here quite safely and have managed to get quite a decent room.

I think perhaps that it was best for me to come by that 12 o'clock train; as I did. I should have been very done up tomorrow had I not done so. These partings are awfully rotten.

The worst thing about War is in my opinion in saying farewell (for a time) to those whom you care for so much at home.

It was much, much harder to leave you this time than it ever has been before although that was bad enough. It must be because I love you more now. It is really

These charms – one enamel, one brass – belonged to Phyllis. In all probability the black cat was given to her by Jack early in the war. The charm to which Jack refers throughout the war was, it is believed, a horseshoe similar to the one shown here which he wore on a string around his neck. After his death, in 1958, Phyllis wore it and was in fact buried wearing it in 1981.

*Pendant watch sent home as souvenir. (**See letter of 14 August 1917**).*

81

A selection of the fine china Jack salvaged from a find near Epehy.
*Each one depicts a month of the year. (**See letter of 12 February 1918**).*

Jack's Military Cross, awarded for conduct at Broodeseinde, during the
*battle known as Passchendaele. (**See letter of 30 October 1917**).*

*2nd Lieutenant Harold Oughtred, East Yorkshire Regiment, elder
brother and former teacher of Jack Oughtred.*

Remains of the original cross which marked the grave of Harold Oughtred at Wancourt.

Standard medallion issued to next-of-kin of fallen soldiers.

Norman Oughtred and Doris Bentham on their wedding day, 22 November 1917.

Standard Field Service Post Card used when in action or otherwise unable to write home.

NOTHING is to be written on this side except the date and signature of the sender. Sentences not required may be erased. If anything else is added the post card will be destroyed.

[Postage must be prepaid on any letter or post card addressed to the sender of this card.]

I am quite well.

I have been admitted into hospital
{ sick } and am going on well.
{ wounded } and hope to be discharged soon.

I am being sent down to the base.

I have received your { letter dated ⎯⎯⎯
telegram „ ⎯⎯⎯
parcel „ ⎯⎯⎯

Letter follows at first opportunity.

I have received no letter from you
{ lately
{ for a long time.

Signature } *Jack*
only }

Date⎯⎯⎯ *20/9/18*

Wt.W65—P.P.918. 8000m. 5-18. C. & Co., Grange Mills, S.W.

85

rather difficult to say how much Phyl I do love you. Words fail me altogether. But I think that you understand what I mean don't you.

I must thank you for the most delightful time that I have had during the last three days; which is nearly all due to you. I think that you have enjoyed it too just a little haven't you.

You said over the phone last night that I must think you a cat or words to that effect. You know you should not say those things really — I mean it. You're an absolute *"Darling"* so there — I never thought at one time that I was ever capable of loving anyone as much as I do you. I think too that you care for me just a little don't you. You can't imagine what a happy sort of feeling that gives me inside somehow. It simply alters everything. I hope "Dear" that you won't be depressed.

What has to be — has to be; I am a bit of a fatalist. I do wish that this rotten old war would finish and that I could come home again once more. It would be simply lovely. No more horrid farewells hanging over you like a cloud.

I was very much tempted to ring you up tonight but I don't suppose I should be able to hear. I have a phone by my bed too. I came down with a Surgeon General in the train — he was very decent indeed. At King's Cross when we got out — he shook hands with me and said "Goodbye my boy — best of luck". Rather sweet of him wasn't it.

Godnight Dearest, With much love from Jack.

ROYAL PAVILION HOTEL, Folkestone, 11 am 16/4/17
My Darling,

I am not leaving here until 4 pm this afternoon; so I shall have a little time to wait. I have just had some more breakfast — they were too slow at the Grosvenor for me to get hardly any at all. They only allow you one solitary roll.

I shall try hard to get back to the T.M.B. but I shall be able to let you know something more definite on that subject shortly.

I don't feel depressed now that we have got on the way. I hope that you will keep your pecker up. It is rather sad that I shall not be able to hear from you for quite a long time; but it can't be helped can it. Every cloud has a silver lining so they say. I must close now for the time so cheers. Dearest Phyl.

With Much Love from Jack.

37 I.B.D., A.P.O., Section 17, B.E.F. 17/4/17
My Darling,

I am very sorry that I could not send you a wire when I landed at Boulogne but we had to go straight from the boat to the train.

I reached the base at about 10.30 pm — pouring with rain it was too — but we struggled up to the camp and eventually managed to get into the Officers Mess. They did not expect us and consequently had no food of any sort — not even bread. Fortunately I recognised one of the waiters here as one of the old B Coy 4th E Yorks. I soon succeeded in getting a few sandwiches for myself and a few others.

Our kit did not turn up so we got three blankets each and slept in a tent 6 in each. So you see we kept quite warm. I simply took my boots off so it was not a long business getting undressed was it. I have seen the Adjutant here this morning and he seems to think I might quite possibly get back to the 150 T.M.B.

I will write you every day for the present — hope it won't bore you. I can see my letters arriving at Swanland ½ Doz. at a time can't you. I hear a rumour here that

Lens and Cambrai have fallen.* I hope that it's true don't you — it would make such a big difference — almost open fighting at last I fancy.

I am not feeling depressed now at all. I thought that I should be alright as soon as I got out again. I shall not forget that little matter we arranged. You know what I mean don't you.

I promise you that I will take care of myself as far as I can — and be really quite a good boy. This crowd I have come out with are rather hot stuff. The charm you gave me long ago still rests round my neck as it always has done. I have great faith in it, mainly because you gave it to me. I can't forget what a Darling you are —absolutely the Dearest Girl in all the world. au revoir.

    With much Love from Jack.

*[*The rumour that Cambrai had fallen was groundless. Cambrai would not be taken until the successful offensives in the autumn of 1918.*]

18/4/17

My Darling Girl,

I have found out I am to be sent up to the 2/7 West Yorkshires. It's awfully rotten luck isn't it. I feel fearfully fed up about it. They only came out in January. However I suppose I shall have to make the best of things.

Anyway I shall have a try at transferring back to the 4th East. I thought that it was quite probable that I might be sent to some other Battalion of the East Yorks but I must confess I never expected to lose them altogether. An Officer Gresham by name is going with me — he also was in the T.M.B.

It is very difficult to write here as there are about 50 people talking at once and it's rather distracting. You know what I mean don't you. Hope this letter won't depress you — don't let it will you Phyllis. It seems an awful long time since I left you. I hope that you are none the worse for those last three days — I am very much at times I fear. But I think that you will forgive me won't you. I love you such a fearful lot and what's more always shall do whatever happens.

    Well I must close now, With Much Love from Jack.

19/4/17

My Darling,

I am still at the Base as you will see from the address.

All round here is nothing but sand hills for miles. Our Camp is pitched on them. Not bad really as it keeps fairly dry — water does not gather much.

Our tent is very feeble; when it rains — which it has done ever since I came here —it simply pours through above my bed. It is alright when one is safely tucked away in one's flea bag — but getting up is rotten. Everything you put on is wet and then of course 6 of us getting up at once rather confuses things.

I have taken off my second star and am once more a Second Lieutenant.

Rather sad isn't it, but after all what does it matter.

I have already taken some steps about my transfer back to the East Yorks, but of course cannot do anything really definite until I join the 2/7 West Yorks.

    Well Goodnight Phyllis, With Love from Jack.

20/4/17

My Darling Phil,

I am still safe at the Base up to the moment. Every morning at 8 am we parade and march off to the training. We are supplied with Bully Beef sandwiches which when you are really hungry aren't half bad.

I have been taking waves of men in the attack today over the parapet, Australians they were mostly. They were all supplied with blank ammunition. Quite a lot get damaged in one way or another. Firing a blank round at too close quarters and running into other people's bayonets.

I hear rumours that my old division has been over the top again last Saturday or Monday. I hope Harold and Norman are alright. I think perhaps you had better keep that bit to yourself. I won't tell my people about it.*

Well I must close now. With Best Love, from Jack.

*[*Jack's reference to his old Division going over the top indicates that he had heard about the Battle of Adinfer Wood, part of the assault on the Hindenburg line. This line was a new and immensely strong series of fortifications behind which the Germans had withdrawn early in the year. Harold, in the 4th Bn, was in another advance a few days later; see below.*]

21/4/17
My Darling,

I have so far escaped being sent up the line. A large number are being sent up tomorrow but I am not included fortunately.

I went tonight to a little place in the adjoining village and they gave us a most astonishing spread. There are no food rations here I assure you. The supply of bread appears to be almost unlimited.

I hear that the lot I am going to join some time or other are right up north — farther so than I ever was before. This of course may be wrong. Anyway I do know that they will not get put into any big show. Nearly all their Officers went sick after they had been in the trenches for the first time. Anyhow I'll do my best to show them how the 4 East Yorks carry on. Rather swank that I'm afraid isn't it.

Well I must close now, hoping to hear from you soon.

With Best Love from Jack.

22/4/17
My Darling Phil,

I have been transferred from the 2/7 West Yorks to the 1st East Yorks. That is of course the regular battalion [*the 4th being Territorials*]. The eight of us that came out together have all been posted to the same. The 1st E.Y. have been badly cut up only recently and are at the moment at rest. [*In the German counter-attack at Adinfer Wood they suffered 287 casualties*].

They are a fighting Division and only go to the line for pushes. So I hear. Rather cheerful in some ways isn't it. However it doesn't matter much as we have got to go through it again with some lot or other.

I see in the papers and hear from other sources that no more wounded are to come back to England unless they are very badly smashed up. Awfully rotten I call it. No point now in getting wounded is there. No more blighties.

With Best Love from Jack.

24/4/17

My Darling.

All goes well with me here at the moment. I have been to the Dentist this morning at No. 1 Canadian General Hospital. I had an awful job to get there and had to interview all kinds of people. However I think that it's worth it as toothache in the line is just about the worst thing I know. I am afraid that I am an awful coward in regard to Dentists. I positively tremble at the sight of the chair and all those instruments.

It seems to be true to some extent about wounded not being sent to England any more unless of course they are very bad.

Posts seem to be rather irregular. My letters to England appear to take at least 4 if not 5 days: rotten isn't it. It's quicker from the front.

I must close now. Write as often as you can won't you.

With Much Love, Yours always, Jack.

25/4/17

My Darling Phyllis.

I was indeed delighted to receive your letter last night. It cheered me up no end.

I promise you that I will do my utmost to take care of myself. Life at present is far too sweet to be thrown away. This world really is at times an absolute topping place — it would not be so at all if you were not in it, believe me.

Your charm still hangs around my neck and I attach a tremendous amount of faith and importance to it.

But please — don't worry very much will you — Darling. It would be very sad indeed if you did. I feel somehow that I shall be alright although I touch wood as I say it. It is strange how one feels these things. I feel almost confident that I shall see you again. By God I hope so too.

I feel often that I am not half good enough for you — I mean it honestly — but I'll try my utmost to make myself so. You know don't you that I love you better than anything else on this earth and what's more always shall do so. You will never find me changed at all in that way — of that I am perfectly sure. It was the best thing I ever did — the day I met you. There would not be many rotters in this world if they ran across girls like you early on.

This Dental business is doing me a little good. All the other Officers down for the 1st East Yorks have gone up today except John Good and myself who are sick for the moment with our teeth. So it has saved me a day or two already you see. I am in no hurry to get up to the line again I assure you.

Well Phyllis Darling, I must close now.

With Much Love, Yours always, Jack.

26/4/17

My Darling Phyllis,

Very many thanks for your letter of the 22nd received today. It is very sweet of you to write so often.

It is rotten not getting back to the T.M.B. but it can't be helped. Anyway I am not going to the 2/7 West Yorkshire. It is rather funny me being sent out to a regular Battalion isn't it. I fear that it will make things rather hard for me to transfer back to the 4th East. The C.O. of the 1st may get rather annoyed if I try as he will probably say that I ought to consider it an honour to belong to the 1st at all.

However we shall see how things turn out.

The terms I.B.D. and A.P.O. stand for the following: Infantry Brigade Depot and Army Post Office. They are not so very easy to guess, so you are not such a hopeless case as you imagine.

My old Division has been over the top — I know this almost for a certainty —the 4th have come off rather lightly on the whole I believe as far as I can gather. I think that you had better keep that bit of news to yourself. I won't tell them at home —no use worrying them. I know I can rely on you in this.

At the railway station here there are a lot of Bosche prisoners working. A wounded and crippled French tommy got out of the Ambulance train and staggered out of the station. One of the Huns made some insulting remarks and spat at him and various other offensive things. Whereupon the Frenchman whipped out his automatic revolver and shot him dead on the spot. Served him jolly well right too in my opinion. Don't you think so.

With Much Love, Yours always, Jack.

29/4/17
My Darling,

Many thanks for your letter of the 24th received last night. I am still at the Base.

I am still paying visits to the Dentist. I am going again — I fancy for the last time — next Tuesday. This is the only reason why I have not gone up to the line. I can put up with being bored for quite a long time when you have an alternative like the front line to contend with. I am not funking it — don't think that but I must confess I am not all all keen about war now — if indeed I ever was. I expect things will be alright when I do get up to the 1st East. They appear to be quite a decent crush on the whole.

You will enjoy having some of your sailors up at Swanland and I'll warrant they do too.

I hear some horrid rumours about the 4th East and their losses. It is so bad that I refuse to believe it although I know quite well that they have had a very rough time. Heard Harold was wounded or worse yesterday. But I think it is all rot so won't pay any more attention to it. Please Phyllis Dear don't tell *anyone* about it will you. I can tell anything to you because I know that it won't go any farther.

By the way I nearly forgot about it — I sent you some hankies the other day. They are not very bon really but I could not find anything else much in the shop. Don't strafe me for sending them will you. I know you asked me not to send you anything, but there you are.

We did have a good time that last night at our house didn't we. I am glad that you enjoyed it just a little too. It makes such a tremendous difference when you do you know. There is absolutely nothing wrong either in it is there now.

I see H. Bottomley says that he will give 2/- to every man in the army if the war is not over in 3 months' time. I think that he will have to float a war loan on his own account. What do you think?

Don't do too much at the Hospital. Let one of us keep fit anyway; although I expect I shall be alright — unless the trenches and places are very wet. Then I am afraid I shall crack up. I am not quite so fit as I was when I came out the first time. My nerves are alright, though; I have no fears on that score — although from all accounts the fighting now is simply terrific. Still, I won't tell you about it — it would only worry you. And I would not do that for worlds.

Well, I must close — I don't seem to be able to stop once I start writing to you. With much love. Yours always, Jack.

30/4/17
My Darling Phyllis,

I did not know until I received your letter whether anything had happened to Harold or not. I had seen men who had come down the line and they said he was either wounded or killed. I hoped so much that it was not true.

The news is too awful for words — it has rather knocked me over for the time. I cannot properly realise that I shall never see him again. Poor old Harold — it's a shame. We have always been together such a lot — ever since I was a kid — he was my form master at School at one time. This war is a terrible business — I never really felt it as much as now.*

I suppose that time will soften the blow although I fear that it is little consolation at present. He died anyway in a good cause and as a soldier. I honestly think that he was quite the straightest and best chap in every way that I have ever met. It seems a strange thing that he should be taken. The will of the All Mighty is quite beyond all human comprehension.

I do not know how I shall write to Mother — I shall have to do it but it will be a terrible business. I can't say how I feel for her now — if it's bad for me how much worse it must be for them both at home. Thank God Ethelwyn and Fred** were there when the wire arrived. I hope that it does not break them up. How I wish that I was at home now — I could for once be of some real use I fancy. Anyway I am sure that all those at home will do their utmost. Please let me know if you can how Mother is — Ring up Ethelwyn anything of that sort — She will tell you.

I wish to thank you — "Dearest" for your letter it was lovely of you — the thought that you are thinking of me has and will help me more than you imagine.

I will close this letter now as I don't for once feel like writing any more.
With Much Love, Yours always, Jack.

*[*Harold Oughtred was 39 years old; he had joined the Artists Rifles in 1914. His home was in Kettleby, near Brigg in Lincolnshire. A brilliant scholar who in two years gained a First in History at Oxford, he had indeed been Jack's teacher at Newton College, Newton Abbot. His presence there probably explains why Jack was sent to Devon after the unfortunate affair with the inkwell at Hymers (see Introduction). The only clue from official records as to how Harold met his death is contained in this entry from the Diary of the 4th Battalion after they advanced at Wancourt, south-east of Arras, early on the morning of April 23, an advance which was designed to breathe new life into the flagging offensive on the Hindenburg Line – which was in any case called off two weeks later:*

"*At 4.30 a.m. the Bn were in a position to advance behind our barrage....At 4.45 a.m the barrage from eighty-four 18-pound guns and thirty 4.5 howitzers opened. Shells fell very short and at once we had serious casualties from them...and it was not long before all officers on the two flank companies ['D' and 'B'; Harold being in 'D'] were either killed or wounded. Enemy machine gun fire in the meantime had begun to tell.*

"*The fact that these companies early lost not only all their officers but also nearly all their NCO leaders threw the Battn into some confusion....*
"*At about 7 am the enemy launched a vigorous counter-attack...when*

he reached his original front line trench the Bn had lost all its Company
Officers....The total casualties were 17 Officers and 352 Other Ranks."

It was quite normal for the infantry to advance close behind a barrage, and casualties were expected, especially in the case of a moving, or "creeping", barrage. Notes on a conference held at Divisional HQ late in the war contain the following memo: "Men should be trained to expect casualties from our Barrage. Unless casualties occur they are too far from the Barrage."

Cecil Slack, in his collected correspondence **Grandfather's Adventures in The Great War**, mentions Harold's death. Writing from the front he describes the Battalion being cut off by a German counter-attack, and continues: "Amongst the killed are Cyril Easton, Harold Oughtred, killed while cheering on his men, and Boyle, an old Hymerian, all splendid fellows." In a post-war note he added the following:

"A rifle had been stuck in the ground where the bodies of Easton, Oughtred and Boyle had been covered over. At a later stage in the war we came back to a position about a mile or so distant from Wancourt where the battle had been fought. The C.O. wished crosses to be placed where these bodies lay and I was given the job of doing it. It meant being there before daylight as although not within rifle range the spot was in full view of the enemy's guns. My small party of men and I found the place as dawn was breaking, but in uncovering the bodies we had to put on our gas masks to partly overcome the stench. I was able to recover some personal items, which in due course, after cleansing treatment, were sent to the relatives. Full daylight came soon and the enemy dropped a shell – but we got the crosses up – and returned safely to the battalion."

**Jack's sister and her husband.]

2/5/17
My Darling Phyllis,

I have just received a letter from Father this morning. They both appear to be absolutely heartbroken. It is an awfully sad business. In fact I cannot find words to describe what I mean. It is far far worse for them than for anyone else I think. Thank God there are still some of us left. I don't think I will say any more about this — as I don't feel as if I could.

I finished at the Dentists yesterday and expect to be sent up the line any time now. I shall not be sorry really to get away either — I am tired of this inaction especially under the present circumstances.

The time is not far distant when I shall have to try my luck again in the line — But I feel somehow that all will be well with me. This feeling I cannot explain but it is so.

I have been put on the job of censoring letters at our Hospital here.

I often think of you and wonder what you are doing. I don't know I am sure what I should do without you. This world indeed would be a very poor place.

This is only a very brief letter I am afraid but I don't feel like writing somehow. But you will understand won't you Phyllis.

With Much Love, Jack.

3/5/17

My darling Phyl,

Thanks ever so much for your letter of the 29th received by the last post yesterday.

I am so glad — more so than I can tell you — to hear that my Mother is keeping up and that she is better now than she was. I feared that the shock of the bad news might cause all kinds of things. When people are getting on in age — you never can tell what will happen in circumstances like these can you.

The old Battalion has been very hard hit, I heard today — only 78 men came back and no Officers at all who were not wounded. Everyone I know seems to have gone — Harold — poor chap — was hit directly he got over the bags together with Capt. C. Easton.* Please keep this to yourself until I find out more particulars won't you "Darling". I hope that he was killed instantly — and did not linger at all.

I should like to tell you how much you have helped me in this terrible business. More indeed than I can ever, ever tell you. On occasions like this, one always turns to those who one loves best. I love you in such a different way from that which I have ever cared for anyone else without exception. It is the kind of feeling that goes down to the rock bottom of everything in me. It's very strange and changes everything in the world for me.

And the thought that you love me too is just the most wonderful thing that ever was. It's nothing much me loving you — who wouldn't — but that you should care for me (Heaven knows why) is simply beautiful. God help me to be worthy of it. My love will last for ever and ever and if need be beyond as well. That is the only thing that can never die.

It is not often Darling that I write like this to you — chiefly because I cannot always express myself — but tonight for once something in me seems to have been let loose and I can find words to tell you how I feel. I must close now "Phyllis Dear" with the hope that our next meeting is not so very far distant.

With Best Love, Jack.

*[Cyril Easton, who died alongside Harold, had earlier been awarded the M.C. He was a chartered accountant, in partnership with Mr. T. Fawley Judge in Hull.]

6/5/17

My Darling Phyllis,

I have just received my orders to go up to the line tomorrow — leaving here at 7.20 am. I do not expect though to get there in one day — I have to spend tomorrow night somewhere on the road. I really have been here quite a long time haven't I. Just three weeks tomorrow since I arrived. I am very glad indeed that I have stopped here so long — as I have missed quite a lot of terrible strafes up at the line. You may be quite — quite sure that I shall do my very best to take care of myself. Life is far too sweet with you in the world to lose it. But I think somehow —Darling — that I shall be quite alright — so do not worry more than you can help.

I often think of you — as I think you must know. Unknowingly perhaps you have carried me through many terrible places, and always will do so. I can't properly tell you how much I care for you — but I think that you will understand won't you.

I heard from an Officer just down from the line that the war is going to be over in 58 days. I hope that it is true don't you.

Anyway things can't go on at the rate they are doing for long. I will write you as soon as I can. I shall not go into the line straight away — but to a re-inforcement camp so that I shall be alright for a few days to come.

With all my love, Yours always, Jack.

7/5/17

My Darling Phyllis,

I have got over a part of my journey up to the line today — far better than I expected. The train went at almost a reckless speed.

There are no Officers here that I know — Good and the others have already gone up to the line — so that my teeth have saved me from something, haven't they? A blessing in disguise.

I will write you again very soon.

With Best Love, Jack.

11/5/17

My Darling Phyllis,

You will be pleased to hear that I am quite well. I have not reached the line yet —in fact I am still quite a long way away.

Two of the Officers who came out with me from England have already been wounded — Gresham and Mansfield.* They got it the first night they were in too. Very lucky for them both as they were not at all serious.

I have got quite a grand billet, very comfy — beds and all that kind of thing. The Lady of the house seems to be a little gone in the head but we manage to get along somehow.

I expect to join my battalion tomorrow sometime; all being well. Anyway I ought to be clear of the line for another three weeks at least.

With Best Love, Yours always, Jack Oughtred.

*[*Gresham and Mansfield had been sent straight to the front line where they faced an immediate German attack, an attempt to re-take a section of the Hindenberg Line taken by the 1st Battalion at Easter.*]

13/5/17

My Darling Phyllis,

I have at last joined up with the 1st E Yorks [*posted to B Coy*]. I arrived here [*Bailleulval*] yesterday afternoon. We are out of the line in rest billets — so that is a good thing isn't it.

They have had a very rough time in — Glad I missed it. Shackles* — who came came out with me has been killed poor chap. They were about 3 miles back when it happened, — he was in his flea bag too when it happened. Awful hard luck. I hope that my good luck will still continue.

My O.C. Company [*Lt Armitage*] is quite a decent kind of chap — when you get to know him. He is an artist by profession I believe. I do not think that we shall be out as long as I thought — but still you can never really tell.

I shall not try for a transfer to the 4th E Yorks for a bit anyway. There are not many left in it that I know really. And after all it does not make much matter what you are in. You have got to go through it sooner or later.

With very best Love, Yours always, Jack.

*[*Shackles had arrived at the Batt. 28.4.17, and is listed in the Bn. Diary as wounded 11.5.17 in a bombardment of the rest-camp at Boiry-Becquerelle. He was the eldest son of Mr. G. L. Shackles of Brough, articled to become a solicitor in the family firm. **The Snapper** reports him as dying later of his wounds.]*

14/5/17
My Darling Phyl,

Very many thanks for your letter of the 6th, which has been forwarded on from the Base and reached me here yesterday.

I had a long letter from Ethelwyn yesterday too. My Mother has indeed been in a terrible way — but I think that they have got over the worst. I think that one of the main things was — that Mother thought Harold was wasted in the army and that he was not appreciated. All the letters that they have received saying how much he will be missed and what a lot of good he did in the world have lifted them quite a lot. Still, it is a shame I think. He was positively brilliant at times. It does me good to talk about it to you — I hope that you don't mind.

They seem to have looked after you very well at the Theatre with the chocs. It only shows that they appreciate you doesn't it.

I wish I was at home to take you about — I am completely fed up with war and every thing connected with it. But I must wait until I come home again.

There is not much difference between this battalion and the 4th — even though it is a regular battalion. There are very few regular Officers. I have not met the Colonel yet as he is away on leave.

Capt. Harrison Broadley is now O.C. my Company. I don't know if he is any relation of the Welton crowd but I rather think so. He does not impress me much at first but he may be alright.*

I have not much news this time things are rather dull.

    With Best Love, Jack.

*[*Harrison Broadley, or "Harrison" or even "W. Barry Broadley" – his name is constantly mis-spelled in the records – appears to have been a son of the recently deceased Conservative M.P. for Howdenshire, Henry Broadley Harrison, previously resident at Welton.]*

16/5/17
My Darling Phyllis,

I was very pleased to receive your letter of the 9th this afternoon.

If at any time I find that I cannot write you a letter I will send you one of those horrible Field Post Cards.

Everyone is very optimistic just now about the war and as far as one can gather from higher sources there does not appear to be much likelihood of it lasting another winter. We could not stand the pace anyway.

I think that the most *unhappy* person at the present time must be the one who is *not* in love. War is such a sordid — ghastly sort of thing — turns one into a kind of wild beast — but love somehow or other seems to keep a spark of something alight — which cannot be touched by war or anything. It is this that carries one through many things.

I write you queer things at times don't I.

    I must close now. With Best Love, Jack.

May 19th 1917

My Darling Phyl,

Many thanks for your letter of the 11th received last night.

I am not in the trenches now — so please do not worry. I have been very lucky so far as had I come up before I should have been sleeping in the same tent as poor Shackles when he was killed in his sleep. Anyway it is a jolly good thing that you are so busy every day until 3 pm. But don't wear yourself to a shadow will you. I often think of you and wonder what you are doing — sometimes at very strange moments.

I have been off on a little joy ride today to a small town near by. There was really not much to do except eat and buy things to take back for others to eat.

I visited the Church and also the citadel. The latter is at present used as a Hospital but is quite an interesting place with its moats and walls and drawbridges.

By the same post as your letter came I received from Mother — she enclosed a copy of Colonel Wilkinson's letters — A very nice letter indeed I think — the Colonel is a topping chap, so sincere and that sort of thing.

I am glad above all things that Harold was appreciated. He seems to have felt in a way that he would not come back — as he wrote and left messages with Aunt Emily (Watson) and Aunt Alice (Davis) for Mother in case he was killed. Rather weird isn't it. But I think one generally knows within one's inmost being whether you are coming back or not. Tonight I feel confident about my return. If ever I am in great danger — I feel somehow that you will know of it too. Funny isn't it but perfectly true — distance is nothing. There are simply things in this world that cannot be explained by logic. They just simply are so.

I wonder if you can imagine how much I want to see, to talk, to kiss you again. Oh My Dearest Girl — I would give anything for a few months with you right now. But of course it is absolutely impossible and I shall have to bottle it up. I am afraid that I am a rather primitive person aren't I.

Well I must close now so I will say Goodnight Darling.

With Best Love, Yours always, Jack.

20/5/17

My Darling,

Thanks very much for your letter of the 12th which arrived tonight. Please do not worry; I am not in the line yet and may not be for a few days.

Up to tonight I have slept on the floor — but today I managed to get a canvas bed made and feel quite comfy now and most certainly higher up in the world. People have a nasty habit of walking on you when you recline on the floor.

Today we held some Brigade sports here. Fortunately for a wonder it was a fine day — so it was not so bad. But sports in large doses are boring things at the best don't you agree.

By the way there are 2 Batt of K.O.Y.L.I. in the Brigade [*the 9th & 10th*]. I do not think however that there is anyone you would know in them.

The Company has again been taken over by Capt. Armitage — Harrison-Broadley having gone to the Field Ambulance. He only stopped with us for four days. He lost his thumb early in the war — since when he had been in East Africa — which does not appear to have agreed with him. Anyway, I don't expect he will return.

I wonder if you are safely tucked away in bed. I hope so. I will meet you in my dreams in a few moments now — as I always do.

With Very Best Love, Forever, Jack.

21/5/17

My Darling Phyllis,

Thanks ever so much for your parcel which arrived this afternoon.

I went yesterday as I told you and after a lot of searching found Norman. I spent the afternoon and evening with him. He looks very well indeed and has a most comfortable camp. It is situated by the side of a moat which runs round a somewhat ancient fort. Very convenient for swimming and that sort of thing.

We went and had dinner in a town close to although the place at which we fed was very much knocked about by shell fire.

They do not appear to be able to find Harold's body at all — he was last seen lying in a shell hole. The ground where he fell was fought over about three times afterwards so that he might have been taken prisoner. Anyway we cannot find out for a certainty what has happened to him. Pease do not let this news about Harold go any farther than yourself will you. I don't want the people at home to know about it at all. As they might imagine all kinds of things, most of which would be unpleasant.

I understand that Col. Wilkinson wants me back again [*in the TMB*] so I don't know what to do.

I came here last night from seeing Norman on an old Lincoln Omnibus full of wounded. It rocked about terribly and they must have had a devil of a time. It's a pity they couldn't have put them into ordinary ambulances but I suppose that there are too many.

I must close now but will write again soon.

  With Very Best Love, Jack.

Sunday 22/5/17

My Darling,

Thanks ever so much for your letter of the 16th received this morning.

The Gresham who has been killed or died of wounds [*29.4.17 as 'B' Coy withdrew under fire*] is the brother of the Gresham who came out with me and was wounded a week or so ago. That makes the second one in that family to get killed in the war. Must be a terrible blow to his family.

You seem to be in a sad way as you say — with the motor broken down and boiler bust. I can quite imagine that you are not keen to trudge down and up that hill every day.

Many strange discoveries were made by Officers of this battalion last time in trenches in the German Dug Outs. Evidence of feminine occupation of the Dug Outs was very obvious, all kinds of garments lying about all over. The details in regard to them I will not go into. But it is perfectly true believe me. The German must run war on very different lines in his trenches to what we do in ours.

I must close now but will write again soon.

  With Best love, Jack.

25/5/17

My Darling Phyllis,

Many thanks for your letter of the 20th which arrived this afternoon.

I am very glad to hear that you are going away shortly for a fortnight at Ilkley. You ought to have a topping time if the weather keeps anything like it is at present. It will do you a world of good to be away from the Hospital for a bit.

You will have another opportunity of wearing your boudoir cap and everything else that you got to match it. I can quite imagine how lovely you would look. I can remember quite well the day when you put that cap on to show me how it fitted what a strong desire I felt to kiss you. But unfortunately we were not alone — sad to relate. I often feel like that as you no doubt know as well as I do. I am afraid that I am rather a wild person. What a terrible life I do lead you at times.

I have been appointed Mess President for our Company since the other man [*either 2Lt Godfrey or 2Lt Case, both of whom have just been admitted to the F.A. (Field Ambulance)*] has Trench Fever as they call it. They frankly admitted that they did not know what was really wrong. I am not very keen on the job as I have had a good deal of it one time or another.

My O.C. [*Harrison Broadley*] has returned from Hospital but he is not much better. I had to guide him to his billet last night. One gets rather fed up with that kind of thing after a time. Do you guess what I mean — I cannot put it plainer in a letter for obvious reasons.

I must close now as I have to get on parade at 4 pm today unfortunately. Goodbye for the present "Darling".

    With Best Love, Jack.

26/5/17

My Darling Phyllis,

We were inspected this afternoon by the Corps Commander. [*Lt-General Sir T. D'O. Snow K.C.B., K.C.M.G.*] He was rather a funny old thing really and seemed to me to be rather too old for his job. It was most frightfully hot and all had to wear steel helmets. You can't imagine how hot these helmets get [*with*] the sun on them — too much so to touch with your fingers with comfort. Imagine having one's head inside that — You literally melt away. We always have to wear them here though — Rotten bit of red tape as we are far beyond the reach of shells.*

A Bosche plane dropped a few bombs in this neighbourhood last night — but they were a long way off. It did not worry us at all as we were playing Bridge at the time. But I can quite understand how rotten it must be to be bombed by Zepps. You can generally judge pretty well when a shell is coming and take precautions but with bombs there is no knowing where they will drop is there.

There is a swallow that has built its nest just above my bed in the roof. It sits there quite peacefully and carries on with its work although I am sure that it does not approve of the late hours that we keep.

You know ever since I first loved you I have found the world quite a s'nice old place haven't you? You make such an awful lot of difference. It's very nice to think about. I *hope* that you believe me — because it's true as anything ever was. You will never never find me change; of that you may be quite sure.

When I am in love I don't half do it and am all in. It's awfully hard to explain oneself about it especially on paper — I think that feelings that go down to the bottom of things always are, don't you. They take an awful lot of dragging out. But you will understand I know.

I must really close now as it is getting late and as Orderly Dog (Officer) I have to go and turn out 5 or 6 guards.

    Goodnight Darling. With Best Love, Yours always, Jack.

*[The 1st Bn Medical Officer, Raine, writing some years later in **The Snapper**, remembered that the Corps Commander on this visit "had nothing better to suggest than that all the men should wear steel helmets, and thus add to their discomfort, already great, in full marching order and in the hot sun....Over a dozen men had sunstroke that day, and needed attention....Fortunately none of them died, but some were very seriously ill."]

29/5/17
My Darling Phyllis,

I managed after all to get permission to go and see Norman last Sunday. I reached the place where I saw him before and to my dismay found that he had departed elsewhere.

I enquired from various people and found out that they had only gone a few kilometres away — so I trudged after them and eventually found them about 2 pm. I had a terrible void below as I had breakfast quite early. They are as usual quite comfy.

The mess was in a pigeon cote — not like ours in England — but a big circular Tower 20 ft high with roof and spire complete. Very nice in this hot weather I assure you. I had another long walk to get back to the main road, — but on arriving there I stopped and got into a Staff Car which soon whisked me home or at least somewhere near it.

Yesterday I met Hal Seed who was down at the CCS [*Casualty Clearing Station*] having his teeth attended to. He has definitely found out now that Harold was hit with a Machine Gun bullet. But that does not explain why he has not yet been found does it.

When he went over with his platoon — 3 men or so of his remained in their trench and he went back to fetch them and thus got hit. I hope that we shall yet be able to get to know something definite soon.

We shall be leaving here *very shortly* in fact I shall not be able to write you again from here — more than that I cannot tell you.

I bought something for you yesterday when I was out. Rather a curious thing perhaps to get — 6 silver spoons — with the arms of various places on them. They are quite pretty — even better than those which I sent home some time ago now. Please don't strafe me will you.

With Very Best Love, Jack.

30/5/17
My Darling,

Many thanks for your letter of the 23rd received last night.

So you think that my last letter was rather wicked — I expect that you will have received some by now that are more so. But it would be nice to see you again even for a few months although of course the longer the better.

You will know where I am when I send you Field P.Cs won't you.

Don't get worried about me. I shall be right enough — although I must confess I don't feel too thrilled at the prospect of things. I must close now.

With Much Love, Jack.

Can you guess what these stand for xxxxx *encore*.

31/5/17

My Darling Phyllis,

I am now in the reserve line — which is of course some way back. [*On 30.5.17 the Bn marched to Boyelles, and on the 31st relieved the 1st Midd'x Reg't in Brigade Support trenches*]. I am quite comfortable and have a little bivouac made of corrugated iron and sack cloth. Very airy indeed believe me.

I slept last night in my flea bag so all is well.

I expect to move farther up very shortly and will write you again when I get there. As far as I can gather it seems to be quite a soft place so there is no need for you to worry really.

All the trees which line the roads have been cut down by the Hun. It makes the country very bare — and also very difficult to find one's way about in it. Rather an extraordinary thing for them to do.

    With Best Love, Jack.

1/6/17

My Darling,

I am now in the line once again — everything however so far has been very quiet — a few German shells floating about but really nothing to get excited about.

I have a little Dug Out which I share with an officer called Carver. We can both lie down together in it — but as it is only 3ft 6ins high standing up is entirely out of the question. It might with luck stop a drop of rain but certainly nothing else much.

With great forethought I bought large quantities of food. We had cold ham and 2 eggs each for breakfast this morning. Fire of course cannot be lit but I have a primus stove.

By the way have you ever heard or read about the Hindenburg line at any time. If you think of that you won't be far off. I see that in *John Bull* it states that the war will be over in 3 months time. I do hope that I don't have to go through another winter.

    With Best Love, Jack.

P.S.   I registered the parcel containing the spoons — I hope you will manage to get them alright. Jack.

Field Post Card post marked 3 June

I am quite well.

Letter follows at first opportunity.

3/6/17

My Darling Phyllis,

Many thanks for yours of the 26th which arrived late last night.

I am still in the Trenches but things in my particular vicinity have been fairly quiet — Haven't had any shells within a 100 yds of me so far.

You ask me how I am. I am very fit thanks although just starting to look very dirty and sadly in need of a wash and shave. But I shan't be able to have them for some time yet. I expect you will be horrified at the thought. I have not as yet collected any creatures on my person. The trenches here seem to be remarkably free from those pests.

I am up nearly all night wandering about looking after the men [*at this time they are engaged in repairing and extending the barbed wire*] which is just as well as I get awfully fed with sitting still all day.

I often think of you during these night hours. I wonder if you know it. Will write again very soon.

Best Love, Yours always, Jack.

4/6/17

My Darling Phyllis,

I saw a most thrilling air fight above my trench only a few minutes ago. They were not more than 150 feet up so that I could see them both very distinctly. Both were playing at each other with their Machine Guns and the Bosche looped the loop twice in succession.

But something hit his engine and he planed down — landing about 700 yards away behind our lines. I saw the two German airman get out and were duly marched off by Tommies. It was quite exciting while it lasted — I fired at him quite a few times.

The German planes are coloured in a most peculiar manner now having bright red bodies — with Green places. Look just like a Dragon fly.

Apart from this little episode we have had an extremely quiet time — in fact positively boring.

I had a wash today using a steel helmet as a basin. It is rather nice to feel moderately clean again.

This letter is very uninteresting I am sure but I haven't much to say today.

With Best Love, Jack.

6/6/17

My Darling Phyllis,

Thanks ever so much for your parcel which arrived yesterday — the contents are intact and not squashed at all.

I spend most of the night walking about. They are not long now though are they? 10 pm to 3.30 am or even less than that and as I don't have dinner or supper or whatever you like to call it until 10 pm — the night soon passes.

I succeeded in making some excellent Fish Cakes yesterday out of Tinned Salmon and ground up Ration biscuits. The biscuits taking the place of the flour, as of course we have not got any of that. It is marvellous what one can do with very little material.

I saw another German plane come down yesterday in flames and the airman fall out of it before it reached the ground. They certainly have plenty of pluck whatever else they may be.

I see that all the men are being put into various groups according to their trades or jobs in civil life. This is I suppose a preparation for demobilisation and peace and all nice things like that.

With Best Love and many kisses, Jack.

7/6/17

My Darling,

I was very pleased to receive your delightfully long and interesting letter of the 31st last night.

You have indeed been having a strenuous time at the Hospital. I am not surprised that after the whist Drive etc you felt tired next morning; walking up the hill too on top of everything.

Let me see, it's just a year ago since you were at Ilkley last isn't it? I was at Kemmel at the time I remember — and we had the Gas attack. How time does fly doesn't it.

I had a very disturbed night last night as the Bosche shelled us from 11 pm to 3 am without ceasing — mostly shrapnel and a few high explosives. He sent about three shells per minute.* We had no casualties at all — but after a time you get rather fed up with the noise and the smell. All the ground round about where the shells are bursting is covered with thick black fumes of the exploded cordite. Makes it impossible to see any distance at all. It is really marvellous the number of shells that can be put over and never give anyone the smallest scratch. I saw the most perfect sunrise this morning that I have so far ever seen.

The early mornings now are beautiful except that they are usually spoilt by the Hun with his shelling.

With Best Love, Jack.

*[On 5.6.17 the Diary recorded "artillery dump behind HQ set afire by enemy shells"]

9/6/17
My Darling Girl
Very many thanks for your two charming letters of 1st and 3rd which arrived this morning. I am very pleased to be able to tell you that I am once again out of the trenches — if only for a brief space of time [back at Boyelles]. I acted as O.C. Company during the tour in the line and managed well enough — no casualties either which is really rather satisfactory.

That Lady who read your hand must have changed your opinion of hand-reading. I am glad to hear that you are going to be married before you are 30. I hope more than I can say that I shall be the lucky man. I would do my best to make you happy as I think you know don't you. I was not aware that I had high ideals and all that sort of thing — but I won't contradict her. Soon be making me quite conceited in my old age you know I don't think.

With Best Love, Jack.

10/6/17
My Darling Phyl,
Very many thanks for your p.c. of the 4th which arrived this morning.

I am enjoying my rest here very much — it's fine to get clean clothes on again and be able to sleep in comfort — even if it is only for a few days. I don't think that I was ever so dirty as when I came out this time. But on close examination I find — much to my relief that I have not collected any creatures.

I have managed to get a bed made of wood and chicken wire — which is most comfortable. You would be surprised how much. Anyway it's heaps better than the ground.

What do you think of this new push in the north at Messines. Splendid isn't it. I know that neighbourhood awfully well — as it is where I was last year at this time — Kemmel you know. The mines we had there — which were blown up the other day — were terrific. I see from the papers that the guns could be heard in England on the coast and even in London.*

They want me to play cricket this afternoon against the N.Fs. I suppose that I shall have to as they are short of players. But it's too hot and I feel too lazy to be keen about it.

There is a swimming bath here fed by a little river — and although I regret to say I can't swim it's rather good sport splashing about in it especially during the hot weather.

I read a most frightful book the other day. I would not even dream of telling you its name — but it is absoutely the limit — it could not be bought in England and the author even does not put his name to it. There is nothing left to imagination — all in plain black and white. I wonder how anyone can write these things really don't you. Some one handed it to me — I didn't buy it — you may be sure. *His Hour* is child's play to it. It is rather annoying me telling you about it and not telling you the name isn't it. I don't know why I did really — but somehow or other I tell you most things don't I?

Won't it be topping when the war is really over — when one can come home and feel that you haven't to return again. War teaches everyone quite a lot I think don't you. You find out the things that really count in life the chief of course is love — not the flabby and wavering kind as I am afraid with many it is in the days of peace —but something that's worth having — that will go through Hell and remain unchanged.

It is much easier to fight and carry on out here if you feel that there is someone at home who does love you — and whom you love ever so much.

    With Best Love and Kisses, Jack.

[The assault on the Wytschaete-Messines ridge – the "push" to which Jack refers –was preceded on 7 June by the detonation at Messines of a series of 19 mines, which more or less blew the ridge away. Two mines failed to detonate; one of these remains buried, and unexploded, to this day.]

11/6/17

My Darling Phyl,

Many thanks for your letter of the 5th received today. I am glad to hear that the weather has changed again for the better.

It seems strange to think of people playing tennis — but of course we are rapidly approaching the summer now, aren't we.

That Waltz Destiny always brings back to me very pleasant memories — doesn't it you too? I should love to dance again although I know quite well that I am a poor hand at it. I am not fishing really.

The Armourer Sgt here is very clever at making souvenirs from shell cases and such like things. I have told him to make something for me. But it will be quite a long time before it's ready — so don't get alarmed.

I played cricket yesterday and took 2 wickets and scored 3 runs. Not a very bright show, was it — but some did not do as well as that.

They are making a collection throughout the Army for the St. Dunstan's Hostel for the Blind — those who have lost their sight through injuries received during the war. What annoys me is that they practically order you to give so much — only a day's pay for Officers and much less for the men. But it's not right I think, do you? Not the amount I am grousing about but the principle of it. It's the job of the government not us. We don't get such a fat lot out of the war in the way of cash.

I will write again soon. Goodnight Dearest Phyl. With Best Love, Jack.

FIELD POST CARD post marked 13 June

I am quite well.
Letter follows at first opportunity.

13/6/17

My Darling Phyllis,

I am once more again in the line — this time in the front Line not in support. The trenches that I am in were German at one time — not so very long ago either.

I am living in an old Machine Gun emplacement. It is a wonderful place and tremendously strong. The walls are 3 ft of concrete strengthened with steel. It's very low inside and has rooms within rooms — if you know what I mean.*

Capt. Armitage and myself and about 10 Other Ranks live in it. The Germans don't half do things thoroughly when they set about it.

So far anyway things have been extremely quiet — but I am afraid that they will not remain so for long.

I have got a trenchboard covered with sandbags to sleep on — which is quite comfy. I have no blankets or anything of that kind — but it's not cold really.

We stand to now at 2.30 am. A frightful time of the morning to be up isn't it. But I am very glad the nights are so short — they are much the worst time I always think.

One of our Officers who went home on leave the other day called in at the Bank and saw Father there and told him exactly where I was.

Goodbye for the present Darling. With Best Love, Jack .

[Jack mentions that he is in a Machine Gun emplacement. The Hindenburg Trench –his current location - was fortified with these strongholds at regular intervals, in a dog-tooth pattern.]

14/6/17

My Darling Phyllis,

Very many thanks for your letter of the 7th received last night.

The Officer Carver who was with me the other day is not a bad sort. He comes from Jamaica and speaks rather funny English.

Douglas Haig says the war is going to end this year. I hope it's true.

Things have not been quite so quiet since I last wrote you — but things are quite normal.* I went out on patrol last night between the hours of 12 pm and 2 am — and wandered about on the Top. I took a Sgt. with me. It is surprising how quickly you can lose your direction out there — all the ground is churned up with shells — one shell hole touching another. The trenches don't smell much here which is a great comfort. I get washed too every morning here and so live quite a civilised life don't I.

There's a dog here that seems to live in the trenches. He once was a German one, a most odd looking creature really — but seems quite at home with shells — never bothers about them a bit; although he has been hit in the back with a piece.

It is most extraordinary how the birds sing here — war does not seem to bother them at all.

I have a very powerful Telescope here. Yesterday towards evening I saw two Bosche with it quite plainly moving along a shallow trench showing themselves from the waist. They wore the ordinary grey uniform with steel hats with sandbag covers. But of course they were really a long way off — 2000 yds at least I should say. Too far to have a pot at them.

We must have a trip round here after the war is over, and all the disagreeable things have been moved away.

With Best Love, Jack.

*[*Things were, indeed, "not so quiet": the enemy was being bombarded with field guns and howitzers; an attack was about to be launched on the Division's right (see next letter), a gas attack on its left – both successful.*]

15/6/17
My Darling Phyl,

I was indeed pleased to receive your parcel last night. I sampled some of the cake at 2 this morning and it proved most excellent.

There was a big strafe on our immediate right flank early this morning — in fact they went over the top. I was very well placed and could see it all. The Germans as usual put up lights of all colours and together with the red flash of the bursting shells it was quite a fine sight, although perhaps rather a horrible one when you know that there are men there. English I mean of course.

We came in for a few of the shells. One hit our emplacement — I was well tucked away inside by that time you may be sure — and put the candle out. But otherwise the event passed off quite harmlessly for us although further down the trench 4 or 5 of the men were wounded.

That Officer — I mentioned Carver — has gone on a Course today — so I have had to move my home for the time being as there is only Capt. Armitage and myself left in the Company now and we cannot both be in the same part of the trench.

With Best Love, Jack.

17/6/17
My Darling Phyllis,

Many thanks for your delightful letter of the 9th which arrived last night. I am very pleased to be able to tell you that I am out of the trenches again [*on the Henin-Croiselles road*]. Things got rather lively at the finish and the Hun was properly stirred up; not without reason as attacks were made on three successive nights.

We of course came in for a lot of his shelling; but did not have any more casualties. As Carver was sent away on his Course I had to go and take over his post; which was considerably nearer the scene of activity and therefore much hotter. I assure you that I was quite pleased to get out of it.

It is great to get some fresh clothes on again and get a decent wash. I managed to get a bath this morning — with the aid of a sponge and a small basin of water. It's better than remaining filthy isn't it.

You give me quite a shock when you say that you feel dizzy and rotten first thing in the morning. I do hope that you are feeling better now. Thank Heaven you went to Ilkley when you did.

But please — Darling — do take care of yourself, and don't work so hard when you return to the Hospital.

With Very Best Love, Jack.

18/6/17
My Darling Phyllis,

Many thanks for your letter of the 11th received late last night.

So the sun is making you brown is it. You must look very s'nice — I hope that you won't let it wear off too quickly. I am like a Hindoo too — as brown as a nut.

Oh — by the way. I have got a bit of good news. On the 21st I am going on a

Course at the III Army School, which is on the seacoast — miles away from the line.

Have you seen that Hal Seed has got the M.C. He has certainly deserved it if anyone has.

I heard from home today. When the King went over Vickers Works at Barrow-in-Furness my brother Bernard was presented to him.* It's rather amusing really —I can imagine how rotten he would feel during the process.

Well, I must close now

With Best Love, Jack.

*[Bernard was a full rugby international, a captain of England. He was to lose a son, Kenneth, in the Second World War – killed at sea off the coast of Norway while serving on HMS Curacao.]

20/6/17
My Darling Phyllis,

Thanks very much for your nice long letter of the 13th received today.

I am very pleased to be able to tell you that I am once again back in the land of civilisation [in rest billets at Berles au Bois].

It is such a relief to see houses with roofs on and little things like that. There are too a few French people about — which is quite a pleasant change from Khaki —although they are rather a strange looking crowd.

We have got quite a nice looking billet — which when it is washed ought to be quite alright. Can you imagine me directing spring cleaning operations. I do it nevertheless — I can't stick a filthy place at any price. To the great joy of our Mess Cook there is a Kitchen Range attached to the place, which makes things much easier as he usually has only a brazier.

I told you in a previous letter that I was going on a 5 Weeks course. Unfortunately that has been knocked on the head. I am a witness for a Court Martial and therefore cannot go away.

Glad to hear that your Father has come safely through the air Raid. It must have been rather a terrible affair. We apparently did not put up any show at all. But aeroplanes are awfully difficult things to get down. I agree with you that it is damnable all those children have been killed. That is the worst of war — those who have the least to do with it suffer as much as any.

With Best Love, Jack.

21/6/17
My Darling Phyllis,

Very many thanks for your lovely long letter of the 15th which came yesterday. It is as you hoped — I am far away from the trenches.

I went for a joy ride yesterday to the place I sent you those P.P.C's of. It was quite pleasant to be able to look at shops again and see a fresh lot of people. One feels rather like a boy out of school for the day. It is such a relief to get away from parades and that kind of thing — even for such a short time.*

Very many thanks in anticipation for the mags you are sending. One gets very short indeed of anything to read out here. Even in the line — you have so many hours on duty and the rest off.

When does Mr. Bentham think the war will finish — is it to be this year of next?

106

Being out here makes you rather optimistic — in fact you have to be — life wouldn't be worth living if you weren't. As it is one lives principally for the arrival of the mail.

With Best Love, to you Jack.

P.S.   Thanks very much indeed Darling for the parcel of magazines and box of cigarettes which have just arrived by the post. It is awfully sweet of you to send them. I was simply fading away for the lack of something to read and also to smoke.

*[Jack's joy-ride would be to the city of Amiens. The Battalion Medical Officer, Raine, writing in **The Snapper**, refers to a regular excursion train run by the French Northern Railway Co. which left Arras about 5 a.m. picked up near the trenches at 6, and proceeded to Amiens for about 11, returning in the evening. "The Mess Sgt. Grice was a regular passenger," he writes, "and so great were his purchases that he had to have the Mess cart meet him upon his return."]*

23/6/17

My Darling Phyllis,

Many thanks for your letter of the 17th which arrived this afternoon

I heard from Norman today and he has given me his Map Reference so I shall try and find him if he's not too far away.

He tells me that he expects to come on leave soon. Lucky Dog isn't he — but of course it's a long time since he had any.

There are rumours about that we may be going up again shortly — but I don't believe it — anyway we haven't gone yet — so there is hope isn't there.

As with you it is fearfully hot here — nearly every afternoon I go and lie about in the orchards. Lazy old thing aren't I.

Best Love and heaps of Kisses, Jack.

25/6/17

My Darling Phyl,

I am still where I was when I last wrote you — a few days at the most and then back once again to the line.

I am getting more and more fed up and tired of this war — as indeed everyone else is, aren't they. I am not a "peace at any price person" — but oh — I would like to see it all over and done with.

All the Officers and NCOs of the Battalion were lectured this morning[by a Major from the 126th Coy, Royal Engineers] on Trenches and how to dig them. Afterwards we all were allotted our bit of ground and had to dig a trench. Frightfully hot work it was too — quite a number took off the greater part of their clothes before they had finished. I collected quite a fine collection of blisters on my hands. We have another go at it tomorrow.

There is an Officer here who is frequently getting letters from Russia. Things appear to be in a terrible state. Quite a lot of strafing and bloodshed going on. The servants too demand higher wages — eight hours per day and once a fortnight the use of all the rooms in the house in order that they may give parties etc. Best to do without them under those circumstance do you think so. It would be a bad job if anything like that happened in England — but of course it never would.

I had a letter from Mother today. She tells me that Edna is going to be married in September. It's going to be a quiet wedding.

Would you like a quiet wedding or otherwise? As one only gets married once in a lifetime why not have a good show I say — of course it doesn't really matter as long as you get married to the Girl you want to. I only wish that we could get married too — it would be awfully s'nice — almost too good to ever come true. If only this rotten war would finish.

I hope that if you ever do take that step — you won't regard yourself as finished and done for. I would do my *very very* best to see that you never regretted it — in any way — whatsoever.

  With Best Love, Jack.

26:6:17
My Darling Phyl,

I was very pleased indeed to receive your letter of the 20th this afternoon. It is *awfully sweet* of you to worry on my account — but I always try to give you the least possible cause for you to do so. I do sometimes fear to tell you too much — if I ever write and tell you I am in the trenches, you may be sure that I shall be out again by the time the letter reaches you.

I will — if it doesn't bore you — write you every day — when I am in the line.

I have rather a disagreeable job to perform tomorrow — Have got to give evidence at a Court Martial against another Officer. An awfully decent chap too — but with a terrible failing for drink. It is such a pity I think don't you —probably finished his career for ever in the Army.

I expect very shortly to return to the line again — but please do not worry as I shall be right enough; of that I am perfectly sure. It is rather extra-ordinary how one knows these things. Most people out here know when their time has come — I have seen it so often.

  Best Love, Jack.

27/6/17
My Darling Phyllis,

I have just finished a most hateful morning — giving evidence I mean of course — in that case I mentioned to you. They were really a very select lot who formed the court — not one Officer who had not got a decoration of some sort. It is rather rotten having to stand up and say most damning things — in the presence of the accused — especially if he's a friend of yours.

We are not going back to exactly the same place in the line as we were in before — although it's not very far anyway.

As long as it keeps fine things will be alright, in the wet here the trenches get into one big sticky muddy mess, and the sides fall in — which is distinctly distressing.

  With Best Love, Jack.

1/7/17
My Darling Phyllis,

I am in the front line [*near Moyenville*] again now as I write.

I have a concrete Dug Out like the one I described to you a short time ago. The trenches were in rather a bad state last night — mud and water up to the knees. I managed to get an hour or so sleep — putting my feet into sandbags — and was fairly comfy under the circumstances.*

Things though on the whole are fairly quiet — a few odd shells in the trench, nothing more.

All the villages here are frightfully knocked about. All the trees have been cut down too.

With Best Love, Jack.

[The Diary's observations on conditions at the front: "Trenches very sticky".]

2/7/17

My Darling Phyllis,

Many thanks for your letter of the 24th received last night. What a long time it has taken. I had not heard from you for 5 days.

I have heard indirectly that Harold has been found by a patrol of the 4 E.Y. about a week ago — they distinguished him by his identification disc. Please do not let them know at home until I get more reliable information.

I hear too that Capt. (Major) T. Morris is missing.

The 4th have been in it again and had a large number of casualties. They are always getting pushed into things aren't they.

I am still in the line and not having a bad time on the whole. I was out wiring from 12 to 3 am last night in No Man's Land. The ground between our lines and theirs is a very strange place. You find old trenches — Dug Outs and lots of other things —some of which are rather gruesome, but enough said.

I have been playing quite a lot of Auction Bridge up here in the trenches; anything to pass the time away.

I had some good sniping at dawn this morning — but I am afraid I did not damage anyone badly — they were just a bit too far away. I will look out for them tomorrow morning though.*

Hope you don't think me too bloodthirsty do you. I am in regard to Huns.

With Best Love, Jack.

[On the previous day the Diary noted: "The Colonel sniped a Bosche who was seen to collapse sideways."]

3/7/17

My Darling Phyl,

Thanks very much for your nice long letter of the 26th and the parcel — which both arrived together last night. The cake and the shortbread arrived intact. It's very sweet of you to send those things.

I am still in the front line. Last night I went out on patrol with 1 NCO and 1 Man and had quite an exciting time. I got quite close to the German lines about 40 yds off and was lying in a shell-hole when I saw a German patrol coming towards me —about 30 strong. At 30 yds from me they opened out into a kind of half moon formation to try and cut me off from my line. I didn't waste any more time you may be sure but set off back and just managed to get round them before they could close on me.

They could see me quite plainly and I could them but they never fired a shot —trying to take me prisoner I suppose. However, rather a nasty moment when I was getting round their flank to get back. Three against thirty is too big odds. Still all is well and I shan't be out tonight.

I will not run so much risk another time — I was a bit too venturesome perhaps, but I will be more careful in future you may be sure.

With Best Love, Jack.

5/7/17

My Darling Phyllis,

I am out of the firing line now and back in reserve in Dug Outs [*at Croisilles*]. Unfortunately our valises have not been sent up — so it's beastly cold at night.

One of the 4th's Officers, Dean by name, was killed on the night of the 3/4th [*he was out on a wiring party*]. It is remarkable but I am the only one left now who came out with the 4th East at Catterick on April 16th. Your charm still carries me through doesn't it. I have great faith in it now too.

I am going up towards the line this afternoon with a working party — An awful bother these working parties.

I feel very optimistic about the war just now — but I think that we shall be able to tell better in about a month's time. More I cannot say, but there is going to be something doing shortly somewhere on the western front.*

I am glad to say that we have had very few casualties in the Company this time in.

With Best Love, Jack.

*[*The "something doing" was the Third Battle of Ypres, which would be fought in the wettest autumn for twenty years.*]

6/7/17

My Darling Phyllis,

Many thanks for your letter of the 29th which arrived yesterday. I was very pleased to see it waiting for me when I returned from my working party.

You seem to be very busy at the Hospital — 37 in your ward — How many are there of you to look after them?

I have not heard as much as you about Harold's body being found. But I should think that my Mother will be relieved to know it in a way — especially as she will know exactly where he is buried. I must find out where it is — and go and see the place — it is quite hard to get any information as I don't know where the 50th Division are exactly.

I have to go on another working party this morning sad to relate — I shall be off in a very few minutes — so I am afraid that it will make this letter rather a short one. I hope however to get back by 5 pm.

With Best Love, Jack.

7/7/17

My Darling Phyllis,

Quite a lot has happened since I wrote you yesterday.

I started on the working party and had got quite a long way when I was sent for and had to return to Batt Head Qts. Capt. Armitage's transfer to the 8th E.Y.R. has come through — so I have been given the command of the Company. Rather good isn't it.

I don't know whether I shall manage to keep it — but I shall certainly have a fight for it — there is hardly any except the present O.C. Company senior to me in the Batt. in regard to gazette — in fact some of them are junior. I must see how things turn out — You may see me with those pips yet. I should get quite a good increase in pay too — which would be very welcome and help things on a bit, wouldn't it? You know what I mean don't you.

I am very sorry that Armitage has gone — just about the bravest chap I've struck out here yet and awfully good to get on with. He asked me if I would transfer with him to the 8th — but of course that is impossible. I think perhaps that it was a jolly good job that I did not get back to the 4th — as they always seem to be getting strafed don't they and have a rotten time.

I still feel very optimistic about the war — especially with this Russian stunt doing so well. I am convinced that it will finish this year — perhaps sooner than any of us realise — let's hope so anyway.

I hope in a few days now to get just a little nearer civilisation. Where I am now —there's absolutely nothing except a YMCA which is in a very knocked about house in the neighbouring village — in fact it's the only house standing up at all. The Hun often shells the place too. They give the troops coming from the line drinks of lime juice [*with plenty of sugar added*] free of charge — no matter how many of them there may be. Those places are absolutely a godsend and they get quite close to the line too.

With Best Love, Jack.

9/7/17
My Darling Phyllis,

Many thanks indeed for your letter of the 2nd received last night.

I am very glad to be able to tell you that I am quite a long way back from the line now — practically out of reach of Hun shells. The camp we have here [*Moyenville, Divisional Reserve*] is quite nice — tents you know.

After being unable to change for 8 days — the thought of a flea bag fills me with joy.

I still am in Command of the Company and am doing my best to remain so. If I keep it for 15 days my name goes in for a Captaincy.

I am so sorry to hear that you are at the Dentists — simply horrible I think — there's nothing I hate or fear more — my knees positively knock together whenever I go and see that horror or horrors.

I can see most exciting times ahead if I have to ride the Company horse, can't you — it's rather amusing to think of me being an O.C. Company.

Goodnight Darling. With Best Love, Jack.

11/7/17
My Darling Phyllis,

Many thanks for your letter of the 4th received last night.

I may have to go up and spend two days with a Battery — 18 Pounders —soon. The idea is I believe to create good feeling between the Infantry and the Artillery.

I heard from my Father today — and he tells me that you're very well.

One of our Officers [*2Lt K. D. Briggs*] has gone to Hospital today as his mind seems to be rather affected — of late he has been talking a lot of utter nonsense — but I think he will recover alright in time.

Jack Ferens is coming out here I understand — it would be amusing if he came to this crush wouldn't it.

With Best Love and lots of kisses, Jack.

12/7/17
My Darling Phyllis,

I am now at the Battery — to which I told you I was going for 2 days.

Unfortunately I go back to the Battalion tomorrow.

I have had quite a good time, have learnt how to fire and Load the gun etc. — which of course may come in useful some day.

The Officers' quarters are awfully comfortable — the Mess especially so — they have got a lot of those sun blinds from a village near by — and so one side of the room can be thrown entirely open — gives things a very summer house effect.

We have not been shelled at all — so it's quite a holiday. I got up here on "George" the Company horse. My word! but I am still stiff and sore this morning. Anyway he did not throw me off — which is something, although I admit I had one or two rather narrow squeaks.

This Russian stunt is going very well isn't it. They seem to be getting along famously — another 10,000 prisoners I hear.

I am going up in a few moments up to the Observation Post from which you can see many miles right back beyond the German trenches — it ought to be interesting.

I'll write you tomorrow and tell you about it.

With Best Love, Jack.

15/7/17

My dearest darling Phyl,

I rode over yesterday to see Norman — he gave me *your message*, not by word of mouth either but the other way as was intended. I think that it is just lovely of you —*awfully* s'nice — I should like very much to send you many messages like that or far better than that to give *them* to you myself. You are indeed an absolute "Darling". I can't say how much you have bucked me up.

I fear that I have not written you for about three days but I have been very busy coming from the Battery and then going over to see Norman.

I am afraid I did run rather a big risk on that patrol — But I will really be more careful this time up. The NCO and man got back safely too.

The Brigadier said I ought to have fired on them and then charged them with the bayonets. I don't think — my life is too valuable to do anything of that kind you may be sure.

Leave is going very well just now — quite a number of Officers are getting away. I may come home sooner than I expected if Leave goes on at the same rate. The thought makes one fearfully excited even now — we would have a good time wouldn't we. It would be a positive paradise while it lasted. Would you be so *very very* strict. I am sure that I would be *awfully good*. Norman tells me that he has had a *very very* good time on leave — and continuously refers to it.

I left Norman's place on my bicycle at 10 pm and it then started to pour with rain. The roads here have no surface at all — and I skidded all over the place, coming to earth altogether 5 times. It was so dark that when I ran across one of the Light Railways I waited and stopped the train when it arrived and put my bicycle on one of the trucks and got inside the engine myself, and proceeded on my way. I got off at a junction and got back to our camp about 12.30 am.

By the way I am no longer in Command of the Company — a regular Captain has turned up from somewhere unfortunately. [*A. F. Cemery, from the VII Corps School.*] Had he not done so I should have kept it and had the glory of 3 pips —the Adjutant assured me of this.

With very best love and lots and lots of kisses, Yours, Jack.

16/7/17

My Darling Phyllis,

I am in the front line. It is quite the most wonderful bit of line that I have ever seen.

Throughout its length — at a depth of about 30 feet — runs a tunnel with rooms off it. It is quite possible to walk 2 miles or more without once getting up into the trench. There are shafts down about every 50 yds or so. You don't half feel safe when you get down there — feel almost brave at times.*

By the time this letter reaches you I shall be out of the line. I hope that those souvenirs arrived safely. I told you the armourer Sgt. was making me something for you — it turns out to be a kind of vase — the lower portion consists of a German Whizz-bang shell case — brass — with the E. Yks badge on it — fitting into the top is a sunflower, each petal being made of brass and joined together in a ring so as to fit in the case.

I will be as careful as possible if I do go out on patrol this time. I hear that they want us to capture a Hun this time in — risky job for the one who gets it to do.

Goodbye for the present Darling. With Best Love and many ? Jack.

*[*The "wonderful bit of line" was the Tunnel Trench, part of the Hindenberg defences; it is described by Raine in* **The Snapper** *as containing "evidences of luxury such as beds, easy chairs, pictures, wall-paper, etc...Further to the north it is said that the tunnel was electrically lit." Raine also points out, however, that when they first took it over dead bodies, German and British, abounded, many crawling with maggots.*]

19/7/17

My Darling Girl,

I had an awful narrow squeak this morning.

I was on duty in the Trench at about 4.15 am — when someone started a show on the Right of us — bombs and shells. Captain Cemery my O.C. Company came up out of his Dug Out and came onto the fire bay. I was standing on the fire step —head and shoulders above the parapet — he was 2 feet away from me in the trench.

At this moment the Hun opened out on us — the first fell just behind us and the next in our bay just to the left of Capt. Cemery.

Cemery was hit in several places and died in about 30 seconds.* I was blown off the fire step into the trench and got a bit of shell in my left shoulder — just about the shoulder blade — it went through my trench coat and tunic and shirt and everything — but it only just cut the skin a bit — so it's nothing to worry about. The M.O. put a little Iodine on it — By Jove it does smart doesn't it — and I am carrying on as before. I believe that my name will appear in casualty lists — but there is no need to get disturbed as I am as fit as a fiddle.

I had a very narrow escape though. Don't want any more like that again. It appears that I shall be able to wear a gold bar.

Your charm saved me again you know — it certainly does bring me marvellous luck — I'll never part with it you may be sure.

I expect that we shall be relieved very shortly now — the sooner the better although except for the show this morning things have been very quiet indeed.

I feel awfully sorry about Capt. Cemery — he was such a decent chap — been out here since 1914 and wounded twice. However what's done is done isn't it.

I am writing home today. You might ring them up — if you wouldn't mind doing it and just tell them that I have only got a scratch and am perfectly fit. I know that they will be rather agitated when they see me in the casualty list.

Hope you don't mind me asking you to do this "Darling". But I know that you will understand. I don't think that I have any more to say this time — so will close now.

With Very Best Love, Jack.

*[*The Diary entry concerning this incident is brief: "Killed Capt. A. F. Cemery. 3 O.R. to F.A.".* **The Snapper** *states that Cemery was a career soldier, joining the Scots Guards as a private in 1910, aged 19. He became a Sergeant in 1913 and later became one of the first NCOs to obtain a commission. He had been severely wounded a year earlier, and had been back with the Bn only twelve hours when killed. Raine notes that Cemery "had only told me two or three days before that he would never come back from the trenches alive, and had a premonition of death. I tried to cheer him up but he could not get rid of the uncanny premonition."*]

20/7/17
My Darling Phyllis,

I am glad to be able to tell you that I am out of the front line now and back in support.

I have quite a nice deep "Dug Out" 20 feet or more — so am quite safe [*in a fortification known as Concrete Reserve*]. I assure you that I was very glad indeed to be relieved — although speaking of the Company as a whole we had not a bad time really.

This afternoon I went to Capt. Cemery's funeral — it was quite close to the line —so I thought I ought to go — although I do hate going to them.

I shall have to write to his people I suppose — rotten job — he had a brother killed at Kut [*Mesopotamia*] in January.

It would be good if I could keep command of the Company wouldn't it. I am now again of course, with Capt. Cemery going under — poor chap.

I hope that some of my letters to you aren't opened by the censor — I don't mean that they have got Military information within — but a much more private and altogether better subject — the best in the world — things that I only want one person on earth to read.

Goodbye for the present Darling. With Best Love and lots of Kisses, Jack.

23/7/17
My Darling Phyllis,

Many thanks for your letter of the 17th which arrived today.

Capt. Broadley is taking over this Company again tomorrow — he has been second-in-Command of the Batt — but someone senior to him has come back again.*

They call the Officers of 'B' Company our "Territorial Brethren" as three of us are terriers. Rather amusing isn't it.

We were having breakfast this morning in our summer house in the trench —when the Hun started to shell us most vigorously. We immediately sought refuge in our "Dug Out" but sad to relate left our breakfast behind. Most ungentlemanly of the Hun to shell us at meals I think don't you?

When Capt. Cemery was killed and I was hit the other day — we weren't 100 yds from a shaft which led down 30 feet or so. There is nothing much to tell you about —generally speaking — except this rotten old war. And I hate writing to you about that. How are you — you never tell me you know.

    With Best Love, Jack.

*[*The officer replacing Broadley as second-in-command and senior Major was Captain Coles, returning from the 8th EYR.*]

25/7/17
My Darling Phyllis,
    Very many thanks for your letter of the 19th received today.

    I am out of the trenches [*back at Moyenville*] but we are still being used for Working parties in the trenches. We have got our kits at last — which is a great comfort.

    I regret to say that I was not altogether free from creatures — just a few. Horrible isn't it — but it can't be helped: it's those dirty Hun Dug Outs.

    I was lying fast asleep this morning at about 10 am — very lazy wasn't it — when the clouds opened and rain poured down. The roof of my little shanty seemed to make a sort of pool which eventually brought down the greater portion of the roof — we both got rather damp — in fact nearly washed out of the place altogether. Amazing, wasn't it — oh, give me a house with a decent roof.

    With Best Love, Jack.

28/7/17
My Darling Girl,
    Very many thanks for your letter of the 22nd and all the good wishes it contains.

    So you are having a slack time at the Hospital — Jolly good job too — you must be about boiled to death in the place with this weather on. I don't know how you manage it. I hope that you will get *10 days off* from the Hospital when I come home. How dare you say that you expect you will be able to get some off — *if I want you to*. *Want you* — I can never see enough of you — only wish I could have you with me always — it would be lovely — afraid *you* might get very bored that's all. I never should.

    I am now quite a long way back [*at St. Leger*] — in tents — nice and cool — We have left the Zone where R.E's spring at you to supply working parties.

    I am rather glad that I went up to the trenches once or twice with working parties as it has given me back my old confidence again. That affair of Cemery and myself shook me up quite a lot — it's surprising really but it did. I don't think that I have ever been quite so close to death before as that morning — just gives you a bit of a jolt for a day or so. I am as fit as anything now — quite merry and bright.

    I got a shock tonight — the Adjutant is going away for the day tomorrow and has told me to act for him. See me ordering the Battalion about — on parade — I hope I don't make a mess of it — still I think it's fairly simple.

    With Best Love and heaps of Kisses, Jack.

31/7/17
My Darling Phyl,
    Very many thanks for your letter of the 25th.

    I feel an awful brute having worried you so. It was just a scratch — nothing more

— honest — But believe me it was a close shave, about 1000 to 1 me coming through with my life at all — and I was hardly touched.

I was standing on the Fire Step head and shoulders above the parapet watching the Hun Raid on our left — Capt. Cemery was standing in the trench — a shell burst actually on the parapet a yard away from me — I measured it afterwards. I must have ducked instinctively — I don't remember much about it — It blew me into the trench almost on top of Capt. Cemery — who was dead even then. My tunic was cut about a bit — I got hit in my back — just about my shoulder on both sides. The Right one was only a bruise, the other on the Left made a bit of a gash and it bled a little — but the Doctor put some Iodine on it — and all was well. It was just a bit stiff for a day or two but it's alright now — I haven't been away from duty for it either.

There's just a scar about an inch long now to show for it. I must say it shook me up a bit for a few days.

We are going in the line again very shortly — never seem to stop out for long do we — I am sorry that my rotten writing has been sending some of my letters to you astray. I will take care that the address is clearer — and will not be mistaken.

I had quite a nice letter from Cemery's people today — I wrote them on behalf of the Officers of the Company.

I had a great day yesterday — I went to Amiens — and that speaks for itself. I was sitting in a café there when who should I see passing but Wilkinson of the 150 T.M.B. We had a great time together. You may remember me telling you about a girl the Prince of Wales ran after — Well, she is still there at the Hotel Gobert.

You would have been amazed to see me as Adjutant the other day — giving orders to the Battalion etc — I didn't make any slips either and got on quite well with the C.O. — although I think personally he is a wash out.

My life in the Battalion is extremely varied — I am frequently changing from one thing to another. I have written to the Records Office at York to ask them if I am a first or a second Lieut. — which is the main thing. But if I had two stars up —I think I would most certainly get a Company permanently and then of course get 3 pips.

Hal Seed I understand was hit in the foot by a shell and has had to have it amputated. Bad job — but it might have been worse.

I must close now, so au revoir "Darling Girl".

With Best Love, Jack.

3/8/17

My Darling Phyllis,

You will be surprised to hear that I am now in Hospital. Can you guess what with — the old complant "Trench Fever". I have been ill since last Tuesday night.

I was sent to the Field Ambulance on Wednesday morning [*1.8.17*] — they kept me there and sent me about 20 miles back to my present home, the 21st Divisional Rest Station. My old temperature has been dashing about rather wildly judging from the chart, from 99 to 103.6. I feel at present as if I have just played about 2 Doz. games of footer all on top of one another.

I am comfy — a bed with sheets — what luxury. My servant [*orderly, or batman*] is in with me too which makes a lot of difference.

With Best Love, Jack.

5/8/17

My Darling Phyl,

I am heaps better now — although I am still in bed. Time does pass so slowly here. There are no nurses or anything in that line — only R.A.M.C. Orderlies, a more undisciplined crew I never struck.

It is an extraordinary thing how Trench Fever can make you feel so rotten —and ache in every joint. Headaches too — nearly drive you crazy at times. The M.O. tells me that the germ is given to people by a certain kind of "chat". It sounds highly likely too — I had quite a large collection of those creatures a short time back.

I really am a lucky beggar — because I hear the Batt. has had a rough time the last few days [*He went to the F.A. the day the Batt. went back to the front line.*]

This Hospital is pitched in a big Orchard. Rather pretty — any amount of fruit in the trees.

My M.O. was up at Ypres winter 1915/1916 — with us — so I know him quite well. Funny isn't it how you run up against people like that.

With *Very Best Love and heaps of Kisses,* Jack

I do want to *kiss* you *so much.*

7/8/17

My Darling Girl,

You must think that my letters are becoming few and far between. But to be quite candid I have been feel very groggy of late. I got up and sat in a deckchair the other afternoon for an hour or so — but haven't been up again — I've been in bed just a week now. There is one good thing though — the line won't see me again for quite a long time — Thank heaven. I was really quite pleased when I found out I'd got it badly. It would be amusing if I landed up in "Blightie" one of these fine days. very little chance of it though I'm afraid.

I couldn't pick you up and carry you now — or damage you in any way. Pity I'm not at home — you would be able to do just what you like with me for once. My kissing apparatus is still in splendid working order though. What a lot of rot I'm writing aren't I. My head must be affected.

Another Officer of the 1st EYR [*2Lt M. B. Stephenson*] arrived here yesterday and is going on to the Corps Rest Station. I want to get to the C.C.S. and then it's even money I get across.

I met here yesterday a chap — Bryden 5 Yks — who was with me last September-October. There were 5 of us who went about together — the other three have all died. Doesn't half bring the war home to you that kind of thing.

My *wound* is better now — only a scar left — I must show it to you sometime but perhaps I'd better not.

Hope to hear from you soon — expect they will arrive in a bunch.

With Very Best Love, Jack.

9/8/17

My Darling Phyll,

I am still at the same Hospital — haven't managed to get myself moved further down yet.

I really do feel heaps better this morning — it's the first time for 4 days that my temperature has been below 100 and now it's 97.2 — a bit too low I believe. They

117

give me all kinds of things to take — but between you and me they don't do much good. My temperature just goes up and down as it likes.

Will write again soon. With Very Best Love and heaps of Kisses, Jack.

11/8/17

My Darling Phyl,

I am still exactly at the same place as I was last time I wrote to you. I have been much better the last two days and have been able to get up for a little while.

I am getting most frightfully fed up with this place — I wish they would move me to a different Hospital. What on earth they have been doing with my mail beats me. I shall strafe them when I see them again.

I know that this is a most uninteresting letter — but I've no news at all.

Hope to hear from you soon. With Very Best Love, Jack.

12/8/17

My Darling Phyl,

I could have positively screamed the place down with joy when I received your letter of the 3rd yesterday afternoon.

Hadn't had any for such a long time and was feeling rather down about it —until yours arrived which bucked me up heaps. I am glad to hear that my letter of the 28th did some good.

I hope that you *do* manage to get the *10 days* off when I come home. I only wish that it was longer — we will have a great time though you may be sure.

It seems ages and ages since I kissed you last, doesn't it. I am positively aching to do so — It would be very s'nice don't you think so.

Goodbye for the present — Darling. With Very Best Love, Jack.

14/8/17

My Darling Phyl,

Many thanks for your letter of the 5th.

Many thanks for your parcel — which arrived yesterday too. I regret to say that the journey and the hot weather proved too much for the cream. The strawberries and cake though were excellent.

I am very glad to hear that the watch pendant arrived safely — what's more that you liked it.

I read that story — "The Big Push in B Ward" in the *Story Teller* you sent me. It is awfully good isn't. I simply roared with laughter when I read it.

I have been allowed to get up today and have actually got dressed — great excitement I assure you. I am rather a white-faced looking thing now, but as they are filling me up with iron pills I'll soon be right.

The Hospital was inspected yesterday by a large crowd of Staff people. A Senior Surgeon addressed a few particularly foolish remarks to me — and said my chart was very interesting and passed on. Do you know I made a great discovery yesterday — I am only *3* off Leave and one of them is in Hospital — so when I do go back I might?! get away pretty soon. I feel quite excited at the prospect. We will have a time — so be warned in time — although I don't think anything *very dreadful* will happen to you — Don't forget those *10 days off* will you.

With Very Best Love and heaps of Kisses, Jack.

18/8/17

My Darling Phyl,

I have not been moved since I last wrote to you — and am feeling a lot better. I get up every day now — and stop up for all meals.

With Very Best Love, Jack.

19/8/17

My Darling Girl,

I was very pleased to receive your letters of the 8th and 10th yesterday — also the parcel containing cigarettes, novel and mags. I am sure it's awfully good of you to send them.

I consider myself awfully lucky to have got down here and missed the line for a bit. It's the first time that I have ever done it — been in a Hospital in France.

So you had a good time at Everthorpe Hall. That's Ben Seed's place isn't it. Yes, it is bad luck about Hal Seed — but still you know it might be a great deal worse, mightn't it.

I don't expect that I shall be here so very much longer — but the Division ought to be going out to rest soon and then of course I *may* get away on leave.

With Very Best Love and heaps of Kisses, Jack.

21/8/17

My Darling Phyl,

I haven't been thrown out of this place yet and sent back to the Battalion but I expect it any time as I am feeling quite fit again now. But you may be sure that I shan't urge them to do so.

They gives me heaps of Burgundy to drink. Rather a nice kind of medicine, I think. Some would do you good, I'm sure. Trying to turn you into a drunkard, aren't I. I don't think.

I had a letter from Norman yesterday. He says he wishes that this war would end and we could get on with something. I do too "By Jove". All these years gone by and nothing really done.

But in spite of it all I have had some very s'nice times since August '14, many of which — I frankly admit — are due to you. You really are a "Darling". I think I love you better every day. Terrible state of affairs, isn't it. I can see you having quite an exciting time when I do come home on leave. Let's hope it's soon.

I must close now as it's just about time for the C.O's tour of inspection.

With write again soon. With Very Best Love, Jack.

23/8/17

My Darling Phyl,

Very many thanks for your letter of the 14th which arrived today.

I am still in Hospital and am rapidly recovering although I have had a headache for 2 or 3 days now — a mild return of the fever, I suppose.

I only wish that you were nursing me. It would be simply lovely. I have a room all to myself too. The woods round here are just the place for a er — quiet walk.

I hear rumours of the Division going out to rest. I hope it's true. Rather a slacker, aren't I. But I am very tired of trenches — and everything connected with them. But I must really get back to the Battalion — mainly because I want to get my leave.

I must close now so goodbye for the moment. With Very Best Love, Jack.

25/8/17

My Darling Girl,

I have just had the M.O. round and am going back to the Battalion this afternoon. I am jolly glad really as I've been away a long time and am perfectly fit now. They are out of the line too, so there is no cause for any worry. Also the Battalion is the only place for me to get leave from — and I want that very *badly*.

By the way in the Gazette of July 26th I relinquish the rank of Lieutenant —have to refund 1/- per day from January 17th 1917 — £9.16.0 altogether. Rather rotten, isn't it, but it's no use grumbling. I ought to get my promotion from the 4th E.Y. any time now and that will be permanent.

I see from the paper that you have been having more Zepp Raids on Hull and district. I really feel very anxious about you — were they near at all? The paper said bombs were dropped on the coast — but you can't trust the papers in these days. I do hope that you're alright and safe and sound.

With Very Best Love and heaps of Kisses, Jack.

[Headed stationery "Corps Officers' Club] **26/8/17**

My Darling Phyl,

Many thanks for your letter of the 19th received today.

I have rejoined the Batt — or rather am at the Transport lines as the Batt is not yet out. I am very pleased to be able to tell you that the Division is going out for a rest — probably a month.

Leave is going strong but I shall not get any at once.

Many congrats on getting your second stripe — it's splendid. I am awfully glad that you've got it. I *hope* that you will get off for as long as you can when I do get leave — won't you, Darling? I'll be *very good*!!

With Very Best Love, Jack.

28/8/17

My Darling Phyl,

I am now miles away behind the lines — in fact only 5 miles away from the place where I was in Hospital [*in huts at Simoncourt*]. We had quite a long march today. I felt rather feeble at the finish.

Things are rather rotten in the Battalion now so I feel rather fed up. My O.C. Company has started on his old business again — I don't want another Court Martial. I do hope that my leave comes soon.

I must close now. Goodnight Darling. With Very Best Love, Jack.

29/8/17

My Darling Girl,

I was delighted to receive three of your letters altogether today — 17th, 22nd and 23rd.

I am very sorry indeed though to hear that you are ill in bed. I feel very anxious. I hope that it's nothing serious, is it "Darling"? Please don't be in too much of a hurry to get up — I know how 'fed up' you can get with bed, but it's worth while in the end.

After not getting to bed until 4 am and then getting up again at 8 am I don't wonder that you felt weary. You are having a busy time at the Hospital too. I suppose it's not much use me saying anything, but please do take care of yourself. I

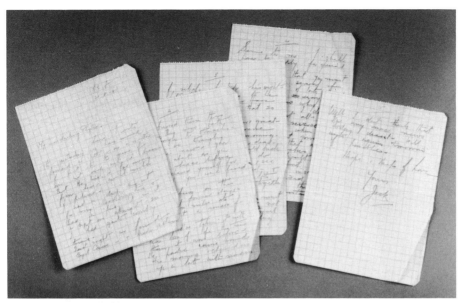

Letter of 30 August 1918, written in pencil on note-paper from the battle zone. His writing remains clearly legible in the most trying conditions.

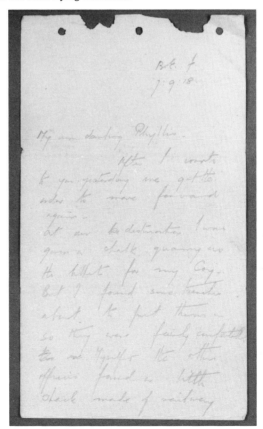

Letter of 7 September 1918, keeping Phyllis up to date with the latest move.

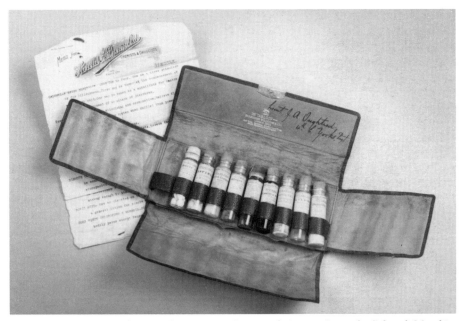

Second page of same letter, which was written in haste on official message form.

Jack Oughtred's own medicine pack, containing Boric acid, Aspirin, Bismuth, Calomel, Morphia, etc. Jack refers to the use of morphine, and tells how it possibly saved one life, in his letters of 9 October and 4 November 1917.

The 1st Battalion Medical Officer,
Capt. R. T. Raine, M.C., R.A.M.C.
(See letter of 28 August 1918).

Capt. Arthur H. Ewing, M.C.
Ewing survived Saulcourt (see letter of
12 April 1918), was shot in the head at
Le Sars six months later, rescued by
Raine, but died shortly afterwards. (See
letter of 28 August 1918).

*Capt. J. H. Keech, M.B.E., M.C.
Keech, who had enlisted in 1897,
survived right through the war, was
shot in the chest three days before
the Armistice, but lived to complete
34 years of military service. (**See
letter of 8 November 1918**).*

*Capt. F. L. Du Moulin, M.C.
Jack considered Du Moulin "too
brave"; **The Snapper** described him
as "brave to a fault". (**See letter of
8 November 1918**).*

124

mean that: you and your health come before anything else.

I wish I could come over and see you. It's awfully rotten when you're ill. I wonder whatever has happened to you. It takes such a long time for letters to reach me generally. I think that it's about time I came home and looked after you. I could take care of you very well I'm sure.

You ought to have a good rest. You have done your bit, I think, and a damned good bit too. My opinion of you is *naturally* rather biased, but I must say that the way you have "carried on" at the Hos. has been jolly fine. I expect I shall get fearfully strafed for saying that, but it's perfectly true.

I count the days until I see you — as I told you in my letter only 3 off leave and two are away on Courses.

I must close now. Heaps of Love, Jack.

2/9/17

My Darling Phyl,

Many thanks for your letter of the 25th which came yesterday.

I am glad to hear that you are alright again — at least fairly so. I am very pleased that you are taking some "beery" stimulant — I am sure that it will do you heaps of good. I know what that Burgundy did for me. How much have you to take every day?

I wrote you two days ago — saying that I expected to come on leave on the 9th or 10th. Well, much as I regret to say it I shall *not* be coming as leave is stopped to all Officers in the Battalion until further notice. Why I cannot tell you in a letter. The General stopped it. How long it will be stopped I don't know. I was so near. I did want to get away now because you said that you were having a week off from the Hospital.

By the way all the French people say the war is going to finish this year —perhaps.

With Best Love, Jack.

6/9/17

My Darling Phyl,

Many thanks for your two letters of the 29th and 30th which arrived today.

I regret to say that leave is still stopped. Anyway, when I do come my people will be home again and I shall be able to see a lot of you. We shall have a very good time together, you may be sure. I can't tell you how eager I am to see you again. It seems just ages ago since I last saw you and kissed you — in the taxi. Do you remember? I do.

I was rather astonished and more than pleased to hear that Doris and Norman are getting married on his next leave. I am jolly glad, aren't you. It's most exciting — and you're going to be a bridesmaid. I hope that I can manage to get leave for it, but I doubt very much if I can. I think that it's an awfully good idea on their part as the war might go on for quite a long time yet. Don't you think so too? What's the good of wasting time?

I too wish that this war was over and done with and you and I could get married too. Goodness knows how long it's going to last. How would you like to get married? I must say that with you it would be awfully s'nice.

I quite realise that it's a most serious business — but with you I am sure it would be simply delightful. You know, Phyl, I am a very poor hand at writing this sort of

125

thing — so easy to speak but very hard to put down on paper.

I don't know what started me on the topic, but hearing that Norman's getting married shortly — one cannot help of thinking of oneself. I shall have to elope with you or something of the sort — I don't think. What do you think of it all? That's the main question. If I could possibly get home for the ceremony it would be tophole.

I hope to go to Amiens tomorrow and have a day's holiday there. The train leaves a station 10 kilos from here at 6.18 am — so I shall have to be up early. It hardly seems worthwhile going, only it's a day off parades etc. — which is a great relief.

I must close now. Goodnight Darling. With heaps of Love, Jack.

8/9/17
My Darling Phyl,

I went yesterday to Amiens as I told you I might, but I had a terrible job getting there and back again. On the whole I don't think that it was worth it. I started from the camp at 4 am and just managed to catch the train at 6.10 am. But the return journey was the worst as I got off the train at 11.30 pm and did not get back to camp until 2 am. I shan't do it again in a hurry.

This afternoon we have had our Brigade Sports. It was frightfully hot for the running. The main turn was a Marathon cross country race — course being 5 miles long. My servant Pte Butcher came in 3rd. Jolly good wasn't it. There must have been quite 400 running altogether from the 4 Battalions. We — the E. Yorks, that is — got eleven out of the first 20 places.

The band — not our own — played all kinds of things — Destiny in particular, which brought back many very pleasant memories. Do you remember that supper dance I had the good fortune to have with you at the Old Hymerians Dance at the City Hotel. Was it not delightfully long? Or perhaps you think that it was too much so. We really had quite a gay winter that year didn't we?

I am sorry to say that Leave has not opened up yet for Officers in this Battalion. There is another reason why I want to get away quickly — but I can't tell you in a letter as the censor might open it and then there would be a row.

It is about a year ago now since I first went into the Somme Show. It's strange how I seem to come through these things, isn't it?

By the way I nearly forgot to tell you — I expect to get a second pip shortly. My name has been forwarded. I hope that it will be permanent this time. I am tired of refunding money to Cox and Co. [*bankers to the East Yorks Regiment*].

With Very Best Love and heaps of Kisses, Jack.

12/9/17
My Darling Phyl,

Many thanks for your letter of the 6th which arrived yesterday.

It is a very sad thing that leave's stopped. I hear that another Officer [*2Lt Stephenson*] is on his way back from Hospital to join the Battalion again — who, sad to relate, comes before me on the leave list.

Yesterday — Tuesday — I went to another Sports Meeting held by the Divisional General [*Divisional Gymkhana at Wagnonlieu*]. It was of course not so good as the one at St. Pol, but quite alright. It was held on an aerodrome. Officers from all the Battalions in this Division were invited, also quite a large number of nurses were present who were all commandeered by the Staff. One of the hangars was cleared and used as a bar room most successfully, while in another similar one refreshments were provided of a somewhat different type.

This afternoon I attended the final rounds of the Brigade Boxing Competition held in our village. Things got rather gory at times.

I think that I may be very shortly where the "fourth" were when I first joined them. More I cannot say. I feel confident that my luck is still good so all is well: it's no use worrying.

That visit you paid to the Munitions Works must have been very interesting. I wonder how the girls stand it. 10 hrs a day takes a bit of keeping up I should say.

    With Best Love, Jack.

14/9/17
My Darling Phyl,

I have just seized this opportunity to write you as I may not have another chance for a few days, so don't worry if you don't hear from me for a bit. I shall be quite alright and in no danger at all, far enough away from the line. As for the future I know that I shall have to go through it again — this is inevitable. You may perhaps guess what I mean — do you? This time however I shall have a Company, so I think that I am slightly better off. I may get a "blighty" but I am sure that it will be nothing more deadly.

I seem to be writing in rather a depressing strain — but I'm not depressed —really. Only one has got to face these things. I only hope that I manage everything successfully. I feel perhaps that it is rather rotten of me to tell you and thus make you worry a little, but I have always made it a habit of telling you everything, so I thought you might as well know.

We had a Brigade field day yesterday and did not get back until 7 pm.* I felt very weary; Carver was in command of the Company and made rather a mess of things — that's the reason why I have got it. My second star is going through according to the 18 Months scheme. It will date from 16/11/16 — so Cox and Co will have the pleasure of paying some cash back to me.

    Goodnight Dearest. With Best Love, Jack.

*[The field day was not an untypical event. Between spells in the line there were all kinds of exercises, including practice attacks. The Bn Diary this day records "2 attacks on enemy, represented by the 10 KOYLI".]

Picture Post Card [place name censored out] 17/9/17
I am [scored out] and having quite a good time — although I am very busy. Am stopping at an Hotel — very comfortable — beautifully clean

    Best Love, Jack.

[The Division was now transferred from XVIII Corps to X Corps (2nd Army) and journeyed by train and on foot to scattered billets north of Hazebrouck. An assault on German lines around Ypres had begun on 31 July and was about to be renewed, on 20 September, the main objective being the Passchendaele Ridge.]

17/9/17
My Darling Phyl,

I was very pleased to receive your letter of the 10th this evening.

It was a bad job, Leave being stopped just as I was going. I can't tell you how fed up I was about it, and am still, but I'm feeling more resigned to it now. The Officer who caused it to be stopped has left the Battalion, so all may yet go well. Still, it will be some time before I get it I fancy.

I got a topping billet for the night at an estaminet close by — everything was beautifully clean: I had to wipe my feet before I went upstairs. It was rather amusing altogether.

Tonight though I've got a huge barn-like room next to the rafters extending over all the other rooms in the house. It looks rather like a place for lots of rats so as I'm sleeping on the floor I shall have to keep a good look out. I don't like creatures of that kind running over me, do you?

Carver — who was second-in-Command of this Company — is going on a Staff job tomorrow as he made a bit of a mess of things the other day. Lucky dog: I wish I was*?

Goodnight Dearest. With Best Love, Jack.

*[*Broadley had now been sent to the U.K. to report to the War Office. Carver had been sent to the reinforcement camp as a musketry instructor.*]

24/9/17
My Darling Phyllis,

Many thanks for yours of the 18th received last night.

So you have guessed my meaning have you ? Well, I am perfectly alright up to the moment, a long way still from the line [*having marched to Thieushoek*] —Thank Heaven. But I don't feel at all uneasy about things. I have been having quite a good time the last day or so in these little towns. I have got a really nice billet now and a bedroom with a bed all of my own. What luxury, isn't it? It is as a matter of fact the very room that Lt-Col. Wilkinson of the 4th had when he was here. Funny, isn't it? The people of the farm remember him quite well. I was in the place where the "Boudoir Cap" came from yesterday.

When *am* I going to get leave — that's the question. I only wish — dear — that I knew the answer. Leave is still closed. I sometimes of late have rather hoped that I could get a "blighty" or something of that sort. I will write you as often as I can —of that you may be sure.

With Best Love, Jack.

Three Picture Post Cards [*origin scratched out*]
25/9/17
My Darling,

I was in this place yesterday — so I just thought I would get a few ppc's and send them to you — I have had to cross off the name of the place unfortunately. I had dinner at the Hotel du Faucon — the one with cross. I am writing you a letter under another cover so will close for now.

Best Love, Jack.

25/9/17
My Darling,

I was very pleased to receive your letter of the 20th this afternoon. I regret to say that Leave is still stopped. It is rotten, isn't it?

It would be simply delightful if I could get home and be best man. With you as bridesmaid it would be lovely.

It's tophole about you and the Hospital. I must say I am not astounded at all. I am awfully glad that they offered you promotion. I always thought that they never appreciated you at all — as they ought to. There are very few that have stuck to the job like you have. I'll dry up about that now, or else you will strafe me, won't you?

I am still out of the line, I am glad to say.

I heard rather a good name for the Ragtime Army — the A.S.C., I mean. Namely "Anglais Sans Courage". Rather good, I think. To hear some of their Officers talk makes me feel a bit sick.

The Mater seems a bit down about Harold, judging from her letter. I don't think, you know, that she will ever get over his death. It must have been a fearful blow. I hope that she won't have any more to bear. No-one will on my account, I feel sure. I always think that Harold died as he would have liked to. Ah well, I won't talk about it; but I can't help thinking of him every now and then.

With Best Love, Jack.

27/9/17

My Darling Phyllis,

I am glad to say that I am still out of the line and in the same old billet as I last described to you.

I have got my two stars up again. Heath, another 4th EYR man in this Company, got one too so we celebrated the return of the wanderers last night.

I went into a town near here yesterday and found the Officer's Club, a really tophole place. It gave me quite a shock to see white table cloths, etc. But there were baths, billiards, hairdressing, reading rooms and everything. All was run by the Army. They are getting quite sensible in their old age, aren't they?

I took charge of the Company this morning in the attack and various other things — horse, spurs and all complete. Some lad, what! As a matter of fact I had rather an anxious time due to the horse galloping about at a most furious rate.

Have you seen these 3-decker aeroplanes — 3 planes in front, I mean? It is absolutely marvellous how they can dive down and only just skim the tops of the houses and trees.

I was talking to an Officer who was in England a short time ago and saw a play called *Three Weeks* by Elinor Glyn. I didn't know that they had put it on the stage. If it's anything like the book I think it's a bit too "hot" for the stage, don't you agree? I honestly do think that it's far better for people to know a bit about things and the world in general as it really is, than to imagine a state of affairs which isn't true at all. Do you agree too, "dear"?

With Best Love, Jack.

29/9/17

My Darling Phyl,

I was very pleased indeed to receive your letter of the 23rd yesterday.

I have some good news at last, the best. *Leave* has started again. Great, isn't it? I can't go at present but might manage it in a fortnight with luck. I am no longer in that billet I described to you but live in a bivouac — 3 of us. [*at Murrumbridgee Camp, near La Clytte*].

There was a bombing Raid here last night. The searchlights were very fine. I only heard one bomb drop and that was a long way off.

I must pray that good fortune gets me home for the wedding. With you as chief bridesmaid and I as best man we should have a great time. Tut-tut, so you've taken to drink, have you? But honestly, I think that some Burgundy every day will do you heaps of good. It's not very nice at first but I think one gets quite to like it after a time. It's rather nice if you just take the chill off it by putting the bottle near the fire a short time. When I was in Hospital I had to drink 2 bottles every day at the least —the M.O. seemed to be very keen about it.

It is time I came home since you have got that explosive feeling. I have too. I remember well the occasions when you had it before. Oh, I can't tell you how much I long to see you again.

With Best Love, Jack.

30/9/17
My Darling,

Very many thanks for your parcel containing pears, cake and two magazines which arrived yesterday. The parcel took rather a long time to come, which proved to be rather too much for the pears.

We had a few more bombs dropped on us last night — but they weren't very near.* I hear that Hull was raided on the night of the 24/25th Sept. I hope that you are safe and sound. I can't tell you how glad I am that you are not on night duty at the Hospital.

I am still living in my bivouac — just two big oilsheets fixed up on two poles, open at both ends. It's very healthy, I assure you, just like going to sleep in an open field.

With Best Love and heaps of Kisses, Jack.

*[Diary: "Considerable aerial activity again during the night".]

1/10/17
My Darling,

Very many thanks for your delightful letter of the 26th which arrived today.

I am very glad to hear too that you came through the air Raid alright, although it must have been very wearing waiting for the relief since it did not go until 5.30 am. You must have been fearfully tired next morning, weren't you.

I do not expect to be able to write you a letter for some days, but will send Field pc's as often as I can.

There is an Officer here who for some reason has not paid his tailor's bill. Everytime the bill reaches him he sends his tailor a Field pc — leaving the words "I am quite well" in. Rather amusing I think.

I saw 3 Generals the other day talking together. Then they all got out cigarettes, but would they light them with one match? No fear — the The third one wouldn't have anything to do with it.

With Best Luck, Jack.

Field Post Card dated 2/10/17, post marked 5/10/17
I am quite well.
Letter follows at first opportunity.

9/10/17

My Darling,

I fear that it is a long time since I last wrote you — nearly a week — but I have been over the top as O.C. and not without some success.

It was quite the hottest stunt that I have ever been in on the whole, although there was not much hand-to-hand fighting. Still, the shelling was simply hellish. We gained all objectives and took heaps of prisoners. They were rather a poor lot and seemed only too glad to be taken.

The Battalion won great fame for itself by the way it carried on. I had the honour to command it in the front line for 24 hours as all communications between Battalion Hd Qtrs and ourselves were severed.

The C.O. congratulated me when we came out — and said quite a lot of nice things. I never was more glad that I had that morphine with me. Before we came out I used it all on various people. Some of the sights I have seen there I'll never forget. I had two of my Officers knocked out, one only a very young Lt just out [*2Lt H. Jarvis, arrived 20.8.17; wounded*]. It seems an awful pity, but it's just fate I suppose. The number of narrow escapes I had are simply marvellous. Still, as I always told you — I would come through and so "Thank God". We were 48 hours without any food or water and had to collect it off the dead — my lips are still cracked and broken with the lack of it. However, I am safe enough now — far away from the line and in a quiet little village to which the remnants of the Battalion were taken by railways, so everything is alright.*

I must thank you very much for your letters and parcel — that tinned Duck and green peas was a godsend as it arrived just as we came out of the line when we were absolutely without anything to eat at all.

You have no idea what a shock I got when I arrived at my billet at 5 am in the morning and was ushered into a bedroom with lovely white sheets. The strangeness of it put me off going to sleep for quite a long time.

Well, it's getting very late and I must to bed. I have had little enough of it recently. I feel as happy as a King to have come through that stunt — it had been weighing on my mind for some time.

Goodnight Dearest. I hope to see you soon. With Best Love, Jack.

*[*Jack had just been through the Battle of Broodseinde, October 3-5, in which the Battalion lost 290 men in assaulting, and taking, a section of the German line west of Reutel. This encounter was a part of the campaign known as the Third Battle of Ypres, or Passchendaele. Lt-Col Waithman, in his War Diary report added a note that "I consider the conduct of all ranks was worthy of praise, and shall have several names to bring to your notice in a separate report." Jack's would be one of these. For further details see Appendix 1.*]

10/10/17

My Darling,

Many thanks indeed for your letter of the 4th received today.

The 4th October was the very day we went into the battle and carried on the attack. I can't say how glad I am that it was such a success — equal to that of the Messines stunt.

I feel an awful rotter not writing to you for so long — because if you don't hear from me you may magine all kinds of things. Still, it couldn't be helped as I was right in the heart of the battle for some days. It is very sweet of you to be so anxious about me. I thought of you many times on the 4th and also on the days that followed. I wonder if you knew it. I thought that my time had come more than once, but I am glad to say that my nerves were as steady as could be.

Anyway the next time the Battalion goes into action I should be left out — as my O.C. Company was this time — so that's alright isn't it.*

I wonder when my leave will come. The O.C. might easily send me off in a few days. If he does I shall just have to come. Still, as I said yesterday, it may pan out alright.

This fitting of the trousseau seems to be a terrible business. Doesn't Doris get very weary. Glad to hear that your Bridesmaid's Dress is going to be a success.

I do hope that things work out so that I get home to be Best man. It would be simply great, with you as Chief Bridesmaid.

Yes, I did not put any water in the Burgundy I took. It didn't seem very strong to me, but you've never had much in that line before, have you? That would make the difference. You would be horrified if you knew how much Rum and Whisky I drank last time in — nearly all neat too. Still, not a word of this to anyone else please, as they might not understand as you do.

I still have the explosive feeling. I've had it for some time now.

Capt. Common — Norman's O.C. — sent me a parcel of tinned stuff from Fortnum and Mason of London. Rather nice of him wasn't it?

I have been very busy writing recommendations for honours for some of the Officers and men I took over the top. It's not an easy thing to do if you want them to get anything. I wonder if I shall get anything this time. I might perhaps, but I don't *care* very much. I've come through, that's the greatest thing.

I've spent most of the last few days sleeping and keeping warm. It's fearfully cold here now — at least I find it so. I've got a touch of rheumatism in my back, which one notices very much when marching. The M.O. can't do anything for it, he says.

The Wesleyan preacher attached to the Battalion was quite close up at the Regimental Aid Post during the show. Jolly good, wasn't it? Never saw anything of the C of E one. the R C padre though went over the top with his men.

Today is your birthday is it not? I have not forgotten, and send you my very best wishes. Something more substantial will arrive as soon as I get into a town. That shop where I bought your Boudoir Cap has been hit by a shell, so that they do not sell anything there now.

I seem to have written a lot about the push and war in general, but I am afraid, dear, that I can't help it, as it's my life now for the moment.

I personally accounted for 5 Huns — Thank God. I never did a better day's work. I have avenged someone. I hope you won't be horrified. It was fair fighting.

Well, I must close now. With My Best Love and heaps of Kisses, Jack.

[Jack was right about missing the next action: in fact the entire battalion missed the battle of Poelcappelle on 9 October, also the first Battle of Paschendaele on 12 October. He himself now went on leave.]

Post Office Telegram made out at Folkestone 1235 pm 13 October 1917
Coming on Leave today should arrive London 2 pm. Jack.

The Grand, Folkestone, 23/10/17

My Own Darling,

I have had a most exciting time so far.

I managed to catch the train at 7.35 am and arrived here at 10 am. We embarked and sailed at 11 am — the sea was *fairly* smooth. There were three leave boats and an escort of 6 T.B.Ds. We must have got halfway across to France when our escort showed great activity and dashed about in a most interesting and alarming manner, forming a screen in front of us. We — the leave boats — stopped altogether while the T.B.Ds went forward. A few minutes later one of them flashed some signal, where-upon our ship turned and went full speed ahead for Folkestone. I bet it hadn't gone so quickly for years. We have to report again at 3 pm — for, I suppose, another attempt. German submarines, I believe. Still, it's pleasant and relieves the monotony.

I met Major Coles — he is O.C. Ship and has a cabin all to himself which I am sharing with him. He also has a car at the other end, so with luck I may spend tonight at Abbeville or Amiens.

I dreamt of you all last night.

Heaps of love, Jack.

24/10/17

My Own Darling Phyl,

I am back once again at the Batt., or rather at the Transport Lines of the same as they are in the line. It was rather a shock to come here as I expected to have gone elsewhere. However I have missed rather a nasty time in the line which is very fortunate.

Parrish — the only Officer left of B Coy after Oct 4 — has I hear been wounded [*on the 22nd*]. I hope that he gets to England. Four of the men I recommended have got the M.M. Nothing has come through about Heller [*Private – soon to be JAO's servant*] as yet.

I can't tell you — dear — how glad I am to be back at last. That tavelling up and down the country is just awful. We had a fearful job to find this camp. I am sharing a tent with the Wesleyan padre and the interruptor. I mean the interpreter. I have managed to get a coke fire going so it's fairly comfy, although sleeping on the ground again is rather a sudden shock, after leave and all its luxuries.

But you know, dear, I really had a glorious leave, just tophole. It all passed too quickly, that's the worst. Pleasant times always do, I think.

I shall never forget — darling — those few days that are now gone by — or that night at 10.15 pm when we became engaged. I don't think — in fact I feel sure — that I never could marry anyone but you. You are just the one and only girl in the world for me. It's perfectly true what I told your father — you are just the best girl in all the world.

My love for you will never alter — although I shall grow older. I'll be just the same Jack to you always. You don't know — perhaps you do, though — how much I long to kiss you again. I must be in a bad state because I have only left you four days ago.

With Very Best Love to You and heaps of Kisses. Yours always, Jack.

B.E.F. 10 Corps Camp 25/10/17

My Darling,

You are my darling now, aren't you. How s'nice it sounds, especially as it's quite true.

133

I have not yet reached my Batt. and have been wandering all over the place. I slept in a tent last night, but managed to borrow some blankets. I do hope that they haven't got any creatures in them, but one must keep warm at all costs. At 3 am we had to rise as the tent showed signs of departing Heavenward. One did next to us —hard luck for the people inside.

Our lot aren't at all where we expected them to be and I hear all kinds of most unpleasant rumours — however I think that I shall have missed it this time.*

I am rapidly getting nearer the war — things are getting very primitive. Had a hard job to get any water to wash in this morning and then three of us used the same.

I am leaving here by lorry in a few moments so I shan't be able to write you a long letter and the room is full of people talking so it's rather hard to write.

With Heaps of Love, Jack.

*[*Jack had indeed missed "a rather nasty time". After ten days' rest and re-organisation the Bn were back in the line by the 21st, close to Polygon Wood and under heavy shellfire, and thence to Reutel on the 23rd – in the second battle of Paschendaele. When the Bn returned from its tour, having spent five days in the front line, 23-27 October, the diary reported 117 casualties: 15 killed, 53 wounded, 4 missing, 6 shellshocked, 25 suffering from trench feet, 14 miscellaneous admissions to Field Ambulance.*]

26/10/17
My own darling Phyllis,

I am very glad to say that I am still at the transport lines in comparative comfort when compared with what they must be going through in the line just now. But really, dear, I never saw such fearful weather. Everything is awash and one big sea of mud. The tent I occupied last night did not prove to be waterproof and I had to make a little tent of my own inside to keep some of the water out.

I received a letter this morning from Howe's father asking for details about his son. He was reported missing believed killed. I shall of course answer at once, although it will be very awkward as I don't know what has become of him myself.

Did the people at the Hospital rag you much when you went back to work last Tuesday? I can't say how much I miss you darling — more than I ever did before and that's saying a good deal. Being engaged is lovely — we have a definite link between us now which is heaps better than formerly. It would have been simply awful if we had had to part this time without being engaged. It was a frightful business parting from you as it was. My fondest hopes and dreams of paradise are well on the way to being realised. However, we have got all that in front of us. I would do my best to be always very s'nice — only I fear that I might kiss you too much. I am afraid I rather exceed the limit in that direction, don't I? It's a case of "You were a good little girl till you met me".

By the way I hear that General Head Qtrs — Haig you know — expects this horrid war to finish in January or before. I myself don't see much chance of it. I wish it would, and I'm sure you do too.

Well, I must say goodnight to "my fiancee" — gives me quite a thrill when I write that.

With very best love, Yours ever, Jack.

28/10/17
My own Darling,

I am going to join the Battalion again today as they are now out of the line [*in*

Divisional Reserve]. I hope that they don't go in again for a bit either as the conditions are if anything worse than when I was last there. The wet of course is responsible for most of the rottenness — the water doesn't seem to sink in or drain away here at all, just stands in big pools and makes everything deep in mud.

I went to a church near here this morning or at least what was left of it after it had been shelled steadily for two years or so. Marvellous, I think, that so much of it has remained. Rather a different church to the one we went to last Sunday. Let me think — we should be just coming out last week at this time. It seems a long time ago now. I've travelled so far since then I suppose. No-one would guess that it's Sunday today here except that there's a bit more strafing than usual. They always seem to celebrate the day that way. It's a very nice feeling to hear a tremendous barrage going on up the line if you are safely tucked away in your "flea bag".

I hope — dear — that you are getting to "peeps" nice and early. You said you would, didn't you? How is the Burgundy getting on. Hope that you are taking lots of it. There is no danger, darling, of you coming to like it too much.

I've been getting to bed by 8 or 9 nearly every night — so that I have a good 12 hours of it. Not that I sleep all that time or anything like it, but it's the only place where you are really warm. My bottle of hairwash was frozen this morning.

I expect to hear some other news about my other pip shortly. I do hope it comes off. The extra pay would help things along no end, wouldn't it!

Being engaged to you — dear — makes such a lot of difference. Even France fails to depress me. I have never been so happy before as I am now. And so I should be — engaged to the best girl in the world. You are a darling, you know. It's just the thing that I have longed and hoped for come true. We are a long way apart now as far as distance goes but my thoughts are ever with you. Really darling, I am more in love than ever. It's very s'nice too — nothing to compare with that feeling anywhere.

Major Coles asked me if I was engaged so I said "Yes". So I expect the C.O. will rag me when he sees me next — as Coles is sure to tell him.

With all my Love and heaps of Kisses. Yours. Jack.

29/10/17
My darling Phyllis,

I have just received your two letters of the 22nd and 23rd. Really, dear, I can't find proper words to tell you how lovely they are — simply tophole. I've read them both through time after time. I have *never* had two such s'nice ones ever before, although I would have cheerfully pawned my soul to have letters like those from you.

I too — dear — feel very lonely indeed. This parting is frightful. You make me far more happy when you say that you are happy too; that is the great thing that matters above all else.

Your trusting me like that is heavenly. I'll do my best to live up to it. I'll trust you — dear — to the end of all time. I'll never doubt you either, and I should never require any explanation about anything you might do — unless of course you choose to tell me on your own. I just worship you — dear — and always shall.

It's such a relief to be able to write and tell you how much I love you without disguising it all, although I never was much good at that was I? I came back to France far far happier this time than ever before, although I should have liked to have stopped with you in England more than I can say. But everything seems just

135

right now, and it's lovely. France — even this part of it — looks brighter.

It's just a week ago now to the minute since I last saw you — may I have that chance again the sooner the better.

By the way I have got some good news. The C.O. gave me command of 'A' Company this morning as a permanent Company Commander — so I ought to get 3 stars up in a week or two. I'll let you know when. That extra pay will be splendid — brings things a bit nearer. I will save too — not half.

Vickers had 'A' Company but made a mess of things in the line and so lost it. I have not heard anything about award of honours — but I have good reason to believe that my name has gone forward. I don't care if I don't get anything very much — nothing matters very much as long as you and I keep alright.

I have now got Pte E. J. Heller as my servant. Supposing he does get the V.C. it will be rather bon. Anyway he is a very good servant which is the main thing after all.

I am very happy tonight as I have heard from you — and if I was with you would be the happiest in the world. We did have a good time, didn't we?

Goodnight dearest. Yours always, Jack.

30/10/17

My own darling Phyllis,

I was delighted to receive your letter of the 25th today. I am glad to say that I am still out at rest. But even here it is cold, but the idea of the line gives me the shivers at the thought of it. Still I shall have to carry on and get through with it. There are rumours of a rest in the near future.

Now then — dearest — I have got some really good news about myself. The Colonel called me into his Mess today just before lunch and pinned the ribbon of the Military Cross on me. He said a lot of nice things. Major Coles was amused at me getting the Cross and engaged all at once. He said, "It's a pity you aren't going on leave, isn't it?" My luck is indeed in now — but I would rather be engaged to you dear than have hundreds of crosses.

Still, dear, it is rather nice. It seems very strange to see it there — but I suppose that in time I shall get accustomed to it. Of course I shan't actually get the cross until I come home next time on leave. When I get it I should like to give it to you to keep. But I am afraid that it will have to go home. You'll understand, dear, I'm sure. I'll send you some of the ribbon though as soon as I get near some shops. M.C. after my name will look quite s'nice, won't it. You must strafe me or I shall get to be a terrible swank perhaps, I don't think.

You seem to be having a busy time answering letters of congratulation. I have had some too but of course letters take a little time to get out to me here.

How does the ring fit? You will have got it back again by now. My ring is feeling quite happy at his new home.

I am getting on quite well with my Company — it's only very small owing to casualties.

The idea of you loving me makes me so very happy that I don't know what to do myself. You're a darling, you know. I love you more every day that passes by, so what shall I be like when I do return, Goodness knows. With a little care on my part though I think that you might manage to survive so don't get uneasy.

Have you seen any more likely houses yet?

We had a simply lovely time during my brief leave, hadn't we? But when we are married it will be heaps and heaps better than that. Never forget — dear — that I who write and love you so very much now will always be the same old Jack. You are just the best friend I have in the world — and that's entirely apart from any other feeling I have for you. I am a very lucky chap — more than anyone can ever realise.

Well, I must close now. Heaps of Love. Yours always, Jack.

31:10:17
My darling Phyllis,

I am glad to say that I am still out of the line and as comfortable as circumstances will permit. But the mud is awful.

Pt. Heller has just got the D.C.M. He is my servant now. 2Lt Parrish, also of B Coy, got the M.C. too. I recommended him so I am very glad. Altogether the Company has got 2 M.Cs, 1 D.C.M. and 5 M.Ms. These are all immediate awards and not those which come up with the rations.

I am enclosing — dear — a little piece of M.C. ribbon. I had to get it from the Quartermaster as there are no shops at all in these parts.

I feel very sorry for the men even back here — they are having a rotten time. Rum of course brightens them up a bit, but the conditions they have to live in are frightful. Still, it can't be helped. They have one blanket each anyway — which is better than nothing at all.

Goodnight dearest. Heaps of Love. Yours always, Jack.

Field Post Card dated 1/11/17
I am quite well.

Letter follows at first opportunity.

2/11/17
My own darling Phyllis,

I am now living in some dugouts — not very near the line — although a few shells come over every now and then [*The Bn. is at Zillebeke, in Brigade Reserve*]. Still, they are heaps warmer and more comfy than the tents we were in before. The Huns bomb us every night with great regularity, but so far they haven't been very near me.

We have nothing much to do here — except a few working parties which other officers take. I think that I am rather good at getting other people to do work —after all, I suppose that it's my job to do that now. [*Working parties are busy salvaging guns, etc. from battlegrounds*].

The Colonel is not up with us this time. Major Coles is in command of the Batt. I think, in fact I'm sure, that I am quite in favour with the C.O. Rather a pleasant change.

I shall be able to manage my Company quite well, I think. The Officers in the Company when I took over weren't very favourable — but I have soon got them into line.

The wedding day [*of Norman and Doris*] must be drawing very near. I am glad to hear that presents still continue to roll in. Very useful things.

I have been to see a 6″ gun battery today, which is just behind us. The concussion is frightful when they go off. I was safely tucked away in my flea-bag last night when they opened out and nearly blew me off the bed.

Darling — I do want to see and kiss you again fearfully badly. Terrible state of affairs, isn't it?

Well, I must close now but will write again tomorrow. Goodnight — dearest. My fiance. Lovely word that.

Heaps of Love. Yours, Jack.

3/11/17

My darling Phyllis,

Many thanks indeed for your nice letter of the 28th which arrived today.

You do seem to be having a lot of letters of congratulations. I remember Lily Scott very well. Please thank her for me. I should see her sometime and tell her I am the luckiest chap in the world.

I am very pleased to hear that you were in bed by 11 pm but I can beat you. I retired last night at 9 pm and slept until 10 am with a few breaks in between to have cups of tea and smoke, as we were all roused at 5 am by two Officers getting up to go on working parties. I am delighted too that you take your "beer" regularly. I hope that soon you won't have anymore of those horrid old pains inside — rotten things; the pains, I mean, not the inside. Mine has been rather disturbed of late owing to this fearful water. I have my temperature taken every day but there is nothing doing.

It's tophole that the Matron and Sister Hollingsworth have got the R.R.C. It's quite a good thing to get too — but there are some who do jolly good work and never get anything. I know one very well.

I have just received a chit from the Adjutant containing news about the contents of which I am sure, darling, you will rejoice with me. I am now a Captain — s'nice, isn't it — especially with my M.C. at the end. What a swank I am getting, ain't I? Anyway the 5/- a day is a sure thing now.

You know, dear, ever since I was lucky enough to become engaged to you good fortune seems to have followed me. Strange, isn't it? Well, I have served a good long time in France and I can't say how glad I am to get my Captaincy for services in the field. I feel that it is a great honour that I should command a Company in the 1st Batt. You understand what I mean, don't you?

So you have got the ring back again, have you? Your finger is a dear tiny one, isn't it? I hope that the ring isn't too slack — but perhaps it's better that way than too tight. Don't you think so?

By the way — dear — do you think that you could have your photo taken in civvies or otherwise. I should like to have one of you ever so much, although I wouldn't turn out the one that has lived in my pocket for so long. I am very attached to it.

Well, dearest, it's getting very late so I must close. Sweet Dreams, Heaps of Love, Yours, Jack.

4/11/17

My darling Phyllis,

I was delighted to receive your letter of the 29th this afternoon. I am quite safe so far and must say I feel quite confident about myself in that direction. I'll touch wood though. You know, Phyl, you are a dear really — saying what you did about being engaged. You have quite lost that feeling of being "finished". Love you. I do, dearest, feel very lonely indeed every now and then. I often think of you — darling

138

— and love you more than ever. I shall never deserve your love. But, believe me dear, you and your love are absolutely beyond price to me — the greatest honour in the world. May God blast me if I ever do anything unworthy of you.

It is a horrible occupation that I have to follow at present. More frightful than I have and shall ever tell you, dear. War gets worse and worse — but I feel sure that I shall be able to carry on as an Officer should. It's a rather curious topic to talk to you about, but it just came out. Do not think that I'm depressed because I'm not. You, I think, understand more what war is like than anyone else at home. Besides, I tell you practically everything, don't I? I have no secrets from you at all. Straight that — I'm not pulling your leg. You have been a dear writing me so often — they cheer me up no end. I look forward to them every time.

It's rather amusing to think of me as a Captain, isn't it? I get 18/- per diem now so I get £328.10.0 in a year. It's not too bad. I ought to save a lot of it. I'll soon finish paying off that War Loan anyway.

I do wish — dear — that this beastly war would finish. Wouldn't it be tophole if we hadn't to part any more. Wait till I do get home for good. I'll just show you how I can get down to it and work. The thought of going through life with you is like a dream of Heaven. We shall have an awfully s'nice time together and I shall be able to show you how much I really do love you. The proof of the pudding is in the eating, isn't it?

I had a very nice letter from [Lt W.W.] Crowe (the Officer who lost his right hand). He is in Hospital. His hand of course has been taken off — he wrote with his left. He seems to be very cheerful and he says that the morphia I gave him saved his life. I am glad to think it has and that I helped him just a little bit. It must be rotten to lose one's right hand. Still, he won't come out again.

I wrote to Company Sgt. Major Tutt's father today. He was my C.S.M. in the stunt and was killed. Horrible letters to write, those.

Well, I must close now — don't be alarmed if you don't hear from me for a day or two.

Goodnight my darling girl. Heaps of love. Yours, Jack.

5/11/17

My own darling Girl,

I am just seizing this chance to tell you that I am alright and quite fit. I am in the front line.

I am giving this to a carrying party who have brought up the tea and are waiting, so I have not got much time.

Considering everything things have been very quiet. I feel quite cheerful and shall be out of this before this letter reaches you. Please — darling — tell my Mother that I am alright.

Heaps of Love. Yours, Jack.

7/11/17

My Darling Phyllis,

I am still quite alright and feeling quite cheerful, although we have been having rather a wearying time. I hope to get this letter away with the ration party which is coming up — or ought to be in a few minutes. We are down to our last biscuit. Bread finished long ago. Terrible state of affairs, isn't it. But we shall survive no doubt. I am not getting any post up here of course. I do miss your letters — dearest

— ever so much. Still, I shall have that pleasure when I get out of this place.

I had a brief note from Norman — he seems to be rather doubtful as to when he will get on leave. Makes things rather awkward for the wedding.

Remember and give my kindest regards to all the family.

Lots of Love. Yours, Jack.

9:11:17

My darling Phyllis,

Many thanks indeed for your two s'nice letters of the 31st and 2nd Nov. They reached me in the line but I could not reply to them then. [*The Bn has retired to Zillebeke*].

I have had rather a rotten time in the line — responsibility is rather wearing, isn't it? I was lucky — Thank Heaven— and had very few casualties, but there were attacks on our Right and Left — not far away. The Hun too tried to raid my left post. I was in my dug-out — 10 yds away — when I heard the bombs and I was out like lightning and opened fire with rifles and Machine Guns. Still, it was very disturbing. Next day we were shelled from 9.10 am till 5 pm.* Imagine it: it simply put years on me. Still — dear — all is well. The worst is coming up to the line and going down again. There is a certain wood there; a wooden track runs through it —1½ miles long, and on each side are limbers, wagons, Motor Lorries, guns, mules, men in one unbroken line all done in — knocked out by shell fire. I never saw such a sight before: they are in one unbroken line on each side of the road and we had to go up that way.

Still, I am out of it now — Thank God. You can imagine, dear, how glad I am to get out.

I had a quiet run out, except the first 1000 yds from the line when I had to run for it in the mud and water. When it's a question of life one can shift. I fell down, tripped up by wire, four times, but I got through.

My pen seems to have run away with me about this. I will stop now, but I couldn't help it as it's so vivid in my mind at the moment.

You are a darling, you know, to say what you do about my getting the M.C. The idea of you being proud of me gives me quite a thrill somehow. I can honestly say that I am of you. Then you say that I have deserved it. I don't really know if I have. There are many who do who never get it. Still, I am frightfully bucked at getting it. It's some return for all the rotten times I've had.

No, I should not have thought for a moment of you consenting — you darling —to become engaged to me because of my M.C. What other people think doesn't really matter a hang. How you should ever come to love me is past belief. It is so delightful that I can hardly ever believe it. It's so very very s'nice.

Anyway, it will show that I am not a "wash out" altogether as a soldier, although I'm sure that you never thought so.

I have received heaps of letters of congratulations from lots of people. They do take a lot of answering. To become engaged to you — the best of all — get the M.C. and my Captaincy in one week is rather swift work isn't it.

My men are in a very feeble state and it's such a small Company now. It's rather a sad sight to see them on parade. They look so few — all that's left. Still, we hope for a rest soon.

I am very sorry to hear that Capt. Wilson Barkworth M.C. has been killed. Poor chap — he was my first O.C. Company, a gentleman through and through. I cannot understand how it is that men like these are taken from the world. They leave it the poorer. Harold's case — there is another. How delighted he would have been at my getting the M.C. But of course he knows all about it — doesn't he? I often feel in times of danger that he is with me. Strange, isn't it? I have never mentioned it to a soul — except to you now — but he went over the top on Oct 4th with me — and kept me safe — and gave me strength and determination to carry on as I should. He was with me again this time up. Don't think I am uncaring — I don't mean it that way — but we have always been such a lot to one another that even death cannot put a stop to it.

I do wish though that this war would finish. We would have a time. I think that you would survive it. I don't think that you will fade away by being kissed and loved, will you? I hope not, anyway, because I shall always do that.

So you have started a bottom drawer. What a lovely thought. I must see if I cannot add to it, but I won't throw any money away and I haven't spent anything since I returned from leave.

Many thanks for your parcel — the apples were tophole. I haven't read the magazines either. I seem to have written you a very lengthy letter, haven't I? It's very late, just about midnight, so I must close.

Goodnight dearest. Heaps of Love. Yours, Jack.

*[At this time attacks were being launched on Polderhoek Chateau, near Passchendaele, bringing an instant response from the German lines: "Enemy barrage immediately opened on our line and back area."]

10/11/17
My darling Phyllis,

I was delighted to receive your letter of the 5th this afternoon.

I was never so astonished in my life when I saw the newspaper cutting you sent me. It's a positive scream. I wonder where they have got all this information from. They intend to marry us straight off, don't they? No long engagement. I think, dear, that they must have confused us with Doris and Norman, don't you think so?

You are a darling to say that I am your best friend. I'll do my best to be always so. That's just the best of it — we were such good friends before we were anything else to each other.

I do love you heaps and heaps. I dont think that it's possible for me to love you more than I do. But I don't know; I feel I love you more every day. It's lovely to think that you love me. It seems so extraordinary — so s'nice and altogether tophole. You are a dear.

It's been raining hard all day here and the place is awash. But I have quite a good mess and a good fire so all is well.

I didn't get any sleep when I was in the line, so I have been making up for lost time. Breakfast in bed — porridge and bacon and 2 eggs is not so bad considering we are in the battle area. We have not been bombed last night and it's too wet tonight.

What do you think of this Russian business? If they make peace we shall have a busy time on this front. There are a lot of rumours flying about. What does Mr. Bentham think about it?

Have you been bombed by the Zepps of late? I hope not.

The Colonel [Lt-Col Waithman, the Bn C.O.] saw my photo etc. in the paper and was very amused. I think he is going to England [*on leave*]. Major Coles was in Command during our last tour in the line [*and took command again during Waithman's absence*].

I haven't been able to find Norman yet or any traces of his Division.

Well, goodnight dearest. Heaps of Love and Kisses. Yours, Jack.

13/11/17

My own darling Phyllis,

Very many thanks for your letter of the 8th which arrived this afternoon. You are a dear to write to me as often as you do. They are always very nice and they buck me up heaps.

I'll promise not to get the V.C. before Xmas. What an idea. I shall not try to run into more danger than I need, you may be sure. Life promises to be far too s'nice to lose at present.

I went for a short route march this morning. The weather was topping, so all was well. My horse (swank) in passing a traction engine became very disturbed. My heart did about 19 to the dozen, but I remained on the animal — much, I admit, to my astonishment.

I am so glad, dear, that you feel the same about being engaged. It must have been rather a shock to you when Mr. Bentham on that ever memorable night consented. You really didn't think he would, did you?

We had indeed a perfectly lovely time for the next six days, hadn't we? I didn't hypnotise you, really. But I was able to show you just a little how much, dear, I do love you. I think that must have done it. I was never so happy ever before, and that was because I felt you were.

I hope that you have lost all your old worries, have you? Never to return.

I'm still living in the hut I described to you last night. You know we really have a very slack time — except when we are in the line.

Well, I must close now. With heaps of Love and Kisses. Yours ever, Jack.

P.S. I hope you haven't got to walk up that road from Ferriby [*North Ferriby Station*] in the dark by yourself ever, have you? Love, Jack.

13/11/17

My own darling Phyllis,

Thanks very much for your letter of the 7th which arrived tonight. I wish to thank you very much too for your congrats.

It is as you say very nice to have a Company of one's own. But you know what pleases me most is the extra pay. It could not have come at a more opportune moment. You have indeed brought me good fortune, haven't you? I shall save lots now, I promise.

I had a joint letter from Elsie and Muriel, which was rather amusing, today. They tell me to buck up and finish the war. Don't I wish I could. The thought of peace, darling, now that I am lucky enough to be engaged to you, is simply delightful. I suppose that it will come along some time, although what with Italy and Russia things look rather black. It's rather strange, isn't it, that whenever we do well against the Hun one of our allies makes a faux pas.

I am now just a little farther away from the scene of activity [*at Micmac Camp, Ouderdom*] and have got a wooden hut to live in which, strange to say, actually keeps out the rain.

I do know that I am writing to the sweetest dearest girl that ever was or will be, one who has no equal in the whole wide world, and absolutely a "darling". *I should like to kiss you.* My word I would. Thank Heaven I never kissed anyone before I met you. All the time of waiting is well worth while.

Well, Goodnight dear. Heaps of Love and Kisses. Yours, Jack.

15:11:17

My darling Phyllis,

I was very pleased indeed to receive yours of the 11th this afternoon. You will know by now that I am safe out of the line again — and am still quite a long way away from it, although I can still hear the rumble of the guns in the distance. No shells here, anyway.

Yes, we did run rather short of food in the line, but you know it doesn't do one much harm if you don't do it too often. I am getting very thin. I shall soon have to have my tunics altered. Nevertheless I feel very fit.

Congratulation on being senior on your ward. Having greatness thrust upon you, you see. You will manage everything alright I am perfectly confident.

By the way, I received the Divisional Commander's Card yesterday. They aren't much, but still one might as well have it as not. I will send it to you when I get it.

I dined out last night with several more at a neighbouring estaminet — an oasis in the desert. One gets rather fed up with one's own mess after a time.

We have not been bombed very much here of late. "The Man with the basket" (Hun plane) has not been over. They throw bombs over just like a man emptying apples out of the basket. I think the name is rather good, don't you?

What a pity, dear, that you can't wear your ring every day. It fits alright now, does it? You are really getting quite attached to it, are you? It is indeed a delightful thought to think that you have *my ring on your finger*. I am a very lucky chap, as Fred told me last time he wrote me. But how lucky I am no-one has the slightest conception except myself. Is *our house* empty yet? Kindest regards to the family and Love to Doris.

Heaps of Love and Kisses. Yours, Jack.

18:11:17

My own darling Phyllis,

I was delighted to receive your letter of the 12th last night and also the parcel which arrived this afternoon.

I regret very much to say that I haven't written to you for 3 days. I haven't been able to get any post away. Don't think though for a moment of the line because I am far away from it and once more in the land of civilisation. It's tophole to see trees and grass again. Have not gone balmy, dear, really. Not more than usual anyway.

I am afraid that I cannot tell you what I am doing, but it makes writing very difficult as we haven't much time on our hands.* Still, all is well with me. Last night I had a nice billet with a real bed — with sheets etc. complete. The one I have tonight is better in some ways although the bedrooms aren't as good.

I do hope, darling, that you haven't got to walk up that road from Ferriby in the dark by yourself. It's a horrible thought.

I *often* think of those few days we had together. The thought of them gives me quite a thrill. They were simply lovely. You are a "dear". It seems years ago since I

143

kissed you. Wait till I come home again. I hope — although it doesn't seem probable — that it will be for good. But you know I feel far happier now — even in France as I am — than I ever was before. Being engaged to you is simply delightful. It just alters everything. I hope that you will last our six months. Is the "bar" still going strong. Well, I am afraid I must tear myself away now and close.

Goodnight dearest. Heaps of Love and Kisses. Yours, Jack.

*[*At this point the Bn was transferred from 2nd Army to the 1st and marched close to a hundred miles down to the Somme via Labecque, Arrewage, Bellevue, Hersin, arriving at York Camp, Ecoivres area, on 21.11.17*].

19:11:17
My darling Phyllis,

I have just heard that I might possibly get a letter away, so hasten to grasp this opportunity to write to you.

I am now in a different billet from the one I had last night. It's a farm and the people are very obliging — do all they can to make you comfy. They really do keep their rooms beautifully clean as they have no carpets, only tiles on the floor.

We have another march before us tomorrow — so far no-one has fallen out. Awfully good that. My horse carries me along very well. Lazy thing, aren't I?

The price of food here though is something frightful. Eggs 5d each. Like eating money isn't it? The French people themselves seem to live very well though.

We have quite a good gramophone in the Company and lots of records. Quite nice to play it occasionally — but one of them especially likes to have it on always, starting at breakfast time. It gets rather wearing after a time.

You do seem to have been having a busy time at the Hospital. It must make a fearful lot of work. I don't wonder you felt like a shadow. Jolly good job that you did pick up someone. It would have been a rotten business walking up there by your lonely own.

Do you remember that time you "strafed" me for not meeting you at the station. A great lack of forethought on my part on that occasion.

Well, I am afraid that I must close now as the Orderly is waiting to collect the letters. Goodnight my darling — my fiancee (I like that last word very much).

Heaps of Love. Yours ever, Jack.

20:11:17
My own darling Phyllis,

Very many thanks indeed for your letter of the 12th which arrived today. I have given the socks etc. to the men and they are very pleased indeed with them. They are lots better than any the Army will serve them out with.

I am stopping in some Miners' houses — quite small places but beautifully clean. The people too are so hospitable — makes a lot of difference, that.

I am sending you a couple of ppc's of the place I am at [*Hersin*]. Rather a swiz that I have got to cross the name out, isn't it? But it's safer.

The Hun put one or two shells into here today. Major Coles was in his Mess having a meal when a shell hit his billet opposite and blew his bed out into the street. Good job he wasn't there, isn't it?

The children still continue to play about in the streets and the civilian people carry on with their every day work. It's rather strange to see them.

Well, sweet dreams. Heaps of Love. Yours. Jack.

144

21:11:17

My darling Phyllis,

Many thanks for your nice and delightfully long letter of the 16th received this afternoon.

We had indeed a groggy time in the line a short time back — but that's past and gone — so let us forget it and trust that we shall land up in a more peaceful place.

I was very amused at your way of describing getting married as a "terrifying thought". I don't think so at all — if you are both in love with each other. But I can quite see what a tremendous change in life it must be for a girl — far more in some ways than the man. For after all she is leaving everything and everyone behind and starting afresh, going off into the world alone with a man. It must be a very nervous time. But all that kind of feeling can be "washed out" if he only loves her enough and is a sport. I trust — dear — that the time may come when I shall prove this to you. I can never tell you how much I do really love you — it's quite beyond me to do that.

The billet I spent last night in was occupied by a Miner, his wife and small daughter aged 9 yrs. They were waiting up for me when I went in — had a cup of coffee ready. Neither of them could speak English so that the conversation had to be carried on in French. A tremendous undertaking on my part — I got stuck heaps of times and had to start all over again. You would have been amused. He had had 3 months on the Trenches and also was in the Verdun battle and was returned to work at the coal mines, so we had quite an interesting if rather broken conversation.

I hear that Jack F[eren]'s Batt. is near here. I must see him and enquire how his platonic friendship is getting on — "dirty dog". Please excuse the last expression, but it suits him.

Well, I must really close now, dear, as it's getting late — but I will write again very soon. Heaps of love. Yours, Jack.

P.S. I am still far away from the line — Jack.

23:11:17

My darling Phyllis,

I was very pleased indeed to receive your nice letter of the 18th today.

You must be having a frightfully busy time with the wedding, although if Norman came home as was expected the actual ceremony will be over.

They do seem to have done very well indeed as regards presents. But, dear, I am sure that you and I will do equally if not better — just see if we don't.

I really have had quite a strenuous day today. For reasons which I cannot state I had to ride up to the line today with the C.O., and other Company Commanders. It was six miles up to the bottom of the Communication trench, where we left our horses, and after wandering about a bit struck a trench called Tired Alley. This trench took us where we had to go and was *5 Miles* long. Imagine it: I ask you. I felt like going down on the duckboards and passing away several times but managed to get there. Everything was beautifully quiet. In fact I think that one has an easier time in the line than out of it. Coming back, as we were all fed up with the trenches, we came over the top which was much quicker — but Oh, I was tired and dirty when I got back again.*

On arriving back at the Camp we were invaded by the 13th E.Y.R. — I think that it was that Battalion. Anyway, Vic Mason was there — we all had tea together.

They appear to be a very merry crowd. There must have been about 7 or 8 Officers from that Batt. altogether. Vic Mason has asked me over for dinner tomorrow night with his Batt. but I don't know whether I'll go or not as it's some way from here. But I'll see what I feel like tomorrow.

Near here is a cinema show which I went to see from 6 pm to 8 pm tonight. It was exceptionally good. I enjoyed it very much indeed, so you see we don't have such a bad time, do we?

I seem to have been done in over my promotion to Lieutenant as Cox & Co. inform me that they have credited my account with £4.2.0 instead of £20- odd. I have written them tonight again on this subject. Rather a swiz, I think, as I refunded £16 in July last. However, my Captain's pay ought to be coming along soon, which will soon make up for that. But I don't believe in losing any money in this show. For what one does in "Pushes" and that kind of thing you get little enough.

I was going to wish you goodnight but as it's 1230 am it will have to be "Good Morning". I hope that you are safely tucked away in your bed by now — and dreaming of me (perhaps, I don't think). I do of you very very often.

I send you many many Kisses. Goodnight and Good Morning, Sweetheat, Heaps of Love, Yours, Jack.

*[*Jack's "strenuous day" is accounted for by this Diary entry: "C.O. and O.Cs Coy reconnoitred route to the trenches with a view to pursuing the enemy should he retire".*]

25:11:17
My darling Phyllis,

I went last night over to dinner with the 13th E.Y.R. together with Major Coles and Capt. Green. We managed — at least the C.O. did the trick — to get the loan of a Staff Car for the night.

Vic was in great form and we had an extremely lively evening. I didn't leave there until 1230 am. There were all kinds of people there — including the G.O.C. of the 31 Division. I enclose my menu card, signed by all the Officers there present.

The dinner was given in the honour of the 1st Battalion. Coles had to make a speech much to his horror, but did quite well.

Jack Ferens is in the Brigade Staff as Intelligence Officer — they have no use for him in the Batt. so he was sent there. Vic Mason has a very poor opinion of him.

I attended the Church parade this morning. It was held in the cinema theatre at 8.30 am — ghastly, isn't it? The hour, I mean, since I didn't get to bed until 2 am or thereabouts.

I have got two new Officers the other day [Lt Topping & 2Lt Stockton] , so now have 5 of them. More Officers than men, almost. A strange state of affairs. How slowly the time passes by — just a month today to Xmas. isn't it? I do hope that we are out of the line for it. Simply putrid spending Xmas in the trenches.

Isn't this latest push in the south topping, the biggest success we have had so far, I think — don't you? I do wish that this war was over. Not a very good spirit, I'm afraid but I'm fed up with it.*

You will have got the marriage service off pat now — haven't you? It's a pity it's such a "terrifying thought". You do seem to be such a fearful long way off. It's rotten us being separated for such ages and ages. It seems years since I last saw you,

146

but we must look forward to the time when we shall see each other again. It's a topping thought that — seeing you again, I mean. You have made this world a very s'nice place for me. I hope that I have brightened it up a bit for you too — have I, dear?

To change the subject, I have also had a letter from my late O.C. Coy, Capt. Armitage, now sec. in Command of the 8th E.Y.R. He congratulated me on my recent good fortune and said all kinds of nice things.

Well, I am afraid that I must close this letter now, but will write again very soon.

Goodnight dearest. Heaps of Love and Kisses. Yours, Jack.

P.S. We seem to be sending some troops to Italy [*in the wake of the Italians' defeat at Caporetto.*] I wonder if *we* will go.

*[*The "latest push in the south" was the assault on Cambrai, the first in the war to use substantial numbers of tanks, over 300 of them. After early success had raised hopes of a breakthrough the attack faltered.*]*

26:11:17

My own darling Phyllis,

I was delighted to receive your letter of the 20th today.

I don't know about my having a very fast fiancee, but I know I've got a very s'nice one. Wouldn't change her for worlds with anyone else.

It was very sad that we couldn't be together for the wedding, wasn't it? I thought of you all on the 22nd — that was to be the day, wasn't it? Still, I feel quite sure that better days are in front of us.

I have some rather important news which is in a way both good and bad. At an early date my address will no longer be B.E.F. but something else — what, I know not. The Alps will be rather cold, won't they?*

This present front is getting too hot, so for that reason I am *very* pleased about it.

Goodnight my dearest girl. Heaps of Love and Kisses. Yours, Jack.

*[*Jack mentions a possible move to the Alps. The Divisional Diary refers to this planned move – and subsequent abrupt cancellation – but briefly.*]*

29:11:17

My darling Phyllis,

Many thanks indeed for your note of the 24th and the piece of Bride cake which I am glad to say has arrived safely and is not squashed at all. I have shared it with practically all the Officers in the Battalion and they wish the happy pair the best of good wishes etc.

I have been for a long ride on horseback this afternoon — about 14 Miles — in order to go to a certain Ordnance Store — as very shortly we shall not be able to make up any of our Kit.

I don't anticipate anything like such a deadly time as we have been having in France and though it will be too rotten for words to send me further away from you I shall have a lot better chance of surviving there than here.

I am afraid that my Mother will be rather cut up about it. I have only hinted at it but it's one of the best things in some ways that could have happened.

Well, I must close now so Goodnight dearest — and I hope that you haven't had any more pains. Heaps of Love. Yours, Jack.

30:11:17

My darling Phyllis,

I was very pleased to receive your letter of the 26th today.

I told you that Jack Ferens is near here. Well, he has invited me and several others of the old 4th East to dine with him at the Club Tonight. I don't care much about it but am going nevertheless.

Thank Doris Pickering very much for her sulphur bag — I'll wear it and drive away all creatures from me. I hope so anyway. I have in times gone by collected quite a lot of these animals.*

To change the subject, I shall not after today be able to write to you or to post my letters for perhaps even a week — at least I don't think so. I shall be farther away than ever. It should be very interesting — at the start, anyway.

Well, dear, I must close. Heaps and Heaps of Love. Yours, Jack.

[On 1.8.17 Phyllis had mentioned that Doris Pickering, having received a tip from "an old Colonel", had made up some sulphur bags for Percy. She promised to send some to Jack. They were little bags filled with flowers of sulphur and worn around the neck as protection against body lice.]

2:12:17

My darling Phyllis,

I regret to say that I haven't been able to write you for 3 days. I did, though, on the 30th but that letter never got away. We have been having a very busy time and I have been for 48 hours without a home.*

The Batt. are now in the line. I, most fortunately, have been left out and am now O.C. Nucleus party — some 14 Officers, 200 O.Rs [*Other Ranks. While Capt. MacMahon took over B Coy, Jack remained with this Nucleus Party at Hamel*].

We have been chased about all over the place. Last night we were all nicely settled down in quite a good billet (fireplace, roof complete) when the Town Mayor came and turned us all out at 11.50 pm and told us to go and spend the night in a cinema nearby. I slept on the stage behind the white screen. I managed to get a few blankets from those left by the men and kept myself from freezing, but I have very grave suspicions that they were inhabited by creatures. However, one must keep warm on these occasions.

The padre is with us too — so you can see that we are carrying on quite respectably.

I must close now. Heaps and Heaps of Love. Yours. Jack.

* [*On 30.11.17 the Batt. left Oppy and entrained at Aubigny for Tincourt, via Peronne. From there they marched to the line.*]

4/12/17

My darling Phyllis,

I've been to a town nearby today with Mansfield as there was nothing to do here.

I enclose a few ppc's of the place [*Peronne*]. The actual damage was done some time ago, but it looks just like that now — only perhaps more people about. I saw about 3 French civilians and many nurses both English and French.

It's rather a swiz that I have got to cross the name off them, but I am afraid that it must be done.

I am quite comfortable here and have an excellent Mess in a wooden hut, but it has a topping fireplace which to keep the fire going eats up a tremendous quantity of wood. There is no coal or anything of that sort. I am going to a cinema show here tonight at 6 pm. As a matter of fact it's the very one I spent a night in a short time ago.

Heaps of Love and Kisses,

Yours Jack.

4:12:17

My darling Phyllis,

I was delighted to receive your letters of the 26th & 28th this morning.

So you gazed with terror at your engagement ring, did you? That's very sad, but I can understand it in a way. However I am glad to hear that my letter bucked you up a bit. You say that I am running the bigger risk marrying you. Good Heavens, it's the other way altogether. It's you who are running the risk. It's *very sweet* of you to say so nevertheless. Please don't say "that perhaps you will improve in time" (except in health). I don't think that you could be s'nicer and dearer than you are —as I *very often* tell myself. As I told your Father, you are just the best girl in the world — I mean it truly — not pulling your leg at all.

My Captaincy has not come through the Gazette and until it does of course I shan't get Captain's pay — but it ought to come through soon, and I shall be ante-dated. If it wouldn't be a trouble to you please keep an eye on the paper and let me know when it comes through. They are very slack in that establishment.

The Batt. are still in the line and I am still out with the nucleus party. They are having rather a groggy time in the line — at least I think so. We haven't really heard anything., They went up — the Officers I mean — in all their best kit. It was rather amusing to see them.

I have got my valise today. The blankets I borrowed from those left by the men proved to be very full of creatures. Horrible, isn't it? I don't want to go into harrowing details but I killed 76 before lunch today in two of my garments, since when I have had a bath — changed every stitch I had on me — so I feel quite free from them. I hope so anyway.

Your last two letters were especially s'nice really. After having read through your letters many times I always burn them. They are too precious to me to let them wander into strange hands.

Goodnight dearest, Heaps of Love and Kisses. Yours, Jack.

5/12/17

My darling Girl,

I am still out of the line with the Nucleus Party. We have simply nothing to do at all as nearly all the men have been sent away under two Officers to a training camp. Only the band and a few people like that left. It is marvellous how tired one can get of having nothing to do.

This village [*Hamel*], although it's only a very tiny one, simply abounds in cinemas erected in barns and huts. It's rather wonderful how they get them put up.

I regret to say that we haven't had any post for two days now — not that it's stopped, but it's all going to the Battalion. We are, so to speak, nobody's child. No-one loves us here. The Town Mayor (who has all the billets under his charge) is always moving us about from house to house.

Do you still have your windows open at night, dear? If it's as cold with you as it is here I don't know how you do it. We had about 20 degrees of frost last night at least. I nearly always think of you at night-time in the trenches — and heaps of other times as well. I remember one incident very well. During our last tour up at Ypres when the Hun bombarded us too much — and the shells came very near — I used always to think and wonder what you were doing. It's strange, but that pulls me together more than anything else. It was just the same too over the top. I really don't know why I am telling you this, but I thought I should like to tell you what a lot you do for me, far more than you imagine.

My being engaged to you is just the one thing I've longed for more than anything else — a dream come true.

I am afraid I am writing rather a lot of rot, but really I haven't gone quite balmy.

Heaps of Love, Yours, Jack.

6/13/17

My darling Phyllis,

I was very pleased indeed to receive your letter of the 29th today.

So glad that you went to see the pictures at the Lyric. Yes, I have been there in the old circus days. If I remember rightly the first lot of pictures I ever saw I saw there. Oh, it's a long time ago now. We were living in Park Holme, Princes Avenue at the time and Alan [*another of Jack's brothers*] took me. I was in the seventh heaven and sat there and ate nougat.

I am still out of the line. I went for a topping ride this morning on horseback. The country round here is ideal for it too. Miles and miles of grass lands, not flat at all but er — undulating, (is that correct). But I do feel stiff now. You would look simply topping on a horse — though of course you always do (I'm not pulling your leg, really dear).

My letters are getting rather scrappy now, but we (14) all live and have our being in one hut, so you can imagine it's rather hard to write decent letters.

I must close now, dear, write again soon. Heaps of Love. Yours, Jack.

7:12:17

My own darling Phyllis,

Many thanks for your very nice and delightfully long letter of the 1st which arrived this afternoon.

That important news I told you of [*the move to Italy*] is all off now completely. I can't say why, but all — even those in high command — were very astonished if not to say annoyed. I don't know myself whether I am sorry or not.

Do you think that you will survive my next leave? You were rather anxious as to the result of that weekend spent at our house, weren't you, you darling?

I am still out of the line and don't expect to be in for some days yet. But of course, no-one can tell.

Sweet dreams, dearest. Heaps of Love and Kisses. Yours, Jack.

11/12/17

My darling Phyllis,

I was delighted to receive your letter of the 4th last night and yours of the 5th today.

I am with the Batt. again now [*in Brigade reserve at Heudecourt*]. We are very squashed up — 2 Coys officers in one small hut. A terrible squeeze, and it is cold.

Today I took the Coy up the line on a working party, and marched many miles. I could tell you — were it not for the censor — heaps of interesting things that have been happening here.

Those cigarettes you sent were very s'nice, also the cream de Menthe pastilles.

I regret to say that I shall spend Xmas in the trenches. Sad, isn't it? I have ordered a Turkey and shall devour same shortly after the actual day.

Think of me during that festive time in the trenches, won't you dear? My thoughts will be with you. What a rotten war this is.

I must close now. Goodnight dearest. Heaps of Love. Yours, Jack.

11/12/17

My darling Phyllis,

I went to a concert party last night in this village, near the line as it is. It was held in a YMCA hut and nearly all the time the Hun was shelling the village round about. Of course our hut wouldn't have stopped anything at all. It was rather strange to see one of the performers singing a song, then all at once hear the whistle of a shell, stop singing and wait for it to burst before carrying on again with the song.

They are a long time in getting my Captaincy through the Gazette, aren't they? I heard that I am still being paid at the old rate, but even then *I'm saving* so that when my back pay as Captain comes in it will improve things wonderfully. So far this month I haven't drawn anything at all either from Field Cashier or the Bank.

Well, I must really close now as I have to be up again at 5 am in the morning — a frightful hour to start the day with, isn't it? Once again goodnight, dearest girl of mine.

Heaps of Love and Kisses. Yours, Jack.

12/12/17

My darling Phyllis,

You will probably be very surprised when you receive this letter as it will no doubt have a stamp on it and will have been posted in England. There are sometimes other means of getting letters through other than the ordinary way.

Now I can tell you a few things we've been doing. We were going to Italy — some units of the Division had already gone, and we were going in 24 hours' time, that is Nov 30th — when the Hun attacked and through the slackness of one division broke through for a mile or so. We were at Oppy, a long way away, but we were rushed into a train and within two hours of receiving the orders were on our way. We passed through Peronne and 8 miles further south.

The southern end of the Cambrai push of the Division was at once pushed up to the line to hold up the Hun. We detrained at Tincourt and then after 2 hours rest marched to the line — some 15 kilos. We didn't know when we started from Oppy what we were in for, and were all in our "glad rags" — white breeches, spurs, etc —and they went into the line like that, some Officers without revolvers even.

All was very quiet indeed though — I don't think that the Hun knew where we were — and I am sure we were in the same position in regard to him.

Before we arrived, our cavalry — English and Indian — had been flung in as the last resort. Quite a fine sight it must have been to see them charging with sword and

151

lance. They got "in the muck" though and suffered heavily.

The Hun cavalry had been through before this and had got round several Battalions — Uhlans you know — capturing many guns, a general or two, etc. Many of the R.F.A. Officers killed in their pyjamas — I saw one walking to Peronne dressed in these garments and a steel hat.

We (our Brigade) soon got the situation in hand and quickly dug tunnels and put up wire [*Diary notes "work done on very primitive trenches"*]. But there were big guns of ours in "No Man's Land" in front of our front line.

Two of our ambulances came up the road and passed by our line altogether but we soon stopped them and they jolly quickly turned around and came back.

I myself haven't been *in* the line at all — but wasn't very far away . I am now at Heudicourt. It's very much knocked about indeed. We are not going to Italy now — of that I am quite sure. But I hope that we are going to have a fairly long rest out of the line shortly after Xmas. As I have told you, I shall be in the line for Xmas, but will be out very likely on the night of the 26th.

So you see we have been having quite an exciting time and fortunately hardly any casualties, and although the quarters the men have to live in are very poor ours aren't any better — but then of course we have our valises. That makes a lot of difference. The place where I had lunch a few days ago at the officers' Club was Peronne. It has great ramparts and a moat all round, although it's such a big place — at least big as towns get in France.

There now, I've been able to tell you more news in this letter on what we've been doing than I have ever been able to before. I do hope that it gets through alright. It's a bit of a risk. I need not ask you not to spread information I've given you —because I know that you would not do so.

I hope — dear — that you won't get fed up with receiving letters from me, will you? This is the second today and two yesterday as well. There is no postage to pay. What a lot of rot I am talking now, ain't I?

Heaps and heaps of love for your darling self. Yours, Jack.

14/12/17

My darling Phyllis,

I was very pleased to receive your letter of the 7th today.

Do you know I haven't been in a civilised town with inhabitants since I came out this time. There isn't one within 40 miles of where I am now. It's rather awful in some ways, you know.

One of my Officers — Coverdale by name — has just gone to England today on special leave as his father is dying. His Mother died just before he came out — he has two sisters; he is the only son. It's a bad job, isn't it? Not much money either in the family. They are of Hull — Holderness Road, I believe. Not a very pleasant Xmas for him. Still, it can't be helped.

You have written me a lot recently — it's very sweet of you, I'm sure. Always *delighted* to get them too.

I will write again very soon. Heaps of Love. Yours, Jack.

15:12:17

My darling Phyllis,

I was delighted to receive your letter of the 9th today and also *your large* parcel. You are a dear to send me such a lot of nice things. We live in a land of absolute desolation — not even an inhabitable house for miles and miles, so you can understand how glad we are to get anything.

We had rather an unpleasant surprise this morning at 9.15 am. I had 'A' Company on parade, inspecting them, etc. when the Hun started to shell us and with the first one laid out 4 men of the Band [*1 killed – Drummer Francis – 4 wounded*] who were in a shelter close by. We cleared the camp of all the men. But several more were hit before all got away. The Orderly Room — a small brick building — was hit and blown to bits.

One man who was killed was going on a month's leave tomorrow, the 16th. Jolly hard luck, wasn't it?

We are still in the same Camp, but you may be sure if they start again we shall very quickly clear out of it. I bet I am one of the first. Anyway, I am not going to entirely "disrobe" tonight — I don't fancy the idea of dashing about in pyjamas at this time of the year.

We have a brazier in this hut — burn wood on it. From time to time it has to be taken out in order that we may be able to breathe and see each other for a bit. The smoke etc. is very annoying, but one must keep warm somehow. That trench coat is worth its weight in gold. When I bought it I thought it was fearfully heavy. Now I hardly notice it. Strange how one gets accustomed to things.

I hope, dear, that you will have as happy a Christmas as possible. It's fearfully rotten to be away from you any time, but if anything it's worse at Xmas time. However, I hope that we shall be together next year at this time. The future holds such a lot of nice and happy times in store, doesn't it?

The idea of Christmas, "Peace and Goodwill" is hardly appropriate nowadays, is it? *I am fed up with the war.*

Please remember me to all the family. I must really close now, so au revoir dearest. I will write again *very soon.*

Heaps of Love. Yours, Jack.

16:12:17

My darling Phyllis,

I have been up the line this morning [*reconnoitring with the C.O.*]. You will be pleased to hear that it's very quiet indeed.

I have got a tophole dug-out there — at least, I mean I shall have when I go into the line. It has four wire beds, stove etc. so you see I shall be quite comfy. Better off anyway than I am here.

An entrance to what proved to be a long passage was found in our Camp yesterday. It's 80ft deep and goes for ½ Mile with large caverns opening off it, enough room to accommodate nearly 2,000 men. Rather a wonderful thing to see.

I've sent some Xmas cards off today — Bruce Bairnsfather ones. Major Coles has just come in bringing some Divisional ones, so I'll send you another one. It's snowing here today — very seasonable, isn't it?

Well, I must close now, dearest. Heaps and Heaps of Love. Yours, Jack.

18:12:17

My darling Phyllis,

I am now in the line — not the front line though. [*'A' Coy has been left at HQ as a counter-attack company.*] I am very comfy as we have a stove and beds etc. Far better off than I was before I came up and in far less danger. I brought up a couple of blankets, so you see I am in the lap of luxury.

It snowed hard here all yesterday and the country is covered this morning. The only thing I have against it is that one is so easily spotted moving about by the Hun.

There are heaps of Bosche souvenirs round here. I've got a Bosche "*Very*" Light pistol — a tremendous size it is, just like a horse pistol of former days. I don't know how I shall get it home.

I've got two Officers up with me who haven't ever been in the line before. It's strange to see how keen they are. I lost that long ago, sad to say.

There is rather a shortage of water here. Quite enough for drinking and that kind of thing but none to spare for washing purposes, so we must simply remain dirty.

Heaps of Love and Kisses. Yours, Jack.

19:12:17

My darling Phyllis,

I was very pleased to receive your letter of the 11th last night. I am very glad indeed that the vase has arrived and that you like it. It did take a fearful lot of making.

I am still in the line but very comfy. If you could see it I'm sure that you would agree. Only that I haven't any windows open here and the door shuts very tight. Terrible of me shutting all the fresh air out. Your way is heaps better, I admit.

Yes, I have any amount of warm clothes. When I get fully dressed — trench-coat and all — the belt of my equipment almost refuses to meet. I dislike getting wrapped up in so many things, but there is nothing else for it if one wants to keep warm at night.

I am very sorry to hear that you have been groggy and had a fit of the blues. I can see that it's time I came home and looked after you (what a life I lead you, don't I?) However, I am glad to hear that it's passed now. How is the "Bar" getting on — I hope that you are still carrying on with it. I am always worrying you about that subject aren't I? Don't think please that I wish to make a drunkard of you — far from it. Not any chance of that if Burgundy is going to be the means. What a lot of rot I am talking.

I received a parcel from the Directors of the London Joint Stock yesterday containing food in various forms. Very good of them really, though it is the first thing that I have ever had from them since I joined. Still, it is a business institution, not a philanthropic one (terrible long word, that).

I am very bucked to hear that you are getting converted a bit with thinking that getting married isn't so very awful after all. A step in the right direction, isn't it?

Surely the war can't go on for another year. If I thought so I should simply fade away. What a lovely time we could have if the war was over, couldn't we? I often think and look forward to the coming days of peace.

Heaps of love. Yours, Jack.

20:12:17

My own darling Phyllis,

I was very pleased indeed to receive your letters of the 13th and 14th tonight.

That notice in the Gazette about me is rather confusing, but the acting rank on the 20th October was when I was made a spare Captain without any command. About a week later I was given A Coy, so they must have put me in again. However, the main thing is that I shall get paid as from the 20th October.

154

I am still in the line and so far (touch wood) have had a very nice quiet time. Of course, it's very cold but we all have very good dug-outs, the men also, and there's heaps of wood to burn if you only look for it. It's been very foggy today, so one could wander about without any danger of being seen by the Hun. I went along an old Hun line of trenches this afternoon. They must have left them in a hurry as there are heaps of things — equipment, rifles, bombs, etc — left behind. Nothing really worth having though, but it was very interesting. I could tell you a lot of interesting things was it not forbidden. Annoying, isn't it?

Have you got any mistletoe yet. I should like to assist you to put it up sometime.

This letter won't go until tomorrow now—the 21st—as the ration party have gone back. Well, I must really close now dear, for the present. Remember me to the family.

Yours, Jack.

22:12:17

My darling Phyllis,

I am in the front line now — at least, my Company is ['*A*' *has relieved* '*D*' *Coy in the line*]. My Head Qtrs are a little farther back. My present dwelling-place isn't quite so good as the last one, but is rapidly improving and will soon be quite habitable. It's a big Nissen Hut built against the side of a railway cutting — fairly safe you see.

This is rather a strange place to spend Xmas in, but I might be lots worse off so I'm not grumbling at all. I think I must hang a sandbag instead of a stocking on Xmas eve. Would be more appropriate to the situation, wouldn't it?

Is the pond frozen at Swanland yet? I hope so, because then you will get some more skating. I enjoyed that little bit we had together last January very much.

I was going to write a long letter to you this time but the padre Crossland has just come in and says that he will take this letter down with him.

Heaps of Love and Kisses. Yours, Jack.

23:12:17

My darling Phyllis,

I was very bucked to receive your letter of the 16th last. night.

I am still in the front line but am not having a bad time at all. I do wish though that it wasn't quite so cold. Last night it was terrible. I am looking fearfully dirty —haven't washed for 3 days now.

Honestly now Phyllis, I liked those Creme de Menthes very much. Don't you believe for a moment that you sent me the wrong things. Of course, you may think that I am being polite again, but I am really speaking the truth.

I had rather a nice letter from Edgar yesterday. He says in one place: "You will have heard all the news about the wedding. The next affair will have to be yours now — *May it be soon.*" I *like* that last sentence *very much*. It would be very very s'nice, don't you think so? You must think that I am never satisfied, but this is far from the case. I've never been happier out here than this time. Were I at home though I should be far happier still. I really don't deserve the extreme good fortune that I've had. I am a *very very lucky* chap. I feel that every day.

Heaps of Love. Yours, Jack.

24/12/17

My own darling Phyllis,

I was very pleased indeed to receive your letter of the 17th last night.

Let me see, it's Xmas Eve tonight, isn't it? I must say that one would never guess it from my present surroundings. However, I shot two partridges today and shall have them for lunch tomorrow instead of Turkey.

It's still most frightfully cold and everything is frozen hard. All my dug-out was white with frost inside this morning when I woke up. We had a fire on all the time too.

Please excuse this short letter but I must close now in order to catch the ration party going down.

Heaps of Love. Yours, Jack.

Christmas Card from 21 Division ("Born 1914, Still Going Strong") dated Xmas 1917

With heartiest good wishes for a happy Xmas.

With Love, Jack.

27:12:17

My own darling Phyllis,

I was very pleased indeed to receive three letters of the 18th, 20th and 21st in the last two days — it's really awfully nice and dear of you to write me such a lot. I can never receive too many and they always buck me up heaps. But tonight I received a small parcel from you. Really I don't know how to thank you enough. It's a lovely case and as a matter of fact the very thing I wanted. I have never possessed such a nice thing before. It's awfully swanky too. I wish to thank you very very much indeed. I am quite in love with it.

I am glad to be able to tell you that I am out of the line now — and a little way behind [*in huts at Longavesnes*]. We have got our valises anyway, but it's most frightfully cold and the snow is about 8 ins deep — everyone is always falling down in the roads.

I hadn't any casualties at all. 2 Lt Wisbey of my Coy though was shot through the sleeve of his tunic — a near thing, wasn't it? Still, it would have been a blighty.

I am sure that you would have had a shock if you could have seen me last night —I was so dirty I looked like a nigger. Hadn't washed for days. Frightful, isn't it? However, I am much cleaner now.

You must please excuse this awful writing but my hands are so cold. Thanking you once again for the lovely case,

Heaps and Heaps of Love and Kisses. Yours, Jack.

28:12:17

My own darling Phyllis,

I was very pleased indeed to receive your letter of the 23rd today.

It's most distressing to know that you didn't hear from me for FIVE days and that it interfered with your sleep. Very sad, that. I feel a horrible wretch my being the cause of worrying you like that. But all the same it's very sweet of you to worry on my account.

I don't want to talk of the weather but it is awful today — snow: I never saw so much. It's so fine that it blows inside the hut we are in. You wake up in the morning and find your valise white over with it. I am very much taken with that topping cigarette case you sent me. It's a beautiful one. Thanks very much for it.

I had quite a nice letter from Capt. Wilkinson of the 150 T.M.B. He is up at Ypres, I think. I will enclose it in this letter.

The worst of this place is that there isn't a town or village inhabited and with shops within 40 Miles. It's frightful, as you can imagine.

156

I am simply flooded out with Officers now — seven in the Company without including myself. I don't know what to do with them at all.

Our men are having their Xmas day tomorrow — one long day of drinking and feeding, starting at breakfast. We have bought them several pigs, oceans of beer and many other things so they ought to have a good time. Our own Xmas dinner hasn't come off yet. We have got the Turkey — that's something.

Goodnight, dearest. Heaps and Heaps of Love. Yours, Jack.

29:12:17
My darling Phyllis,

I was simply delighted to receive your letter of the 24th today. You really are a darling to write me as often as you do.

I am very glad to hear that the Divisional Xmas Card has arrived. It's not so bad, but did you notice that they have missed off the 3rd Battle of Ypres from the list of battles that this Division has been engaged in?

The Men have been celebrating their Xmas today and have had a great time. For my Company we managed to get plates and benches and forms. The special feeding started at breakfast and has continued all the day. I sampled the Xmas Pudding, beer etc — quite good, especially the Pudding. At dinner time Major Coles came in and wished them all the best and we drank our respective healths. Quite a jolly time. The NCOs waited on the men and gave them heaps of food. Tonight they are having a concert of sorts — a lot of local talent I should think, so it might be very amusing, although rather like a fourth-rate Music Hall.

I am very sorry that my Xmas present hasn't reached you yet. It's most annoying. I've written them about it again. I did want you to get it in time.

Well, I am afraid that I must close now, dearest Girl, but only for a brief space of time. I will write again *very soon*. Heaps and Heaps and Heaps of Love and Kisses. Yours, Jack.

31:12:17
My darling Phyllis,

I am still having a very quiet time here and am doing nothing very much.

I regret to say that that Officer of this Company who went home on leave on account of his Father's health arrived just in time before his Father died. I don't know what his two sisters will do. Coverdale is his name.

I went to the C of E service yesterday — parade of course. It was held in a hangar of an aerodrome and my word but it was cold. I was nearly frozen to death.

The old rumour — the important news I told you of a month or so ago — is now very strong again. Whether anything will come of it though I can't say. I am not very keen now either — as I hear that those who have gone have had rather a rotten time — huts of mud, and shortage of rations.

I've just had some terrible news. You see we were having our Xmas or New Year's dinner tonight — whatever you like to call it. Our Turkey, costing 41 francs, has been foully attacked by a cat, losing in the engagement one leg and a portion of breast. Frightful, isn't it? I am sure I don't know what to do. We shall have to be content with the remains. It's a sad life at times. Our Cook is in a very distracted state about it.

They are asking for a lot of men for Commissions now — doesn't matter if they are suitable or not. I have got ½ dozen through already but I don't see where the next one is coming from.

Heaps and Heaps of Love. Yours, Jack.

1918

2/1/18

My darling Phyllis,

I was very pleased to receive your letter of the 27th tonight.

My fiancee seems to have been having a very gay time — dancing and having a fling round generally. But I don't really see why you should regard it as wicked of you, just because I am in France. I am very pleased — honestly — that you have been having a jolly old time. You do far too much work for my liking, although I know that you enjoy it.

Today the Brig-General presented a lot of Medal ribbons to the various NCOs and men who had won them. Thank Heaven it wasn't to the Officers or I should have been dragged in — a horrible business in some ways.

So you have been having your hands read again. I didn't know that Auntie Lizzie read hands at all.* However, all she says about you I think is very nice. *I am delighted* to hear that you are going to live to be quite old — it would be simply frightful if you didn't. As you say, I am in for it — and *very very glad* I am of it too — you know I have complete faith in you, trust you absolutely. I hope — no, I feel, if I may say so — that you do really trust me. In my opinion there is no halfway in this kind of business. It must be absolute, complete, in the best sense of the word. Don't you agree? As you know perhaps, most fellows knock about a good deal — more I cannot say to you — but I, through no merit of my own, never have done. I often wonder why — I always seem to have had an idea at the back of my mind that I should perhaps one day meet you, and so have not done some things which at times all regret.

I seem to have got rather tangled up, don' I? I never thought that I had ideals but I suppose I have in a way, although I call them by a different name. Some things are done, others aren't. At least, that is so with me. It's a game. There is no danger of me having a fling with anyone else — of that you may be quite sure. It's very seldom that you are out of my thoughts. You know I feel sure that in the times to come we shall have a very happy time indeed. I look forward to it with the greatest delight, don't you? Well, I really must really say goodnight now, dearest.

Heaps of Love and Kisses. Yours, Jack.

*[*Aunt Lizzie was a surviving sister of Phyllis' grandfather, the late William Jackson, founder of the Hull grocery and bakery firm.*]

3:1:18

My own darling Phyllis,

I am afraid that this will have to be a short letter as I haven't much real news. Everyone practically has gone to the Divisional Concert party, so it's nice and quiet just for once.

You will think I am sure that my last night's letter was rather a strange one. I am afraid that I got rather tangled up, but I simply wanted to tell you that I trust you to the end of the world. But of course you knew that long ago, didn't you?

Although I am far away from you the distance doesn't seem so great this time. War used to harden me so — I mean kind of dry up or keep all your feelings locked away, but this time everything is changed. France — it sounds rather impossible — is a much brighter place.

One Captain [*Green*] has gone to England to Aldershot on a three Months Course — Lucky dog, isn't he?

Well, I must really close this letter now and wish my best friend — and fiancée —the dearest and sweetest girl in the world — goodnight, and the s'nicest of dreams.

With Heaps and Heaps of Love. Yours, Jack.

5:1:18

My darling Phyllis,

I am somewhat nearer the line than when I last wrote you, but nevertheless I am fairly comfortable [*in Brigade Reserve at Saulcourt*]. There are altogether eleven of us in this hut — our beds are arranged in tiers: 6 beds on one level and then another six on top. It certainly saves space.

Does the date of this letter remind you of anything? January 5th 1916. Two years ago — the date on the locket is Jan 6th 1916, isn't it? It was just a day wrong — the date, I mean. But I shall never forget that night, will you? I remember quite well what a job I had to get you to accept that locket, hadn't I?

The C.O., Colonel Trimble, M.C., who is at the moment on leave, has I see been awarded the D.S.O. in the New Year's Honours. Very good, isn't it? He is quite a nice sort, really, but he never talks about anything except the Army. Gets rather wearing after a time. The late C.O. Colonel Waithman, who went home in November, has got a D.S.O. too. Rather good, although the Battalion won him it — not he himself. However, I must be careful what I say.

Heaps and Heaps of Love. Yours, Jack.

7:1:18

My darling Phyllis,

I was delighted to receive your two nice letters of the 30th and 31st last night. I intended to write to you yesterday — don't think me a wretch — but I was really very busy. I had to take a party of 100 men up to the front line to dig a sap.* We set out at 2 pm, and didn't get back until 11 pm. This morning I left here at 10 am to look over the line with the C.O. and other Coy Commanders. It's started to thaw and the roads are like glass — awful, isn't it? The trenches too are full of water —about two feet at the worst part. So it looks as if we were in for rather a poor time very shortly. My own dug-out isn't so bad but the men will have a very poor time I'm thinking. I have only just got back again and have had to change every stitch of clothing as I was wet through.

It's *very sweet* of you, dear, to say that you wish I was with you to share the times you are having just now. Still, there's the future — we will have heaps of *very* s'nice times some day. We have nearly been engaged three Months now, haven't we? What an age that seems — and of that only 6 days have we been together, the happiest six days I have ever spent in my life. Oh for the war to finish. England, home and beauty for me — the touter the sweeter.

I must say that I think that I am very well — no chance of getting to E.F.A. worse luck.

Well, au revoir, dearest. Heaps and Heaps of Love. Yours, Jack.

*[*A sap is a communication trench between support trenches and front line.*]

Field Service Post Card dated 8:1:18, post marked 9 Jan 18
I am quite well.
Letter follows at first opportunity.

9:1:18
My darling Phyllis,
   I am once again in the front line [*near Epehy*] — but things aren't so bad really.
We had a very heavy fall of snow yesterday so that everything is just the same as it
was before the thaw. My Head Qtrs are in a deep dug-out. 50 steps. It's a tunnel as a
matter of fact. All kinds of people are in it — T.M.B., ourselves, Dressing Stations
and some Officers of another Batt.
   We had a rather nasty time coming in as when we got to a certain cross-roads not
far off our trenches the Hun saw us and opened out with Artillery. Several fell on the
road. I hadn't any casualties except the guide but other Companies were not so lucky.
   I do hate writing to you about the war and that sort of thing, but it's all I see
nowadays.
   Leave is still going very well. I feel very optimistic about my own. I can see myself
getting away sometime towards the end of February, which is lots better than I ever
dreamed of. We will really have an awfully s'nice time, won't we? Of course I admit
it's rather early to talk about such things, but one must look forward to something
nice, otherwise things would be rotten.
   The only trouble is that I can't keep my feet warm. Most distressing, I assure you.
With all this snow I have to change my socks once every two hours at least to keep
dry. But this frost is a lot better than wet and rain. I came up to the trenches to look
around during the thaw and they were — as I believe I told you — several feet in
water.
   Well, I must close now, dear, but will write again tomorrow without fail.
      Heaps and Heaps of Love. Yours, Jack.

10:1:18
My darling Phyllis,
   I was very pleased indeed to receive your letter of the 2nd yesterday.
   It has just started to thaw again and everything is in a most frightful mess
—trenches full of water and the sides all falling in.*
   By the way, what about peace? There is a very strong feeling out here that it's not
far off. It's rather surprising how everyone seems to think that. Of course, I don't
suppose we know much about it really. Those 25,000 Bosche refusing to go west is
excellent, I think; don't you?
   Rather a curious thing happened to two Officers this morning. They had a coke
brazier in their little dug-out and the fumes from the coke affected them to such an
extent that when they went outside into the air both of them passed away for the
time, gassed slightly. Horrid, isn't it? But one must keep warm somehow.
   Well, I must close now, dearest. Heaps and Heaps of Love. Yours, Jack.

*[*Diary: "trenches in very bad state after rain"*].

11:1:18
My darling Phyllis,
   I was more than delighted to receive your letters of the 3rd and 4th last night.

*Jack mentions Coles more than any
other officer, apart from his
brothers. From October 1917, when
the two travelled back from leave
together, they saw a lot of each
other. (**See letter of 10 May 1918**).*

*[Major, acting Lt-Colonel, James
Hugh Coles was a Bristol man,
educated at Eton. A career soldier
formerly with the Lancashire
Fusiliers, he saw service in India,
was wounded in France in October
1914, spent some time with the
Special Reserve Bn in England, and
returned to France early in 1916. He
left a wife and three children].*

*Captain A. F. Cemery, who died at
Jack's side. (**See letter of 19 July
1917**).*

161

Lt.-Col. E. Laverack. **See letters of 27 March and 2 April 1917.**

Capt. Cyril Easton, M.C., who died alongside Harold Oughtred at Wancourt, 23 April 1917.
(See letter of 3 May 1917).

After the Armistice Jack entertained hopes of being sent to Blighty to fetch the Battalion colours from Withernsea – but it was not to be. ***(See letter of 2 December 1918)****. Note Capt. Cyril Slack, 3rd from left.*

One of the guns captured during the Battle of Epehy, displayed at Beverley Barracks. ***(See letter of 20 September 1918)****.*

163

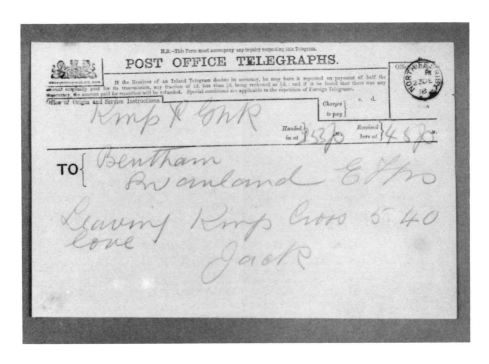

The final telegram from King's Cross station, 23 December 1918.

OUGHTRED-BENTHAM. — 23rd October, at Hessle, John Alwyn Oughtred, M.C., 4th Battalion, youngest son of Mr. and Mrs. Oughtred, Davenport Avenue, Hessle, to Phyllis, younger daughter of Mr. and Mrs. Bentham, Swanland.

Notice of Jack & Phyllis' marriage in **The Snapper.**

The wedding, which took place at Hessle on 23 October 1919.
The re-touching of the photograph has effectively disguised Jack.
Note the three wound-stripes on his sleeve: these were awarded for wounds sustained in action.

It was indeed very sad about our Turkey, but no-one noticed that it was minus one leg. We had several people in too from other Companies. However, all went off very well and the next day after I was invited in to another Company to take part in another show of the same sort.

This morning "Barbara" (codename for the Major General) came round the trenches. He [*Campbell*] is only quite a small man and the water in places nearly reached his waist. He was, I must say, very pleasant. People of that sort, you know, generally find fault: it's what they get paid for, I suppose.

I am wearing big gum boots, thigh — India rubber boots, you know, very like the kind of thing the men who work in the sewers wear at home. You must have seen them some time or other.

Heaps and Heaps of Love and Kisses. Yours, Jack.

13:1:18

My darling Phyllis,

I was very pleased indeed to receive your letter of the 6th. It was a *very nice* one. You will, I know, be pleased to know that I am out of the line again [*in support at Epehy*]. We have quite a nice cellar with a stove and beds of wire.

I am *quite* sure that I shall never have any cause to regret trusting you. I do, you know, completely. Yes, wouldn't it be s'nice if we could have an evening together sometime. We had some very nice ones last time I was on leave, didn't we? I think that it's simply lovely of you to tell me that you always want me very much — and more especially when you're feeling fed up. It's really very sweet of you, dear. I always want you too — oh, ever so much. You know, I honestly think that we care for each *other heaps*. It's a good old world after all, isn't it? War has made us realise how good peace is, hasn't it?

I am very glad you managed so well in the operation theatre. I think personally that it must be rather a gruesome business — very interesting, though, I admit.

I saw two Bosche planes brought down this morning. Rather a fine sight — anti-aircraft guns did it. It's a beautiful day for them — so clear and frosty. Grand day for a round of golf.*

Heaps and Heaps of Love. Yours, Jack.

*[*Diary:* "*German triplane attacked one of our obs balloons near Heudicourt and brought it down in flames. Plane shot down by rifle and machine gun fire. Plane intact, occupant capt. (2Lt). Fokker triplane with 110 h.p. engine.*"]

14:1:18

My darling Phyllis,

Many thanks for your nice letter of the 7th which I was very bucked to receive last night.

I do hope that you won't walk up the hill by your lonely self in the dark. However, with this afternoon stunt you will be able to stop longer in bed in the morning and make a decent breakfast.

So "Destiny" is still being played, is it? It's funny what memories it recalls to us both, isn't it? I wish I could have a few dances with you. I shall never forget that delightfully long supper dance — 1½ hours we had together at the Hymerians at the City Hotel — will you?

Please give my love to Doris and remember me to the rest of the family.

Heaps and Heaps of Love. Yours, Jack.

15:1:18

My darling Phyllis,

I can't tell you how pleased I was to get your letter of the 8th yesterday. The mince pies were excellent.

I am still living in my coal cellar. I really like it very much. I haven't been so comfortable for a long time. Of course, candles have to be burnt all day, but we've got plenty of them, so that's alright. The Hun shelled us late last night with heavy stuff — 8 inch — which was very annoying. A partially demolished house nearby has almost entirely disappeared during the night.

By Jove, if I could only salve some of the machinery and other things that are lying about here — and sell it — I should be worth quite a lot. Must be thousands of pounds' worth rusting away. Seems such a frightful waste.

Please, dear, don't think that just because the weather's rotten and we are in the line that we're having a very bad time. I don't know how it is but we get so accustomed to being wet and always out in the open that one doesn't feel this severe weather anything like as much as you would suppose. The only great trouble, you know, is Frost Bite and Trench Feet. You know, dear, I do feel awfully lonely so often — it is such a long time since we saw each other. I've got heaps of things to tell you. I don't think that you are ever out of my thoughts altogether.

Well, I must really close now, dearest, but will, needless to say, write again very soon.

Heaps and Heaps of Love. Yours, Jack.

16:1:18

My darling Phyllis,

You know I was simply delighted to receive your letter of the 9th last night. You've written to me practically every day now for a long time. They have bucked me up heaps.

You may be quite sure that I will take care of myself as much as possible and not run any needless risks. It's all a matter of luck — say what you will.

I expect to leave my coal cellar soon — very sad, isn't it? All the snow has gone now and it's turned to rain. Still, it might be far worse.

So you do remember Jan 5th 1916. I am afraid that I was rather rough on that occasion. You must have thought me rather a wretch, didn't you? But, dear, it *was nice* — though we've had some heaps better times since, haven't we?

You know, isn't it awful? I haven't kissed you for simply ages — perhaps I am rather too exacting in that way, am I? But it's not so very bad, is it?

Will write again tomorrow, dearest. Heaps and Heaps of Love. Yours, Jack.

17:1:18

My darling Phyllis,

I am now again in the front line in the same place as I was before. Unfortunately the tide in the trench — mud and water, you know — has risen to such an extent that my old dug-out is completely flooded out. However, I have found a temporary home elsewhere. It is quite impossible to get along the trenches at all —you have to walk over the top.

One man last night had to be pulled out with ropes — he got stuck so fast in mud in the trench. That's getting past a joke, isn't it? It's still raining. We shall soon be Torpedoed.

I expect to go on a Course on the Lewis Gun (7 days) on the 23rd down at Paris Plage. I hope it comes off as I shall be quite glad to get away from this mud for a bit.

What do you think of these increased rates of pay? Jolly good, I think. I shall get another 1/- a day out of it, paid as from October 1st. The ones who do best are the 2Lts — 2/6 extra a day.

Heaps and Heaps of Love. Yours, Jack.

18:1:18

My own darling Phyllis,

I was very bucked to receive three letters — the 10th, 11th and 12th — from you last night.

Leave is still going very well. I am 8th on the list now — so with luck I might get away in 6 weeks or so. I'm not half looking forward to it. As we haven't seen each other for such ages and ages and ages I shall be absolutely at boiling point when I do — I must really be careful (of course, not too careful) because I really do want you dearest to survive and live for oh, simply ages. It would be "drefful" if you didn't. What a lot of rot I'm writing, aren't I?

It was awfully sweet of you to tell me that you do so long to see me again. I liked that portion of the letter very much indeed. I felt so frightfully bucked that I didn't know what to do with myself for sometime after reading it.

Things aren't turning out so badly as I expected. Of course, it's quite impossible to walk along the trenches. The Hun must be in the same state as he never shoots at you much when you walk about in the open.

Heaps and Heaps of Love. Yours, Jack.

19:1:18

My own darling Phyllis,

I am sorry to say that there wasn't any English Mail in yesterday at all — very disappointing.

I am still in the line and things honestly ain't so bad. In this dug-out there are two other Company Commanders besides myself, so we have quite a cheerful time. It's the men — worse luck — that are having the rotten time.

A friend of mine in this Batt., and also of the 4th — Capt. Speath by name —had a very busy time on his leave to England. He was introduced engaged and married all in 14 days. Rather quick work that, wasn't it? Hadn't met the lady before either. A bit too rapid, I think.*

I'm afraid darling that this is a rather uninteresting letter, but I really haven't got much news, and the Hun is at the moment shelling our dug-outs which is rather distracting.

Heaps and Heaps of Love. Yours, Jack.

*[The story of Captain Speath is referred to again in a letter dated 10.7.18. There is some confusion as to whether this is Speath, Sleath or indeed Heath. the Diary entries are no help: like Jack, they use various spellings.]

21:1:18

My darling Phyllis,

I was delighted to receive your letters of 13th and 14th last night and the 15th this morning.

Very many thanks too for your parcel of socks, soap and magazines. I gave the first two items to the men this morning. They were very pleased indeed to get them.

Jolly glad to hear that you're feeling so well. If dancing suits you I hope that you will have lots more of them. You are going the pace smoking, what? But I understand: you can't go on working for ever without having a fling sometimes. I feel like that often. I am going into P[*eronne*] tonight for dinner, just to get rid of the monotony of things for a bit. But we'll both be able to let off a bit of steam when I get home, shan't we.

I came out of the trenches yesterday and am quite a long way back [*in billets at Haut Allaines*]. We travelled in a Light Railway in open trucks: it was lots better than marching. But as we were waiting to get on at the end near the trenches the Hun started to shell us with quite heavy stuff. It was most unpleasant. The first one burst about 30 yds off me. I wasn't thinking of the war at all, so it was rather a shock at first. No-one was hit. How they all missed I don't know.

I leave the Batt. on the 23rd for Paris Plage. Well, I must close now, dearest, but will write tomorrow without fail. I must be off now into P[*eronne*] as I do want a bath so badly.

Heaps and Heaps of Love. Yours, Jack.

22:1:18

My darling Phyllis,

I was very glad indeed to receive your letter of the 16th this afternoon. I had quite a good time in ---- [*Peronne*] last night. There are just a few inhabitants (about 12 I think) and about two shops.

It was a very beautiful moonlit night and it was pretty weird walking along those streets without hearing another sound except the noise of your own footsteps. Nothing hardly except broken and empty houses. It does seem a shame. I guess when the original inhabitants of the houses come back they will get a bit of a shock.

I have got quite a decent hut here now, only the Officers of my Company in it, so I am really quite comfy. It is really marvellous with what a little you are satisfied with out here.

I am going away tomorrow on my Course and shall be away for 10 or 12 days if not more. You may be sure that I shan't hurry back again. It's not a very good time of the year for the seaside, but I shall have quite a decent time no doubt.

Heaps and Heaps of Love. Yours, Jack.

E.F.C., OFFICERS REST HOUSE AND MESS, 23/1/18

My darling Phyllis,

I have started and have got so far on the journey. I am now at the place where I bought that pendant watch for you.

It all looks very much the same. I was very glad to get here. So far my journey has been made in a cattle truck, and a very slow one at that. However, I am going from here in a French passenger train, so ought to do rather better. It leaves at 6.18 pm.

I shan't try to get through to my destination tonight, but am going to put up at some hotel or other at my next stopping place. I have dreams of white sheets and that sort of thing. Whether it will come off or not I don't know.

My servant Heller is with me. I've let him off to have a rush round. I hope that he comes back in time for the train.

Heaps and Heaps of Love. Yours, Jack.

Lewis Gun School, Le Touquet, 24/1/18

My darling Phyllis,

I arrived here this morning about 11 am. It's quite a long way from the station, so that when I got off the train at 11 pm I gave up all idea of getting here the same night. 7 kilometres and all my kit with me.

Unfortunately the Officers' Club shut up at 10 pm and they would not allow any more people to come in after that time. So I spent the night in the YMCA close by —any amount of blankets and a bed. I went to the Club for breakfast — it's a huge place. WAAC waitresses too. I am afraid that this Course is going to be very boring.

Heaps and Heaps of Love. Yours, Jack.

25:1:18

My darling Phyllis,

I have had rather a more interesting day today on the whole. All this morning we were out doing tactical schemes, which as every one can have his own solution of the problem naturally prove to be rather amusing. It's all imagination of course. You are told for instance that you've got to attack such and such a place with a Company or Battalion — or whatever it may be — and you've got to work out what formation you would use and where you would place all your men. We carried on with this for about 3 hours, advancing all the time. I quite enjoyed it, although we were late for lunch.

This letter won't get away tonight so I'll go and see the show and finish it tomorrow. Goodnight dearest.

Saturday. I went to the show in the YMCA given by the Staff. It was really very good indeed. One of them dressed himself up as a girl and I must say quite looked the part, only his hands and feet gave him away: much too large.

I was one of a crowd this morning who watched a miniature attack being made —without artillery of course. It was quite a good show — bombs, Lewis Gun and rifles only were used. That's the kind of war I like: not much danger attached to it.

Heaps and Heaps of Love. Yours, Jack.

Etaples, 27:1:18

My darling Phyllis,

I went into Paris Plage yesterday. Everything looked delightful and it was perfectly warm, really most strange weather for January. I visited a picture show —nearly had the place to myself too.

We finished at 11 am today so I speedily left the Camp and made my way here in order to catch the Field Cashier and draw some cash. I just had enough for lunch. The suspense waiting to see what the bill would be was rather awful. I didn't catch the Cashier either, so I simply haven't got a farthing on me now — a terrible state of affairs, isn't it?

This is an awfully nice club. It was given by a Mr. Knott of Newcastle, late owner of the Prince's line, in memory of his two sons who were both killed out here.

I think they are starting to run this war on quite civilised lines now. I mean providing Clubs, etc. I haven't met anyone I know yet, but there's an Officer of the 12 N.F. of the 21st Division who is at the same Course and we go about a great deal together.

This is an awfully interesting letter — positively thrilling in places, isn't it? I will really try and do better next time — so goodbye for the present dearest,
Heaps and Heaps of Love. Yours, Jack.

Lewis Gun School, Le Touquet, 27:1:18
My darling Phyllis,

After I wrote this afternoon I caught the train and went over to Paris Plage. I sort of wandered about a bit and then went into a Picture Palace — shocking thing to do on a Sunday. You know, I think that Frenchmen on the whole are a very odd-looking lot, so effeminate. That's hardly diplomatic, is it? But I don't think that that sort of thing suits men myself, do you? However, I suppose that it's all a question of taste.

Owing to lack of funds we were unable to have any tea but bought some chocs instead and then set off and walked home through the woods and over the links.

Well, I must close and be off to bed, so goodnight dearest, the sweetest of dreams. Mine I am sure will be of you.
Heaps and Heaps of Love and Kisses. Yours, Jack.

28:1:18
My darling Phyllis,

I have had quite an interesting day today. The squad I'm in were marched away into the woods and then given a certain Magnetic bearing to march on, the total march distance being 1600 yds. It was really rather amusing, but what it has to do with Lewis Guns I fail to see.

There is a written exam coming off tomorrow. I am very glad too, as in these oral tests I can never get the right thing out when I want to.

I was talking today to an Officer of one of the Brigades in Norman's Division. They are out at rest now, up North not far from St. Omer. I was round there just before I came home on leave last October. Tophole billets too. Quite the best that I have ever had.

There is one great thing in favour of this place and that is that we get the English papers everyday. It's very good to be in touch with civilisation again.
Heaps and Heaps of Love. Yours, Jack.

Officers' Club, Etaples, 30/1/18
My darling Phyllis,

I finished my Lewis Gun Course at 12 Midday today. My train leaves at 6.18 am. I shall if I can stop somewhere on the way — possibly Amiens.

I shall be back with the Batt. in a couple of days now. They may take some finding as I believe they have moved from the place where I left them. [To Templeux la Fosse].

You know I do so long to see you again. I always feel like that but it's just a wee bit worse tonight.
Heaps and Heaps of Love and Kisses. Yours, Jack.

B.E.F. 1/2/18
My darling Phyllis,

I got back to the Battalion again this afternoon and found your letters of the 17th, 18th, 20th and 21st. We are in tents with a Mess made of corrugated iron sheeting.

It will be rather a pleasant change going in in the afternoon at the Hospital. I am very glad that you're not walking up that hill in the dark by yourself.

I hear from various people who have been on leave that food is very short or hard to get in England. Is this so? I expect that we must get it all, as we always have any amount. Not fair that, at all.

By the way, Carver has rejoined us again today. He has been away for 3 Months instructing. I don't know if you remember me telling you about him. He comes from Jamaica. His wife is a nurse at Boulogne. Well, he has just got 3 Months leave to go over to Jamaica to see his people — some leave that, isn't it. But what I think is rotten — he's got to pay his own fare. It's a bad show altogether, as he has been in this country for over two years. I do think that the Army might have treated him a little better.

Heaps and Heaps of Love. Yours, Jack.

2/2/18

My darling Phyllis,

I was very pleased indeed to receive your letter of the 27th this afternoon. I am very sorry to say that I can't find any trace of that Pork Pie you were so good as to send me. It must have been sent onto me at the School, although I told them here not to do so.

Yes, I feel very sorry for Hal Seed too. It must be awful losing a foot. I haven't seen him for a long time.

I have had a very busy afternoon making a new fireplace in the hut and I regret to say it's far worse than it was before. Smokes frightfully. We all get driven out of the Mess every few minutes.

I am quite a long way from the line — in fact miles away from anywhere, so I'm safe enough. This is rather a poor letter, dear, but it's the smoke: I've constantly got to go outside to breathe.

Heaps and Heaps of Love. Yours, Jack.

4:2:18

My darling Phyllis,

I am very sorry to say that I didn't hear from you today — rotten old post again. I have had a very quiet day today — carrying on with the digging.* As Major Coles is away I am at the moment Sec in Command and shall have to go up the line tomorrow to have a look round and gather information.

This will have to be a short letter as it's getting late, but I will write again tomorrow.

Goodnight dearest, sweetest of dreams. Heaps of Love. Yours, Jack.

*[The Batt were engaged in work on the Green Line, a defensive trench designed to contain the Germans when they launch the expected Spring Offensive].

5/2/18

My own darling Phyllis,

I had a grand mail today — simply great. Six letters from you — namely the 22nd, 24th, 25th, 26th, 29th and 30th. Some list that, isn't it? The first four had been sent down to the Base and then re-addressed and sent back to the Battalion again.

I am so glad that you liked my letter of the 24th and also that it bucked you up

172

— that's the great thing. I wouldn't have you depressed for worlds. You know I feel very lonely sometimes. The feeling sort of comes over you all at once, every now and then. I really think I'm more in love than ever. It's rapidly getting worse and worse — so you see what you're in for.

I am very concerned to hear that your cough isn't any better and that you haven't slept for nights. You must have a rest or something. I am very glad that my Mother made you promise to take Scott's Emulsion. though I hope it doesn't make you sick. I always was considered to be very delicate and my Mother always made me take it. It's very good stuff — sickly, it's true.*

I had a very long ride today on horse-back — about 17 kilometres. Where to I cannot say, but I feel most awfully stiff now — absolutely all over.

Yes, I still burn your letters as I said I would. I read them over many times, especially some of the *very s'nicest* parts, but the fire is the only safe place for them out here.

I am glad that your Father has come through these air Raids in town alright. It must be rather worrying for you all. Very annoying for him, I should think.

It's very interesting to hear that Col. Wilkinson is getting married. Who's the girl? I did hear but have forgotten.

Don't strafe me for what I am going to say, will you? But please do take care of yourself a bit. You seem to be worked to death, what with walking up and down that hill and then Hospital. I wish I was at home to take care of you. Please give my love to Doris and remember me to the rest of the family.

Heaps and Heaps of Love. Yours, Jack.

*[*Scott's Emulsion* was widely advertised as "*Nature's Body-Building Food*". It claimed to be recommended by doctors in case of: coughs, colds, consumption, whooping cough, bronchitis, pneumonia, influenza, measles and rickets – and wasting.]

8:2:18
My own darling Phyllis,

It was as I feared — I couldn't get a letter away to you yesterday.

I am now once again in the trenches, in the same old place. My Company Head Qtrs are the deep dug-out that I think I have described to you before, so you see I am really very comfy. Got quite a nice bed and had about 4 hours sleep last night, so feel very fit today. The trenches too have been improved a lot since we left [*Diary: "trenches in very good condition"*]. The men are much more comfortable.

We unfortunately got shelled a bit coming in, but I personally hadn't any casualties. Other Coys were not so lucky. You know, it is a strange feeling being shelled in an open road with nowhere to take shelter. Simply have to push on and get out of it.

My word, but I am looking forward to leave. I've got that funny feeling inside that I shall simply explode if I don't see you *very very* soon. I can see that you'll have a job to keep me properly in hand. Nothing like giving you due warning, is there?

Heaps and Heaps of Love. Yours, Jack.

10:2:18
My darling Phyllis,

I was very bucked to receive your letter of the 3rd last night. Directly I saw that it was written in pencil I said, Good Heavens, she's ill in bed. You assure you me that you're not ill. Still, I have my doubts.

Many thanks for the Pork Pie which arrived yesterday. It has done some travelling all over France. It has proved rather too much for the Pie, so I am afraid that it will have to be scrapped.

Who do you think is coming to have a look round the line this morning? Lord Nunburnholme.* I think I shall have to make an effort and get washed today.

When we get out of the line I shall go and ask the C.O. if there's any reason why I shouldn't go on leave. I shall have to be diplomatic about, it, shan't I?

I do hope that by the time this letter arrives you'll be feeling heaps better.

Heaps and Heaps of Love. Yours, Jack.

*[Lord Nunburnholme was a Wilson, a member of the family who owned the shipping line of the same name.]

12:2:18
My darling Phyllis,

You will be glad to hear that I am out of the trenches again.

I am in that same old cellar that I mentioned a month ago [in Brigade Support at Epehy] I was very lucky in the line — hadn't any casualties at all.

We have quite a lot of work to do by day — digging, you know — but all the night off, so everyone gets a chance of getting down and having a good sleep. Leave is going strong. One Officer to go yet before me.

A most exciting thing has just happened — the men have dug out a lot of plates etc. buried by French inhabitants. I must go and see them.

To continue my letter again, we got heaps of ordinary plates — soup and otherwise — but there are about a dozen which have pictures on them and appear to me rather quaint and possibly old. I wish I knew something about china. However, I will send them to you to judge. They will be a good souvenir.

Amongst other things we got a flower boat. I don't think it's silver, but it may be silver plate, so if it washes alright and polishes up a bit don't be surprised to see it arrive. There are too a lot of vases, odd coffee and tea cups, also several tea pots, all china of some kind, but I don't think they will be worth bothering with. I was hoping that something really valuable would turn up — notes or something like that, but nothing was doing.

Heaps and Heaps of Love. Yours, Jack.

13:2:18
My darling Phyllis,

I was very pleased indeed to receive your letter of the 6th last night and am *glad* to hear that you're well enough to go back to work again, though I personally think that you have too much work.

I hope that your photos turn out better this time than last. I should like to have one very much indeed. Your photo in its case which you gave me about January 1916 is still my constant companion. In fact ever since it arrived by post at Railway Dug-Outs, Ypres, it has always occupied my top left-hand breast pocket.

By the way, referring to the crockery I found today, I have had some of the plates washed and told my Quarter Master Sgt to have a box made to fit the ones I am sending to you. They are really quite pretty. That silver flower or fruit dish is very much tarnished by the weather. I am sending it to be properly cleaned. Trying to make an addition to our bottom drawer, you see. I do hope that no-one pinches it on the way over.

It's very strange though to have tea out of thin tea cups — you see light through them easily — and pukker tea pots and so on. I've given the Wesleyan padre a couple of the plates depicting the months of the year. He seemed very bucked.

I am still living in my coal cellar but hope to change it for more congenial quarters soon.

Well, I must close now, so au revoir. Heaps and Heaps of Love, Jack.

14/2/18

My darling Phyllis,

I was very pleased indeed to receive your letters of the 8th and 9th last night.

I am sorry to hear that you have had another attack of neuralgia. There's nothing worse, I think. It must have been rotten. However, I'm glad that you're better again.

By the way, I had the Adjutant into dinner last night and after having fed him pretty well I asked if there was any chance of my going on leave in the near future. He said, "Oh yes, you might go any time now." I shall keep him to it.

The wooden box made for the plates came up with the rations last night so I speedily packed the plates in it and sent them off. I have sent that dish to Curtis. It's silver plate alright on top with brass underneath.

You know, I do think that it's awful bad luck you having to go to the Hospital on Sunday.

Heaps and Heaps of Love. Yours, Jack.

16:2:18

My darling Phyllis,

I was very pleased indeed to receive your letter of the 10th this afternoon. It was an especially s'nice one.

I am very glad indeed that you're really feeling fit again. We will make up for lost time when I come on leave and do heaps of theatres etc. and other much nicer things.

I went to see the pictures yesterday. I was quite thrilled with a picture entitled "Bullets and Brown Eyes". The Hero and Heroine didn't half get on with the business.

Quite a lot of Officers are going home on this 6 Months rest in England. I stand a very good chance the next time this comes round.

Heaps and Heaps of Love. Yours, Jack.

[*The Battalion, having travelled by train from Saulcourt, is now at Haut Allaines, about three miles north of Peronne*].

17:2:18

My darling Phyllis,

Very many thanks for your parcel which arrived today. I have been very hard up for something to read too.

I haven't done anything thrilling since I wrote you yesterday. Church this morning at 10 am. This afternoon I went out for a short walk. The village near here is in a frightful state — hardly one brick left on top of another. It does seem to be an awful waste.

People coming off leave all say how hard it is to get food. Is this so or is it an exaggeration. We are never short. Isn't this an exciting letter? I am so sorry, but I haven't much news today.

Heaps and Heaps of Love. Yours, Jack.

18:2:18

My darling Phyllis,

Many thanks indeed for your letter of the 12th which arrived this afternoon.

The Adjutant told me he was going to ask the C.O. if I couldn't go on leave almost at once. He is going to find out today. I don't suppose the C.O. will object — it's Brigade that are the trouble.

Last night the Hun planes came over and bombed us. They got far too near for my liking. 2 or 3 dropped only 100 yds away. One Officer of this Batt. was out dining with some other Mess not very far away from here and a bomb dropped very close, a piece coming through the side of the hut. All in the hut at once went outside to see what was doing. When they returned a lock of hair was to be seen on the table, which turned out to belong to the officer of ours. The piece of bomb had just grazed his head and snipped off a bit of his hair. Rather a narrow squeak, wasn't it? If it had been ½ inch lower it would have done him in.

Well I must close now, dear. Heaps and Heaps of Love. Yours, Jack.

19:2:18

My darling Phyllis,

I was very pleased to receive your letter of the 13th today. We have had a very busy time today as lots of generals and people of that sort have been floating around. I missed them, I am glad to say. They always strafe one about something or other. That's what they are paid for, I suppose.*

I haven't heard any more news about leave yet, but I am keeping the Adjutant at it. I feel *very bucked* indeed at the prospect of seeing you again very shortly. I fear that you're in for a terrible time — well, perhaps not as bad as that.

Heaps and Heaps of Love. Yours, Jack.

*[*The tour of inspection was made by the Army Commander (General Gough), the Corps Commander (Gen. Congreve), the Divisional Commander (Gen. Campbell) and the Brigade Commander (Gen. Headlam)*].

20/2/18

My darling Phyllis,

I have slightly changed my place of habitation since I last wrote you, but it's the right way — further away from the line.* We have bell tents to sleep in, but have an excellent Mess. It was originally an outhouse but has been much improved and we have put in today a stove which, Thank Heaven, doesn't smoke.

The country round here has in days now gone by been very heavily fought over. There are abundant signs of this. One of my Officers, Woodhead by name, who is doing a Course in Pigeons, told me today that at a certain place near here today an old Bosche dug-out was opened up — and sat at a table in the room down below was a dead Bosche with his head in his hands.

There are some very extensive marshes here and heaps of ducks and other game. We succeeded in bagging a couple — a great addition.

It is very cold here today. Shortly after lunch I saw the C.O. and Major Coles in the forest sawing and chopping wood. The men were amazed that a Colonel should do such a thing. He looks quite a nut with his D.S.O. and M.C. up.

Heaps and Heaps of Love. Yours, Jack.

*[*The Batt has moved to a camp near Brie, south of Peronne, relieving the 19th Entrenching Batt. (10th Royal Dublin Fusiliers) for work on the Brie-Estrees Light Railway under the guidance of a Canadian outfit.*]

24/2/18
My darling Phyllis,

Very many thanks for your letter of the 18th received this afternoon.

I regret to say that I didn't write to you yesterday, but I was really very busy every bit of the day. One of my men hit a German bomb with his pick yesterday and was quite severely wounded — stretcher case anyway. Another walking through the long grass ran his foot onto an old French bayonet and he's gone to F.A. too. I'm coming to the conclusion that old battle fields aren't too healthy.

I must say I haven't any scruples about taking that old china at all. The original owners would never get them. Those things must have been buried for 3 years at least. I had to mark the plates I sent you as "Surplus Kit". Rather an effort of imagination, isn't it?

I shall simply fade away if I don't see you soon.

Heaps and Heaps of Love. Yours, Jack.

26:2:18
My darling Phyllis,

Everything has gone on very much the same since I last wrote you. We managed to finish work on our railway early today and get back here for lunch, which was much better for the men. A new Officer has been posted to my Coy, another of these cavalry Sgt. Majors with 20 years' service. It seems rather strange to me to have such people under me.

These old battlefields round here are very interesting in some ways, but you occasionally run across rather gruesome sights. I often wonder what can possibly be done with all this ground after the war's over.

I censored a most extraordinary letter today. I never repeat things as a rule but this one was so strange. He said, "The man that killed Dad has joined the Batt."

My one great thought now is leave. It does seem such a long time since we parted on Ferriby station, doesn't it? I had a terrible pain inside for a long time after. I wanted you *very much* this morning, though for that matter I always do, as of course you know.

Heaps and Heaps of Kisses for yourself. Yours, Jack.

27:2:18
My own darling Phyllis,

I was delighted to receive your letters of the 21st and 22nd this afternoon, but I am most awfully sorry to hear that you felt so rotten at the Hospital the other day. I don't see at all what you have to be ashamed about though — personally I think it was very plucky of you to try and last out.

I have been up to the line today. We went the greater part of the way by bus. Things seemed to be very quiet, only a few shells knocking about.

Well, hoping to see you very soon — "The touter the sweeter" in fact,

Heaps and Heaps of Love and Kisses. Yours, Jack.

[*On this day the Batt. returned to Haut Allaines to rejoin the Brigade. Later, however, they were ordered to take up battle positions, and travelled by Light Railway*

177

to Saulcourt. The Germans' preparations for the coming offensive were quite evident by this time, according to Wyrall in his history of the East Yorkshire Regiment.]

28/2/18
My darling Phyllis,

This I am afraid will have to be a very short letter because I believe something is doing — what I don't know — but we have got to be prepared for all kinds of things so I've got a fearful lot to do. But please don't feel uneasy at all about me. I think that it's mostly "wind up".

I was talking to the Staff Captain today — I had him in my Mess as a matter of fact — and he said that the General had no objection to Officers going on leave anytime between 4 or 5 Months. So you see I shan't be long now.

I heard a most extraordinary thing today. A certain Chinese battalion (labour) out here was examined by an M.O. to ascertain their general health and would you believe it about 50% of them were women. It's rather astonishing, isn't it?

And how are you now? I do hope, dear, that you haven't had any more of those groggy times. I like that Photo you sent me very much. I think it's very good of you. It is reposing quite safely in my left breast pocket.

Heaps and Heaps of Love. Yours, Jack.

1:3:18
My darling Phyllis,

I regret to say that there wasn't any mail in today but I hope for better luck tomorrow.

We have moved forward a bit since I last wrote. We came up on one of those Light Railways in trucks and, by Jove, but it was cold. My trench coat stood up on its own when I took it off. During our many halts, when the engine was trying to get sufficient steam up, I sat on its boiler and managed to get thawed a bit in places.

But we are quite comfortable now. We reached our present habitation at 2 am and 10 minutes later our Cook produced an excellent dinner. It's really marvellous how they manage it, I think.

I have been for a long tramp across country this morning — not for pleasure —looking and taking notes of the ground with a view to other possibilities.*

There is an old French cemetery a few yards away from this hut and the Bosche have opened nearly all the tombs and graves. I can't see what on earth they have done it for. Looking for loot perhaps.

Heaps and Heaps of Love. Yours, Jack.

*[*The "tramp across country" was in order to reconnoitre approaches to Epehy and Chapel Hill, Epehy being prepared for defence against the expected attack.*]

2:3:18
My darling Phyllis,

Many thanks for your letter of the 23rd received this afternoon.

I also had a short note from Curtis and Sons saying that the Dish has arrived safely. They say that it will repair alright although it may take some time to do.

The number of men going on leave now is simply tremendous — 40 are going today and a similar lot tomorrow. They are down to 7½ Months now — never been anything like that before.

Well, I must close now, dearest, hoping to see you soon.
Heaps and Heaps of Love. Yours, Jack.

4/3/18
My darling Phyllis,

I was very pleased indeed to receive your letter of the 26th today.

We have had a day off working parties today. We do it every other day, you know. It's as well too as it's a rotten day — snow, rain and wind.

Two of the new Officers I have got were through Mons and have the 1914 star of course. They are very interesting to talk to about the great retreat and appear to be on the whole fairly truthful. These 'old soldiers' are terrible people for exaggerating things, but I suppose that we all do that a bit.

As I said yesterday I expect to come sometime between the 12th and 15th.

Well, I must close now, dearest, as I have got to attend a lecture by the Brig -General in a few minutes [*'Diary: "Lecture on Raids and the coming German offensive."*]. Cheerio.
Heaps and Heaps of Love. Yours, Jack.

5:3:18
My darling Phyllis,

I was delighted to receive your letter of the 27th and parcel of the 1st today. Thanks very much indeed — the Pork Pie is a great addition: they are very handy kinds of things, don't take any preparing. And I'm glad to have something to read again. Can't get anything here in that way. An American comes into this Mess everyday with the Continental *Daily Mail*. They are a very amusing lot.

Two more Officers went on leave last night. I think that I shall go in the next allotment.

I haven't been doing anything exciting myself since I last wrote. We went on our usual digging party at 8 am this morning — it was cold too, but later on was quite warm and pleasant. By giving the men piece work we soon were finished and got back here again at 1 pm, finished practically for the day.

I've had to send a couple of men down to Base to do odd jobs there as they are absolutely balmy, or weak-minded. One man says he was put in the Army for losing time while working at munitions. A bad state of affairs, isn't it?
Heaps and Heaps of Love. Yours, Jack.

6:3:18
My darling Phyllis,

Many thanks for your letter of the 1st received today. I am having the Adjutant in to dinner tonight so will try and get it out of him — after feeding him well.

My second-in-command, Lt Bolton, has just got the job of Town Mayor of this village we are now in [*Saulcourt*] — or at least the piece of ground where the village originally was. I am very sorry to lose him, but I am glad that he has got such a good job. He's safe anyway.*

We were busy digging again this morning, but rather too near the line for my liking, in full view of the Hun. But there was a grand ground mist which hid us very well. Fine weather is very nice in some ways but the Hun always wants to get on with the war then.

I was awakened this morning at 4.30 am by the guns. Someone feeling a bit

179

bored with life fired the S.O.S. to see what would happen. Anyway, nothing came off in regard to our "friends" on the other side.

I must close this letter now, dear. Will write again very soon.

Heaps and Heaps of Love. Yours, Jack.

*[*Lt Bolton replaced as Town Mayor the previous incumbent who was found drunk when the Batt. arrived a few nights previously.*]*

8:3:18

My darling Phyllis,

There wasn't any mail in today, which was very sad. However, I shall be seeing you myself in a few days now. I'm trying to fix up with one of the Officers in the Bde Staff for a lift in a car down to Boulogne.

There's nothing at all exciting happening here — digging every day as usual.* It's surprising how fearfully hot it gets in the daytime, quite like summer.

I had quite a dinner party last night here — an Officer from South America, an African and a U.S.A. Officer. So you can imagine we had a very lively time indeed.

You know, I rather think that I ought to go out and get my M.C. this time — that is, of course, if we can fit it in with other arrangements. I might manage a few days' extra leave for it if I'm lucky. I should have to apply to the War Office for an Investiture.

It's very exciting news that leave is getting so near. I feel like boiling over at present, so beware.

Heaps and Heaps of Love. Yours, Jack.

*[*According to a later account 'A' & 'B' Coys were going into the line each night in case the enemy should attack. Jack makes no mention of this.*]*

9:3:18

My own darling Phyllis,

I was very pleased to receive your letters of the 3rd and 4th today.

There is a great chance that I shall arrive before this letter reaches you, but I'll chance it all the same. I'll write you as soon as I land.

You must come and spend the night at Hessle — that's just for a start. You will, won't you, if you possibly can? And then we can fix up all kinds of things. I haven't seen you for such ages and ages I don't want to miss a minute. It will be 14 days this time — the longer the better.

Heaps and Heaps of Love. Yours, Jack.

11:3:18

My own darling Phyllis,

I'm afraid, dear, that my letter written to you earlier on this evening was a very hurried one, but I was determined to catch the post. I delayed writing it until I found out definitely that I wasn't coming on the 14th. You know I feel rather sick with myself for telling you that and having to wash it all out again. But I really did feel so sure. I really "got my rag out" with the Adjutant but he said that it wasn't his fault and that he'd do his utmost to get me away as soon as possible. I'll see that he keeps his word. You know, you wouldn't perhaps believe it but I can at times be quite a determined person.

180

Norman will be in Town tonight, won't he? Lucky chap, I think, to get leave so quickly — no such luck for the "Poor blinkin' Infantry". I was looking forward to seeing you almost any time — and I want to fearfully badly. Well, I must close now, dearest, hoping to see you soon.

Heaps and Heaps of Love. Yours, Jack.

12:3:18
My darling Phyllis,

I was very pleased to receive your letter of the 8th today. I have no further news about the leave question, and can't have until some of the officers come back from courses, etc.

I was going away from here today — back to the war again so to speak — but it has been washed out so far.

By the way, what I told you about those Chinese women is perfectly true.

I have just come away from a lecture given by the Brig-General on Egypt. And very interesting it was too. He has spent a lot of time in the Sudan ruling over some tribes there and has some very strange and peculiar things to talk about, many of which are as interesting as they are unprintable. One Chief he knows there had 600 wives — and a very jealous chap he was too. Guess he'd have to have roll call every now and then, wouldn't he?

Will write again tomorrow. Heaps and Heaps of Love. Yours, Jack.

13:3:18
My darling Phyllis,

I was delighted to receive your letter of the 9th this afternoon. It is a bad job about my leave, isn't it? We are so short, and then although this front is quite quiet at present you never know what may be happening shortly. The papers talk a great deal about the coming German Offensive — make rather too much of it, I think —but no doubt it's coming and in many ways a jolly good thing too, because we'll give those Bosche such a thin time as they've never had in their lives before. A real good reverse might do far more to finish this war than anything else.

Good Heavens, what a fearful lot of shop I'm talking. But I've had all this kind of stuff pumped into me by the C.O. and Brig-Gen etc. to raise our "esprit de corps" I suppose.

I'm afraid that the news of my leave being stopped again will depress you rather. It did me a lot, for a time, but I've recovered now.

Well, I must close now, dearest, hoping in spite of all things to see you very soon.

Heaps and Heaps of Love. Yours, Jack.

14:3:18
My darling Phyllis,

We started today very early indeed. I was peacefully sleeping at about 5.30 am when an orderly dashed in with a "chit" telling me to take up positions at once, which we did and very quickly too, being on the way out at 5.45 am, men and everything complete.

Of course, for the last week or so we never got really properly undressed, simply taken off tunic and boots. [*Men were allowed to loosen their belts. Otherwise, it was full kit – boots, puttees and all.*]*

However nothing happened at all. In fact I've never seen things quieter — may they keep so. It's a jolly good thing though to be thoroughly prepared.

I have some rather good news. I had the Adjutant in to dinner again last night and he told me that providing sufficient Officers came back from courses etc I should go on leave on the 20th. I'm afraid that you will feel rather dubious about it. Still, the third time's supposed to be lucky, isn't it. I am positively frantic to get away.

The Colonel being away Major Coles is in command. I'm sure that he will allow me to go if he possibly can. As you see we are not in the line and I rather think too that we shan't be in for a day or two.

Well, I must close now, dearest, hoping that you're keeping fit and well and that I may see you very very soon.

Heaps and Heaps of Love. Yours, Jack.

*[*The expected German offensive appeared to be beginning. The Bn Diary for the 14th reveals that 2 captured Germans stated the attack to be imminent, at which news 'A' & 'B' Coy were put into line, 'C' & 'D' made ready to move at 15 minutes' notice.*

The Snapper *notes that Col. Trimble "had been looking worn and tired for some time" – hence his absence.*]

4/4/18

[*Jack has had his fortnight's leave, starting 19.3.18, and is now returning to the front. He has no knowledge of what has become of his battalion.*]

My own darling Phyllis,

I am now on my way across the channel, and am going to give this letter to the steward to post in England when this ship returns.

I have got quite a nice berth, sharing a room with Foster. I am sitting on it (my berth) now as a matter of fact, so please excuse wobbly writing.

Aunt Emily met me at King's Cross, after which we went to the Great Northern Hotel and had some food. But you will no doubt hear full details from her. Wilde got off at Peterborough. We managed without the aid of meal tickets to get quite a lot of sandwiches at Doncaster.

Well, the 14 days has soon passed, hasn't it? But it has been a simply lovely time. I've never had a better, and although I am going back to France I feel awfully happy. It was a most fearful rend parting from you. I had a horrid pain inside somewhere, but I tried my very best to hide it as much as possible. I think that the worst thing about war is having to leave those I love so much. I can't help telling you again what an awfully s'nice happy leave I've had. You do make a tremendous difference —turn this world into a topping old spot.

I feel very lonely tonight without Miss Phyllis. I hope that the Months will simply fly by until we are together once more.

The more I see of you the more convinced I am that you're just the sweetest and dearest girl there is anywhere — and I love you so much that I can't find words to express it properly at all.

Well, I must close now so goodbye for the present, dearest, and Heaps and Heaps of Love. Yours, Jack.

6/4/18

My own darling Phyllis,

I am still in the rest Camp and there doesn't seem to be much prospect of my going any farther just at present. I'm not at all sorry either, as I see that the battle started again — must be very unhealthy up there at present.*

I couldn't face the prospect of sleeping in a bare tent with doubtful blankets, so I set to find a billet. I selected some likely looking houses in the vicinity and tried my luck at each one. After about the seventh attempt I was completely successful and managed to get a very nice room with bed, sheets and all complete — a fire too when I went to bed.

There are a tremendous lot of Americans here now. They are a very hearty lot too. A lot of them carry revolvers about with them as we would wear a Sam Browne belt.

I haven't heard any news of the Battalion and haven't the faintest idea where the Division is either. I went down into the Town yesterday. I always thought that Amiens was pretty hot stuff, but really dear this place isn't safe at all. I must confess that I never saw anything like it.

I met Lloyd of Brough here yesterday. He has been here 11 days already. If you remember we passed him in Paragon Street early on in my leave.

Foster is here with me. I lost him yesterday afternoon for about two hours and when I found him again he'd spent £4 and had nothing to show for it. I don't mean that he had been doing anything he shouldn't — far from it. I'll take care he doesn't today anyway.

It does seem a frightful long time since I left you at Paragon Station.

If I should get orders for a sudden move today I'll let you know.

Heaps and Heaps of Love. Yours, Jack.

*[It is uncertain to which action the 1st paragraph refers here: the Germans were advancing at this time on the Somme, the Marne and the Lys. The 1st East Yorks were involved, about 4 April, in a fierce battle at Saulcourt, near Epehy. See Appendix 2.]

No. 1 A Rest camp 7/4/18
My own darling Phyllis,

I am glad to say that I haven't been sent any further on and am still at the Base.

I have been trying to find out some news about my Division, but have not succeeded so far. I see that the Division that was on our left at the commencement of the battle is posted up as non-existent. It seems rather incredible to me, but of course it may be so.

I haven't anything to do here at all — no duties, I mean. I have to report twice a day in case orders have come through for a move — and all the rest of the time you can please yourself what you do.

I have been talking to a lot of American Officers recently. They get a lot more pay than we do — a 2 Lt gets 150 dollars a month and a Captain 220 dollars, just over £50. Pretty good, isn't it? But of course everything costs more in the U.S.A., doesn't it?

You will be back again at the Hospital today, won't you? What a long time it seems since I kissed you. It will be a lot longer before I do again, worse luck.

Well, I must close now, dearest, for the present.

Heaps and Heaps of Love. Yours, Jack.

YMCA headed note-paper 8/4/18
My own darling Phyllis,

I have just received my orders and leave here by train at 10 pm tonight. I just thought I would drop you a line as it may be some time before I have such another

183

opportunity. On the whole I think that I am very glad that I am going. I will write as soon as ever I can.

Must close now, dearest. Heaps and Heaps of Love. Yours, Jack.

11/4/18
My darling Phyllis,

I have just received orders to join the Batt. Will write again as soon as possible. Things don't look too gay.

Goodbye for the present, dearest. Heaps and Heaps of Love. Yours, Jack.

11:4:18
My own darling Phyllis,

I have not found the Battalion yet, but am at the Divisional Reinforcement Camp, and they don't know where the Division is either.

Things are in a very disturbed state here — civilians leaving their places wholesale. I never saw such a bad sight in my life before, carrying all their belongings with them too. One continuous stream of them.

I hear terrible rumours of the casualties of the Batt. It looks as if Mansfield has gone poor chap — and lots of others too. Capt Heath as well. As soon as I hear definitely I'll tell you full particulars. It's a rotten business. There doesn't seem to be any batt. left at all as far as I can see.*

I can see that it may be very hard for me to get letters off. So if you don't hear for a while please don't get uneasy.

Heaps and Heaps of Love. Yours, Jack.

*[*Jack mentions Captain Heath. According to the Diary – with its equally unreliable spelling – Capt. **Sleath** went on a Lewis Gun course on 13.3.18 and may well have missed the action at Saulcourt. On his return he took over 'C' Coy of the Composite Battalion which was formed from, amongst others, the remnants of the shattered 1st.*]

12:4:18
My own darling Phyllis,

I had a long trip on a motor lorry last night and landed up at last at our Nucleus Camp. This morning I am going on to the Transport lines. I don't think that the batt. is in the line, but not very far off it.

As far as I can make out only three officers are left who went through the show down south. Major Coles, Capt. Ewing (Adjutant) and Capt. Stephenson. All the rest have been killed, wounded or captured. However, I'll let you have a list later.

I think that Norman is round here somewhere. I was talking to a man of the 4th yesterday. They seem to have had a very bad time.

Heaps and Heaps of Love. Yours, Jack.

12:4:18 2 pm
My own darling Phyllis,

I was very bucked indeed to receive your letter of the 7th today as soon as I arrived at the Transport. I have to rejoin the Batt. today. It looks as if we might be in for something, but it's no use getting agitated about it.

All the Officers of my Coy were killed or wounded. The four that survived are Major Coles, Capts Ewing, Stephenson and Heath. A Bosche came up to Coles

184

and Ewing and asked them to surrender, but Ewing shot him and they both ran for it and got away. Poor Mansfield was hit by a Machine Gun bullet in the leg and bled to death. Must have cut some artery or some sort.*

Things are [*not*] very cheerful here but I feel very optimistic on the whole.

I must close now, dearest, as I have got to go to the Batt.

Heaps and Heaps of Love. Yours, Jack.

*[*According to the report in* **The Snapper** *Mansfield was hit in the femural artery by a bullet fired from an attacking aircraft, and was reported as bleeding to death within seconds.*]

13/4/18
My own darling Phyllis,

I am not in the front line trenches and so far haven't had a bad time. The only thing is that we are very short of rations. However, we shall no doubt survive.

There is a terrible change in the Batt. — only about 5 of the old Officers left — A Coy had only 10 men left after the show, but of course we have been made up to strength again now. All the faces seem fresh. You do miss the old ones. A lot of pukka Captains and Majors have arrived during my absence and I regret to say that as they are very much senior to me one of them has taken over 'A' Coy so I am now sec-in-Command of the same [*under Capt. E. B. Robinson*]. This of course doesn't affect my rank at all — I'm still a Captain — but I can't help feeling very fed up with it. After I've commanded a Coy out here for six months and with some success, to drop back again to 2-in-Command is disgusting. Major Coles said that he is very sorry and that he had always been very satisfied with everything I'd done. I might manage to get a soft job somewhere now. But after all the great thing is to survive.

That fortnight's leave was the most delightfully happy time that I've ever had. I am always perfectly happy when I'm with you. It's a sad case, isn't it? (I don't think). I think that apart from you being an absolute darling, you're a thorough sport. I can imagine you saying "no" but so it is nevertheless.

I must try and find Norman when I get out of this line as I'm sure he's about here somewhere. I am going to send this letter down with the ration party tonight. There is no communication by day.

Heaps and Heaps of Love. Yours, Jack.

[*The 1st, clearly reinforced, have been brought north to take over in the line north of Wytschaete, Ypres sector. According to Wyrall the line on the ridge there was "a series of strongly fortified lower storeys of farms and shell-hole positions" rather than the usual series of trenches.*]

14/4/18
My own darling Phyllis,

I was delighted and cheered up no end by receiving your two letters of the 8th and 9th this morning. I am glad to hear too that some of mine have arrived. I am sure that the Steward never posted that letter of mine — I gave him quite a good tip too.

It is sad about Mansfield's Father. I had heard a rumour about it, but nothing definite. I miss poor Mansfield *very* much. He was just about my best friend in the Battalion. He seems to have died in about 5 seconds.*

I am of course still in the line and during the last 24 hours have been taking things very quietly. We had very little to eat — I had a round of bread and a drink of water. I think that with that and the cold it brought on an attack of Trench fever. Last night I wandered a bit — but have had a lot of Quinine which has bucked me up a lot, and then too more rations have arrived. I've completely lost my double chin anyway.

In my present capacity I haven't very much to do and no responsibility which under the circumstances is just as well.

I am still feeling very fed up about having to hand over A Coy to Robinson, though he is a great friend of mine. He's sorry himself too. However, I suppose that it's the fortune of war. But it's rather a dirty trick in some ways. Still I won't say any more about it as it won't help matters.

Your letter today, dear, did buck me up. This war would be far worse for me, dear, without you and that's an honest fact. I've got a tremendous lot to be thankful for.

This writing of mine is awful, isn't it? But I am sat on the floor with the pad on my knee.

    With Very Best Love. Yours, Jack.

*[Regarding Mansfield's death, **The Snapper** reported that "his father in England, upon hearing the news, was so ovecome with grief that he died almost at once."]

B.E.F. 23/4/18

[On 21.4.18 Jack, with a Lt Smith, was sent away with a fresh Nucleus Party.]
My own darling Phyllis,

I was very pleased indeed to receive your two letters of the 15th and 16th this morning.

I feel rather better now as compared with yesterday, but am still rather groggy. That last turn in the line was simply appalling — I was in as you know the Battle of the 16th when the Germans tried to break through. They very nearly did it too. They got on one flank within 500 yds of our Batt. Hd Qtrs. I had a Coy of all kinds of mixed people, but managed to hold him until nightfall when the Scotch [7th Seaforth, and a Black Watch Bn.] counter-attacked and drove him back. We didn't suffer very much from shelling but the Machine Gun fire [particularly from North House until it was recaptured by Jack's own 'B' Coy] was terrific. Every Hun seems to have a M.G. The last few days though before being relieved he got onto us with big stuff — 9 in. etc. — and in many places completely changed the landscape.

The slight touch of gas I got — some 4 days ago now — with all the fumes of explosives it's very hard to detect. I felt a tickling feeling in my throat and nose as if someone had tied a rope round my chest. I can tell you I soon put my gas helmet on. I felt very groggy for some hours after and have done ever since although I am rapidly getting better. I shall miss a tour in the line this time anyway. If things go on at this rate though I shan't last long. It affects me more now than it ever did before.

It's a bad job about Foster but I have great hopes that after all he is only a prisoner. A lot of his men were taken prisoner anyway.*

I've written you quite a lot of letters, dear, but I feel sure that a lot of them have been lost. [This would account for the gap in the sequence of letters between 14 and 23 April.]

I am very sorry to hear that you've been groggy too. What a couple we are. What have you been doing to make yourself so? I hope that you're better now though. You seem to have been worked *far too hard* at the Hospital, I think. It must be rotten to be so short-handed. It's not good enough.

That Crown Derby cup, saucer and plate that you bought the other day sound very nice. They must be lovely. I should like to see them very much.

Well, I must close now, dearest, to catch the mail. Will write again tomorrow. I shall be quite safe for a week at least.

Heaps and Heaps of Love. Yours, Jack.

*   [*Early on the morning of the 16th the Germans advanced after a gas attack and a very heavy bombardment. Some ground was lost, including the ruined village of Wytschaete, but this was regained in a counter-attack next day which cost 216 casualties. Private Heller died. Nearby Passchendaele Ridge was lost, barely five months after it had been taken. According to* **The Snapper** *2Lt Heaton Foster "fought like a Trojan" but with most of his platoon killed he was taken prisoner.*]

23/4/18
My own darling Phyllis,

I was very pleased to receive your letters of the 18th and 19th and also the parcel this morning. They bucked me up a lot.

I feel just a wee bit better this morning. An American doctor has given me a lot of pills to take — Bismuth, I think. I shall soon be fit again now. That damned gas is responsible.

Did I tell you that I got a bullet through my scarf and another through my trench coat? Far too near to be pleasant. I can't quite realise those last few days I spent up there. Seems rather like a rotten dream. Thank God I am not going up the line again for a bit.

Our M.O. went about with stretcher bearers and a Red Cross flag attending to the wounded during the fighting — and all the pains he got for his flag was a German Machine Gun turned onto him. The Bosche are dirty dogs. The more one sees of them the more you hate them.

I was very sorry to hear about Pier Van Oppen. It seems only such a short time since we saw him.*

Captain Robinson, M.C., my O.C. Coy is one of those very fussy kind of people. Very wearing if you see much of them. However, we get along quite well and I expect that there will be some more vacancies soon. Any way, I assure you that I am not going to trouble myself very much about things. Intend to have as soft a time as possible.

I must confess that it's a great surprise to me to be sat safely here — miles behind the line writing to you. I never thought that I should come through that show alive for a moment. I still feel rather dazed with it all.

We had a tophole time during that 14 days leave. Gives me quite a thrill when I think of it. Our waitress at the Station Hotel Grill must miss us, I'm sure.

Heaps and heaps of Love. Yours, Jack.

*   [*Both Jack and Phyllis seem to know Pier Van Oppen, although there is no other mention of him in the letters. He died 16.4.18 in hospital in Boulogne, aged 31.*]

No. 8 Red Cross Hospital, Boulogne, 27/4/18
My own darling Phyllis,

I am afraid that you will think me a wretch. I haven't written you for several days, but I've been travelling from place to place the whole time. As you see, I am now at the Base.

I arrived at this Hospital at 2 pm yesterday. It's quite a comfortable place —though of course I've been in bed ever since I arrived and am having nothing else much but milk. This place is right on the sea front. I can see the Hospital ships go out every now and then. I wonder if I shall be lucky enough to get across. The C.C.S. I came through was packed with wounded — hadn't anything like enough beds for them. [*See letter dated 12.12.18*]

I received your letter of the 15th before I left. It was a very s'nice one indeed. I don't know why you call it balmy.

   With Very Best Love, Yours, Jack.

28/4/18
My own darling Phyllis,

Nothing very much has happened since I wrote you yesterday. I am of course still in bed and feel more or less the same. Quite a number are being sent over to England today, but I am not one of those lucky ones.

I assure you, dear, I am very thankful to be down here as up at Kemmel they seem to be having a very thin time indeed. My Battalion would be in the front line of the attack so expect they will have had a pretty bad knocking.*

I am in No.6 Ward — a little room with three beds in — and through the window you can look right out to sea. Rather aggravating to see the Hospital Ships go over to England every day.

The English papers come over every day. Arrive in the evening of the day they are issued. I like to hear how things are going, especially now.

   Will write again tomorrow. With Very Best Love. Yours, Jack.

*[*The Battalion has more or less been wiped out again at this second battle of Kemmel. The Germans attacked 25.4.18 after a heavy bombardment with H.E. and gas shells, inflicting heavy losses. Coles died, shot through the head as the officers and men at HQ retreated under heavy fire; most of the other officers – 15 in all – were reported missing. The* **Snapper** *account states that out of a force of 500 officers and men there were 29 survivors, including walking wounded; many of the casualties, however, were prisoners.*]

29:4:18
My own darling,

I am afraid that I haven't really much news to tell you today dear. I am still in bed and am feeling very much better.

In the last show I was in — the 16th March [*he means April*] — we took up a lot of the A IV boys — 19 yrs old. They had come out as a draft and of course never seen a shot fired before. For the first 3 days in the trenches it was quite quiet but on the 4th day when the Hun attacked it was simply appalling. I'd never seen such a barrage before, ever. I felt very sorry for these new people — must have been a terrible shock to them. They carried on very well, but later on I found two of them lying in the bottom of the trench in tears. Strain and excitement too much for them, I

188

suppose. Seems rather a shame to me to rush fresh men like that from England into a battle straight away.*

I must close now for the moment as an orderly has just brought some lunch in. Lunch, did I say? I mean milk and bread and butter.

I am longing to see you again, dearest. It's rather rotten when I know perfectly well I can't. I shall have to keep myself in hand — no good looking for what you can't have just at present, is it? But what wouldn't I give to see and kiss you again just right now.

Very best Love. Yours, Jack.

*[Jack mentions the new recruits. A **Snapper** report spoke of them thus: "A few... couldn't stand it, but the great majority fought splendidly, and dealt very promptly with the Germans who got into the trench."]

4/5/18
My own darling Phyllis,

I was ever so pleased to receive your letter of the 1st yesterday.

The Gas — Phosgene, I think — hardly affected me at all except in the "tummy" and I couldn't get milk or anything of that kind with the Battalion —only the ordinary army rations, and they gave me a "horrible pain" and sad to relate I became quite feak and weeble and so here I am.

I got up in a dressing-gown yesterday — but after ½ hour I really felt so tired I crept back to bed. Isn't it absurd?

I didn't know that anything has happened to Slack. Glad he's a prisoner. His worries are finished with anyway. Rollitt, Robson, Slack and I came out together in January 1916. So far we are alive and kicking. Strange, isn't it? Mother's letter, which arrived yesterday too, tells me his Father has given £50 as a Thanksgiving for his son's safety.

I am glad that Doris has heard from Norman and that he's alright. I wrote him myself several times but so far have had no retaliation. Well, I must close now, dearest.

With Very Best Love and Heaps of Kisses. Yours, Jack.

7:5:18
My own darling Phyllis,

There was no mail in last night which was very sad. The thick fog that came on in the afternoon was no doubt responsible.

Do you know, dear, I'm still in bed. Awful, isn't it? I feel as if I should explode this morning if I am not careful.

The Hospital seems to be getting rid of as many patients as possible today —looks like a push coming off somewhere, doesn't it? I see that Amiens Cathedral is getting very much knocked about by the Hun shells. It is a shame, but nothing is spared in war now, is it?

There is some prospect of sick leave from here — of course, the leave to be spent in England. I can't very well approach the M.O. on the subject, so I'll just have to await developments. I've just been thinking what a horrible lot of time I'm practically wasting with this war on. Three years up to the present, simply standing still.

How is our Baronial Mansion progressing? I wanted you fearfully badly this morning — it was really quite a bad attack. It's not quite so bad now, though. Have to take a very firm hand with myself.

Well, I will try and write a better letter tomorrow. This one is so thrilling in places, isn't it?

With Very Best Love. Yours, Jack.

Post Office Telegraph from Eltham, 9.50 a.m. 10 May 1918
Am at Royal Herbert Hospital Woolwich, Jack.

Royal Herbert Hospital, Woolwich, 10/5/18
My own darling Phyllis,

It seems rather hard to believe that I am in England. I arrived at this Hospital at 9 pm last night.

The Channel was as smooth as a pond. I was a stretcher case — it's an awfully funny feeling being carried on a stretcher.

I feel very fit today. I shan't be very long in this place, I'm sure. Everything is very comfortable. I'm in a big ward with 30 beds in.

When I do get clear of Hospital I get 3 WEEKS LEAVE. I'm simply fading away for the want of some s'love.

I heard also from Capt. Stephenson 1 EYR just before I left. The Battalion have been practically wiped out — all that came back were 3 Officers (2 Lts) and 32 O.Rs. Major Coles was shot clean through the forehead — and the day after the D.S.O. came through. Seems damned hard, doesn't it? Stephenson, of course, wasn't in it. This happened when the Hun attacked Kemmel on the 25th.*

It is awful isn't it? But of course, quite a lot of them may be prisoners. I hope so anyway.

I hope, darling, that you aren't frightfully busy at the Hospital. What about some leave? I have thought of all kinds of schemes.

Aunt Emily is coming to see me tomorrow. She has just wired me to that effect.

Heaps and Heaps of Love. Yours, Jack.

*[Lt Howard, writing in **The Snapper** some years later, listed Keech, Raine, and himself as the three officers to survive the slaughter at Kemmel. Stephenson had indeed missed it. He was left out, having had such a bad time with 'D' Coy on the previous tour.]

[After his sick leave, Jack was sent to Stafford to take various training courses until passed fit for action.]

No. 1 Officers School of Instruction, Q Lines, Brocton Camp, Stafford, June 3 1918
My own dear Phyllis,

I have met several Officers I know here today — some of the 4th and one of the 1st. I hear to my great astonishment and joy that the weekend at Hull is quite possible. So prepare yourself, dear, for my speedy arrival. The fare with ½ fare voucher is 17/6. I leave here at 1.34 pm Saturday, getting to Hull at 7.50 pm, leaving again ... [letter incomplete]

June 4th 1918

My own darling Phyllis,

I have had a rather busier time today. This morning we had 2 hours drill, giving words of command and saluting, starting right at the beginning of things again. The army is a strange place, isn't it?

I feel quite fit today, no return of the old trouble. That brandy treatment soon settled the question.

Yesterday I met Captain Case of the 1st. He was wounded on the Passchendael Ridge in October. He hadn't heard any news of the Batt. and got rather a shock from what I told him.

There are a lot of Cavalry Officers — some from India — here learning the job of the P.B. [*Poor Bloody*] Infantry. Rather hard on them. Most beautifully arrayed too with epaulets of ringed mail on their shoulders — just like a fishing net, same idea.

Well, sweetheart, I must close now — will write again soon.

Heaps and Heaps of Love. Yours, Jack.

June 12th 1918

My own darling Phyllis,

We had an exam in drill this morning — the first of many. I got through it alright. One Officer goes out as an Instructor and another to pick out any faults that he may make. It's rather amusing.

Do you know, dear, I got a horrible shock yesterday. Every Officer has to give a lecture to his group on any subject he may choose. My turn comes on Saturday morning. I think I shall hold forth on Patrolling — scouting, etc. Can't say that I am looking forward to it.

Now that your photo has returned to its home again I feel much more at ease. Strange, isn't it dear? But it's been with me everywhere, just as the charm you gave me has.

Heaps and Heaps of Love and Lots of Kisses. Yours, Jack.

June 13th 1918

My own darling Phyllis,

I was very pleased indeed to receive your letter of the 12th this morning.

I really feel very well. No return of the old complaint. How is your neuralgia, dear? You never mention it, you know. I had a set or two at tennis yesterday. Felt very strange to be playing once more. The German prisoners made the Court and watched as we played. I saw a funeral of one of them today. Gave him full military honours — flag (German), sounded the "last Post" and fired a volley over his grave.

Your blue dress has had a hard life of it dear. As you say, all the *packing* must have spoilt it rather!! It must be rather a trial. But at some *future time* I've got to mend all the things I tear.

Heaps and Heaps of Love. Yours, Jack.

June 14th 1918

My own darling Phyllis,

Very many thanks for your letter of the 13th which arrived this morning.

We had two hours drill this morning — very boring it was too. No more this week, anyway. I am still T.T. I really hardly miss it at all. I thought I should just at first.

I'm afraid I shan't be able to write tomorrow, dearest, but will on Sunday.
Heaps and Heaps of Love. Yours, Jack.

16/6/18
My own darling Phyllis,
I was delighted to receive your letter of the 14th this morning.

I feel greatly relieved at having got my lecture over. I nearly faded away with horror at the prospect, but wrote out a few notes. I found much to my astonishment, I had quite a lot to say, but one can't help feeling that some of the audience know far more about it than you do.

I am looking forward to seeing you next Saturday, dear, *very much*. Seems a long time since I have done. I'm simply aching to s'love you again and play "BEARS" etc!!!

Thanks very much for the list of Officers. I hadn't seen it. They are all from the 1st. Wisbey and Coverdale were both in my Company — very glad indeed that they are safe. [*Both were posted missing at first.*] Jolly decent chaps, both of them. Nearly all the Officers seem to have been made prisoners — I wonder how it happened. [*See letter of 9 August, in which he hears the details.*]
Heaps and Heaps of Love. Yours. Jack.

June 19th 1918
My own darling Phyllis,
Many thanks for your two letters of the 15th and 17th.

We had a most energetic time this morning, doing another attack: rifles, blank ammunition. We had to cycle some 4 miles. Very heavy going in the heather. I was properly blown at the objective — so was everybody for that matter. After which we pushed back to Camp again.

Well, I don't think that I've any more news today, dearest. Will write again tomorrow. Quite a lengthy effort this. Hope that the weekend comes along *quickly*!
Heaps and Heaps of Love. Yours, Jack.

25/6/18
My own darling Phyllis,
I was very pleased indeed to receive your letter of the 24th this morning. I am glad to say that I feel much better this morning — temperature 100.2 Last night at 7 pm it was 103. I'm on milk diet. Quite like old times again.

I hope that you haven't caught anything, have you dear? Because really you had quite a good chance of doing so from me, hadn't you?

Well, I most close now, dearest. Heaps and Heaps of Love. Yours, Jack.

26:6:18
My own darling Phyllis,
I am glad to say that I'm much better today, feeling more like my old self again, temperature only 99.2 You know, dear, it's left me with a feeling as if I want all my joints oiling. I'm so fearfully stiff.

I heard from Mearns [*3rd Batt., Hornsea*] yesterday, and he says that 20 Officers of the 4th and 500 men are down with this "flu". I do hope, darling, that you haven't caught it. I'm afraid that you must have done from me. It's a miracle if you haven't anyway.

I had a copy of the E.Y.R. magazine sent to me. There's a photo of Major Coles in it, so I'll send if to you as I think you'd like to see it. Has the blue dress survived the actions of the weekend? I'm sure it (the dress) was treated most gently, wasn't it?

Have been trying to find a way by which I can make £500 a year at once!! Nothing doing at the moment though, sad to relate.

Heaps and Heaps of Love. Yours, Jack.

28/6/18
My own darling Phyllis,

I was delighted to receive your letter of the 26th this morning — a *very* s'nice one too.

So you've decided not to buy those chairs, have you? No doubt you're quite right. Be able to go on the "bust" with the cheque I sent you, won't you? £8 for a chair is a trifle expensive, but it all depends upon the chair.

'A' Group here has gone away today — broken up. Capt. Case goes back to France a week on Sunday. Had the School photo taken yesterday — like your Hospital one, circular effort. I couldn't keep a straight face.

Hope you're keeping fit, sweetheart. Will write of course tomorrow.

Heaps and Heaps of Love. Yours, Jack.

June 30th 1918
My own darling Phyllis,

I was very pleased indeed to receive your letter of the 28th this morning.

I am sorry that Vic [*Mason*] has been taken worse. Muriel seemed so optimistic last Sunday, didn't she? Hope he managed to pull through.

Only six days now, dearest, before we see each other again. I'm simply aching to see you again — shall fade away if I don't soon. It seems to get worse and worse dear, every time I have to leave you. Thank Heaven it isn't for long — if it were I don't know what I should do. You are such a darling. I never want to leave you a bit!!

Heaps and Heaps of Love. Yours, Jack.

July 4th 1918
My own darling Phyllis,

I was very pleased to receive your letter of the 2nd this morning.

I am really quite well now, honestly. Quite equal to playing *Bears* or anything of that kind. I hope shortly to prove this to you.

It seems simply ages since I've seen you. I want to s'love you very very badly. Quite a hopeless case, you see. I won't write tomorrow, dearest, as I shall be with you before it arrives — so goodbye until Saturday, dear. Cheerio.

Heaps and Heaps of Love. Yours, Jack.

July 8th 1918
My own darling Phyllis,

I landed up here safe and sound this morning and honsetly I don't feel so very tired at all. Had a good 3 hours' sleep at Crewe — no soldiers on draft filling all the carriages up this week — but it was fearfully close. I was simply boiled in my British warm.

Don't the weekends simply fly by, dear? But they are always very s'nice. I think that on the whole you came through the last quite well, don't you? The dress is still more or less intact. I am a villain — I do lead you a life!!!

I didn't do so badly in the Musketry and Lewis Gun exams as I got 70% and 78% respectively. I was rather surprised as to the result of the Musketry.

Heaps and Heaps of Love. Yours, Jack.

July 9th 1918
My own darling Phyllis,

I've just finished a most strenuous morning. We went over the retreat of the 5th Army — on a small scale, of course. Lewis Guns, rifles, etc. We were the British. The Germans were represented by other Officers carrying red flags. It's very amusing to play at it like that.

I do hope that you've not been run off your legs so much this week. Do they still ache? I feel rather disgusted with myself, because you didn't get much chance of rest on Sunday, did you — anything but!! But I certainly succeeded in bringing a little colour back into your cheeks again, didn't I, villain that I am?

Heaps and Heaps of Love. Yours, Jack.

July 10th 1918
My own darling Phyllis,

I hope that you're feeling better now, though I don't see how you can be as I expect you are still having a hard time at the Hospital. You do stick to your job, don't you? Very few who have kept on with it as long as you.

It's quite true, dear, what you say. There's always France in the background, like a cloud. Don't I just wish that I could stop in this country. I've no desire to start my travels over again.

I noticed in the paper that Capt. W. F. Heath [*Sleath, according to* **The Snapper**: *so Sleath is probably his correct name after all!*] is reported a prisoner of war. He was in the 1st — captured at Kemmel. He was the one who got introduced, engaged and married in 14 days. [*see letter dated 19.1.18*].

I must close now, dear. Please remember me to the family.

Cheerio. Heaps and Heaps of Love. Yours, Jack.

July 11th 1918
My own darling Phyllis,

I was delighted to receive your s'nice long letter of the 9th this morning.

I had a letter from Mrs. Foster today enclosing one which she wrote to me in France and was returned to her, asking me about her son. She seems very cheerful about it, thinks there is a chance of him being a prisoner. I'm sure he's not, worse luck. But I can't tell her so. It's going to be rather a hard letter to write, I can see. However, it must be done.

I haven't much news today, dearest. Heaps and Heaps of Love. Yours, Jack.

July 12th 1919
My own darling Phyllis,

I was very pleased to receive your letter of the 10th and was fearfully bucked after I'd read it. It's simply tophole of you being able to get that time off. We'll have a great time at Scarborough.

You must have got a shock when Sister asked if you were going to get married!!

You villain, saying "it's not as bad as all that".

We had an exam in Administration the other day. Much to my surprise I got 87%. My luck's in, evidently.

Cheerio. Heaps and Heaps of Love. Yours, Jack.

61 Mellor Rd., Western Park, Leicester, 14:7:18   [*His brother Edgar's house*]
My own darling Phyllis,

Many thanks for your letter of the 11th received yesterday and the one of the 12th this morning.

They have fixed up for us all at Scarborough — got rooms in Langdale Road. I don't know where that is — do you? Father refuses to go to an Hotel as the idea of being strictly rationed appals him.

We shall be able to get lots of s'love in too, shan't we? I'm sure that there will be heaps of opportunities. I will really try to be fairly *good*. You know I was sorry that I didn't give you any chance for a rest last Sunday, but I'm afraid that you are quite right — I should probably do just the same again if I got the chance. I really can't help it when I'm with you. I feel as if I must s'love you or I shall explode.

I've a lot more examinations coming off next week. One on LAW on Monday morning — never was a strong subject with me.

I've written that note to Mrs. Foster — told her all I know and explained fully how it was, that 2 Lt Foster's Platoon was captured. She seems to think that he may be a prisoner so of course I've had to say so too. What else could I do?

Well, I must close now, dearest. All here send their love.

Heaps and Heaps of Love. Yours, Jack.

16:7:18
My own darling Phyllis,

I was very pleased indeed to receive your letter of the 14th this morning — and am delighted to hear that you have an extra Nurse coming so that everything will now be right for your holiday.

We've had an awful day today — I nearly passed away cycling home — and I'm practically reduced to a grease spot. Another of these tactical schemes, you know. The C.O. was with us too, so we had to go in for a lot of "eye wash" which was really rather trying.

I've no more news now, dearest. Hope you're keeping fit. Will write again tomorrow.

Heaps and Heaps of Love. Yours, Jack.

17:7:18
My own darling Phyllis,

I've finished the last examination today — "Tactics". I feel quite relieved to have got them all over at last. I've written to the 4th E.Y.R. for my meat and sugar coupons for my leave. Never do to forget those, would it?

I'm looking forward to the weekend very much indeed. I do hope that nothing happens to interfere with the Scarborough touch. I feel fearfully bucked about it all. We'll have a lovely time. You won't be too strict, will you?

Well, I don't think that I've any more news today, dearest. Hope to hear from you tomorrow.

Heaps and Heaps of Love. Yours, Jack.

22:7:18

My own darling Phyllis,

I landed back here after quite an uneventful journey.

I enjoyed the weekend ever so much, dear, though the time seemed to pass so quickly. However, we haven't many days to get over before we see each other again, Thank Heavens.

I only wish, darling, that we could get married before I went back to the front —but of course it's impossble, though Heaven knows I'm only *too willing*. The unfortunate part is that as soon as the war is over I'm without a job. No screw or anything very much. It's rather sad when you come to think of it, and one must look ahead to the future.

However, we can talk it over at Scarboro' a lot better than in a letter, can't we?

Heaps and Heaps of Love. Yours, Jack.

July 24th 1918

My own darling Phyllis,

I was very pleased to receive your letter of the 22nd this morning.

I don't honestly see a way how I can be stopped going back to France. If I did you may be sure that I would take it. However, we'll discuss it together in a day now.

I heard from Mearns this morning. He sent me my warrant and several other things. The date I have to embark is the 5th August.

We are having a final dinner tonight. The C.O. and all instructors are invited, after which there is a concert. I can see that the evening will be rather a lively one — too much so. I wonder how many of them will want putting to bed.

Well, goodbye for the present, dearest. See you on Friday at Scarboro'.

Heaps and Heaps of Love. Yours, Jack.

Post Office Telegram dated 6 Aug 1918 1120 am Folkestone

Sail at 2.15 sea rather rough Love Jack.

E.F.C., OFFICERS REST HOUSE AND MESS 6:8:18

My own darling Phyllis,

I landed here quite safely this afternoon and in spite of the rough sea I'm none the worse. I was careful to remain on deck all the time.

I am in a Camp at Boulogne now and shall be here for the night anyway, though I shall probably move on to my Base at Etaples tomorrow. I shall be quite comfy here — a little room all to myself, a canvas bed, 4 blankets. My kit has been sent on. I do hope that the blankets aren't full of creatures. The only sad thing is I haven't got a towel in my pack, so how I am going to get washed rather beats me. I must make friends with someone or other and borrow one.

As the boat came in to the harbour it passed the Hospital No. 8 that I was in last April and strange to say the Hospital ship I went over on was in Harbour too.

Oh my darling, I feel so lonely without you, and miss you awfully. It's rather a hard life when I've got to leave you like that — please, dear, don't think that I am very depressed, but leaving you this time was far worse than ever before, though Heaven knows that was bad enough.

I only wish I could give you a slight idea of what a darling girl you are. But words fail me altogether. I love you now as I never did before and that's saying something.

It really gives me quite a pain to be away from you. However, we must cheer up as there are lots and lots of lovely times in front of us, I'm sure. I'll do my best to take care of myself because I want to see you again very badly in the future — I hope not far distant — to be with you always.

Heaps and Heaps of Love. Yours, Jack.

F. Depot, A.P.O., S17, B.E.F., 7:8:18

My own darling Phyllis,

I reached here this afternoon and to my great surprise found a lot of Officers I know very well — Capt. Green of the Yorks, Sutton and Brown E. Yorks. and would you believe it Jack Ferens also. I was surprised to see him. Capt. Green was at Brocton with me. That chap Helmsing has gone sick with Scabies. Gough of Gough and Davy is also resting here for the time. What Officers and men there are left of the 4th are here too. The regiment has been broken up, I hear. I hope that they re-form it.*

It's awful, darling, not hearing from you. I can't do without s'love nowadays. I wish I could see you now if only for a few minutes. But it's no good wishing that, is it, because it's impossible.

Well, I must close now, dearest. Will write again tomorrow.

Heaps and Heaps of Love. Yours, Jack.

*[*The 1st Battalion had left the action at Wytschaete and Kemmel, late in April, with its fighting strength reduced to 3 officers and 29 other ranks. Some reinforcements joined, but when the fragmented 64th Infantry Brigade formed a 64th Composite Battalion the 1st East Yorks contributed one officer and 100 other ranks to form a Company, leaving themselves barely a hundred men altogether. Resting on the Marne in June, the Battalion was then rebuilt and re-organised. By late July it was at Beaumont-Hamel, contributing to the counter-offensive which was to see the war to its conclusion three months later. Much of the action to which Jack refers over the next three months, is related in a little more detail in Appendices 3 & 4. These contain accounts he wrote up some years after the war for the* **Snapper**.]

E.F.C. OFFICERS REST HOUSE AND MESS, 9:8:18

My own darling Phyllis,

I move on again at 1230 noon today entraining at Le Gare Centrale. But it will be quite a short run and then I shall be at my own Base. I hope to meet someone I know there. I've just had an excellent breakfast — and white bread once more.

I believe we were subjected to an air Raid last night. I just heard one explosion and then I went to sleep again.

I managed to borrow a towel, so I did get a wash and am quite a clean boy again now.

I have been in this Camp before. I had to march a draft up here when I returned from leave in October 1917 and then Major Coles and I motored away next morning.

Heaps and Heaps of Love. Yours, Jack.

F.I.B. Depot, A.P.O. S17, B.E.F., 9:8:18

My own darling Phyllis,

I am very glad to say that I haven't been moved on since I last wrote you and am having quite a pleasant time with nothing much to do.

Isn't the war news good today — 7,000 prisoners and 100 guns. I expect that they have improved on that too. It's a strange thing, but in England you always get the latest war news before we do out here.

I hear that the Zepps the other night passed right over Hull. Thank Heaven they didn't drop any bombs near you. Some of the Officers coming back off leave on that 8.5 train from Hull were held up so long on the line by the Raid that they missed the 7.50 from Victoria — not that they would be at all sorry.

This afternoon at 3 pm I'm going to have a look round Paris Plage with Lt. Sutton (Rollitt married his sister, you know).

It's rather surprising how many people here seem to think that the war — the fighting anyway — will be over by about October. I hope that they are right, but I can't see it myself.

I met one of the Company Sergeant Majors of the 1st last night. He says that there isn't an E.Y. Officer in them now at all — all Officers from other regiments. He was wounded on the 25th April. It appears that the Hun came round the right and captured the Battalion Head Qtrs first and completely cut off the Battalion, which accounts for so many of them being taken prisoner, doesn't it? I have often wondered how it was.

Goodbye for the present, dearest. Heaps and Heaps of Love. Yours, Jack.

F.I.B.D., A.P.O. S17, B.E.F., 10:8:18
My own darling Phyllis,

I am still resting here quite peacefully. I went down to Paris Plage yesterday afternoon — a lot of the shops have been shot up since I was there. I suppose this night bombing by the Hun is responsible.

The village here has had a very rough time. Some complete streets have been razed to the ground. None of the civilian inhabitants remain in the village during the night but go out in boats on the river, into the fields and so on.

I often think, dear of all the tophole times we've had in the last 3 months. I'll never forget that week at Scarborough. I think that you quite lost the "lonely feeling" before the end, didn't you?

I was rather a wretch making you row me about that lake. Hard life, wasn't it? Do you remember the reeds? Nice friendly things, reeds, I think. Don't you? And so useful!!! I think that I could convince you of it now if you were here. Not by words alone either!!

Cheerio. Heaps and Heaps of Love. Yours, Jack.

E.F.C. 10:8:18
My own darling Phyllis,

I have just received my orders to proceed to join my unit tomorrow at 9 am. It's the 1st East Yorks again. I'm very pleased about it — much nicer going back to people one knows.

Will write tomorrow if I can. Heaps and Heaps of Love. Yours, Jack.

1st East Yorks, B.E.F., Sunday 11/8/18
My own darling Phyllis,

I have not yet reached the Battalion as they are in the line [*Mailly-Maillet sector, opposite Beaumont-Hamel, where they have been since late July*], but am at the moment with the divisional wing in quite a peaceful village.

I had as usual rather a wearisome journey, which would have been a very much longer one had I not left the train and come on here by a friendly motor lorry. There are several officers I know, so I don't feel like a stranger in a strange land at all.

Last night at the Base from 10.30 pm to Midnight we had an air Raid. About 50 bombs were dropped in all, but none very near to me Thank Heaven. A lot of shrapnel from the anti-aircraft guns.

Capt. Stephenson, I hear, has gone home on six months — but was awarded the D.S.O., and M.C. Jolly good, isn't it? If anyone deserved it he did.

We keep hearing almost astonishing rumours about the great success of the push. It will affect the war a lot, quite the most successful thing that we have ever done — and, thank goodness, it shows up to the present no signs of slowing down.*

I've got quite a nice tent pitched in an orchard — though there isn't a bed in it or anything of that sort. Nevertheless, I shall be quite comfortable. It's well I brought that cork mattress along with me — that's better than lying on the ground. One's hip bone gets in the way so, I find.

I don't think I've any more news. Heaps and Heaps of Love. Yours, Jack.

*[*The great success Jack refers to is the Battle of Amiens, begun on 8 August, a turning-point in the war and the beginning of sustained Allied advances.*]

1st East Yorks, B.E.F. 12:8:18
My own darling Phyllis,

I am going to the Battalion nucleus party this afternoon — they are in the same village only a few hundred yards away. I think on the whole it will be better than this.

I walked round to see them but among the officers there are none that I know. A Major Browne, E.Y.R., is in charge.*

There are only about 4 Officers of the old lot left now. It only shows what a rotten time they have been having. They are at the moment in the line [*and constantly on the move, mostly forward*]. Of course at present I am miles away from them. I can only just hear the guns at night.

I was quite correct in saying that Gordon Allen [*Lt T. G. Allen, O.C. 'D' Coy*] is with them. At present they only have three Captains with the Battalion, so that looks quite hopeful in regard to me getting a Company again.

A big German plane was brought down here the night before last. It must have been a huge thing as it had 9 men on board, 4 of whom were officers. It was brought down by one of our single-seaters and caught fire. Several of the German crew jumped out to avoid the flames, but their parachutes caught fire too. I won't go into details but they were rather a rotten sight. One of them had the Iron Cross 1st Class. I saw several photos etc taken from him. He has been quite a good looking chap.

It's a such a quiet village this, you'd never think that there was a war on at all. Any amount of French inhabitants. It's never been actually in the war Zone. I was through here in August 1916.

Heaps and Heaps of Love. Yours, Jack.

*[*Major W.S. Browne was deputising for Lt-Col F. L. Du Moulin of the Royal Sussex Regiment, who took over the Battalion when the previous C.O., Lt-Col. W. H. Alexander, returned to England on the verge of a breakdown.*]

13:8:18

My own darling Phyllis,

I have now joined the nucleus party and have not up to the present received any orders about going any nearer the line. And I assure you I'm in no hurry. I have a tent in an orchard to sleep in and our Mess is in an old Barn.

Major Browne seems to be quite a decent sort, a regular officer I believe, but the Battalion has altered — fresh men as well as officers. We have no parades to do here at all as there aren't any men. So I'm having a very lazy life.

Talking about that German plane that I told you of. It is said that one of the crew was a woman. Seems very extraordinary, I think, don't you?

Heaps and Heaps of Love. Yours, Jack.

14:8:18

My own darling Phyllis,

I have just received my orders to rejoin the Battalion in the line and have to go in a few minutes. I'll write you a longer letter when I get there. Please don't worry about me dearest. I'm sure that I shall be alright. Your charm is still with me so all is well.

Heaps and Heaps of Love. Yours, Jack.

14:8:18   8 pm

My own darling Phyllis,

I have now reached the transport lines after a long trip, 17 kilometres in the Mess Cart. At 8 o'clock tonight I am going up to join the Battalion in the line.

It's very strange, but there is a Captain here of the Somerset Light Infantry who it turns out went to Newton College. I was there myself, you know. I very seldom meet anyone who was there, as they mostly came from the South.

I hear that Watt of Hessle is with this Battalion [*In 'C' Coy*]. Do you know him —he's rather small.* I think with luck I may get a Company here. I shall be very fed up if I don't.

I'll do my best, I promise you, to take care of myself — as I simply must get back to you sometime. I think that my special treatment was very successful. Have you lost all the "roses" yet?

Well, I must close now *dearest*. Heaps and Heaps of Love. Yours, Jack.

*[*Meeting up with Watt of Hessle was an interesting coincidence: Watt's grand-daughter would one day marry Jack and Phyllis' grandson.*]

20:8:18

My own darling Phyllis,

I was delighted to receive your letter of the 16th today. By Jove, but it does brighten things up hearing from you.*

I fear that we may be leaving here [*the villages of Acheux and Arqueves*] sometime today and going back to the war again.

You know, dear, I do so wish we could get married next time I'm home. I want you so badly. I quite admit though if you look ahead beyond the war the prospects aren't very bright as to how to get the necessary cash to live on. But how long is this war going on for? If it's for some years yet I think that we ought to snatch what happiness we can out of it, don't you?

No sign of my wandering "pip" returning. I hate being messed about like this. Honestly, I'm sorry I ever came back to this battalion. I can't stick the C.O. at any price. Du Moulin is his name. Treats all the officers as if they were infants in arms —only been out 5 Months I believe too. However, I am safe and sound — that's the great thing. Because I'm coming back to continue the treatment, you may be sure.

I hear that Mr. Manley's son of Hessle has been killed in an aeroplane.

Well, I must close now, dearest. Heaps and Heaps of Love. Yours, Jack.

[Jack would indeed soon be returning to the line. At this time each battalion rotated its four companies thus: one in the front line, one in close support, one in the battle line, and one with Battalion H.Q. in reserve. 'A' Coy had been in action as recently as August 15, towards Beaucourt and Miraumont. The Battalion had suffered casualties amounting to a dozen killed and some 75 wounded or missing, and had moved back a few miles to rest. Now it prepared to take part in an attack on Beaucourt and clear a section of the north bank of the river Ancre. See Appendix 2.]

23/8/18

My own darling Phyllis,

I have just been through another stunt — am quite alright —though we've had a rotten time [*the attack on Miraumont*].

Captain Watson was wounded and afterwards died.*

I am still in the trenches but some way back from the front [*just north of Beaumont Hamel*]. Hope to move out before long. Awfully sorry that I couldn't write you the last two days. I am once again in Command of 'A' Coy.

I am giving this letter to the padre to post so it will have to be a very brief one.

During the last two days I have had some narrow escapes. But I'm feeling quite well now.

Heaps and Heaps of Love. Yours, Jack.

[Watson was killed at the crossing of the Ancre, a lengthy and difficult business undertaken in great heat with the Germans having managed to flood the valley, creating terribly boggy conditions.]

24:8:18

My own darling Phyllis,

I have been over the top again since I last wrote you. It wasn't so bad. My Company came off best in regard to casualties. That makes the sixth time over the top since I rejoined the Battalion. Very few officers left now.*

I'm feeling rather done in myself — just feel as if I couldn't go another yard but after some sleep I shall feel better.

I'm in the front line now and I've actually got a shelter to sleep in. The last few nights I've slept in shell holes — very well too — only it was nearly always interrupted by someone — the Hun generally.**

This is an awfully scrappy letter Sweetheart but as soon as I get out of this I'll make amends.

I've done such a lot the last few days. Your charm still keeps me safe and sound. It's marvellous. I thought of you a lot last night during the attack. I wonder if you knew. It seems like 6 Months since I left you dearest. Oh, but I do so want to see you again. I've got such a lot of things to tell you.

War is horrible, isn't it?

No, try as I will I can't write to you in a natural way tonight. Everything I say seems so hard and disconnected. It's the effect of all this fighting, I think.

We haven't had any mail for days. I do so miss your letters, dear.

Well, I must close now darling — I will write tomorrow if possible. You are a dear.

Heaps and Heaps of Love. Yours, Jack.

*[On the night of 23/24 August the Bn had crossed the Ancre and took the village of Grandcourt. During this action, the Bn Diary reports, Brigadier-General McCullough was wounded, and Du Moulin took command. Jack, writing after the war, remembers that McCullough was reconnoitring a forward position on the far bank of the river, neglected to report his intentions, and was bayoneted by a private of the D.L.I. who mistook him for a German.
**Jack speaks of sleeping in shell-holes; he later wrote of having drunk large quantities of water from them – "with no ill effects".]

Field Service Post Card dated 25/8/18, post marked 27/8/18

I am quite well.

Letter follows at first opportunity.

27:8:18

My own darling Phyllis,

I've just been through the worst 24 hours that I've ever had [attacking through the recently taken village of Le Sars].

We attacked again at 7 am on the 26th — without any artillery support. The German Machine guns and snipers were awful, just mowed the grass down. We had to dash from shell hole to shell hole. It took us about 1 hour to reach our own front line. Some continued the advance straight on, but I got a party and worked down the trench which the Hun were in as well as we.

After going a long way we ran into them, capturing 2 Machine Guns and 35 men — Allen was with me. We tried to hold the trench — shooting a lot of the retreating Huns — But we got simply blown out of it by artillery and had to retire.* Shortly after we got a few more men together and counter-attacked —Allen, Ewing, the Adjutant and I. The first to drop was Ewing — shot through the head — Allen went down too — killed and I was hit on the buckle of the belt of my trench coat. Thank God it didn't go in — as it would have hit me right in the "Tummy" — Just left a little mark that's all.

My word but I was lucky. Everyone thought I'd got a fatal one. It's simply marvellous how I escaped — I'll send you the belt — After that I wasn't much use at all and lay in a shell hole — The Hun then attacked and we had to retire — I ran like the devil — I admit it — so did everyone — and we held a line farther back.

Later that night we were relieved and have moved a little farther back in dugouts — out of the 20 officers who went in only 6 came out — the C.O. myself and 4 more. One Company is only 25 strong.

Both my officers were wounded. I do feel thankful to have got out of it alright so far.

We've had a very rough time indeed the last few days. We've done so many attacks that I've only a very confused idea about them now. I do hope that I haven't

202

to do anymore stunts! I don't think I could.

I haven't had a wash or shave for a week — look a terrible sight — clothes all torn to ribbons.

We receive no letters up here at all — so expect that there will be quite a lot waiting for me when I do get out — oh I wish I could see you — I've got lots of things to tell you. This letter seems to be more like a diary — than anything else doesn't it — dear — But I thought that you would like to know all about it — I must confess yesterday I never thought I should see you again — that charm of yours has worked again hasn't it.

This show was worse than the Ypres October one — sheer murder I call it — The men are simply "done to the world" — physically and morally.

I don't think I've any more news today dearest so will close — Write again tomorrow.

Heaps and Heaps of Love. Yours, Jack.

*[*After being forced to retire from the captured trench the party had to leave behind not only the captured machine guns but also their own Stokes Gun, which the Germans now used against them as they withdrew along the trench.*

The day was not a success. **The Snapper** *reported that "the only tangible result of our day's operations was to prove that the German resistance was thickening, and that it was necessary to have artillery preparation and assistance for further advances." Jack's own comment, writing later, was that "it was a most disastrous day without much point. I think that this was the most senseless waste of life and energy I have ever seen." See Appendix 3.*]

28:8:18
My own darling Phyllis,

I was delighted to receive three letters from you — 20th, 21st and 22nd last night. The first post I've had for a long time.

Last night we were relieved and have come some little way back [*although still under shell-fire*]. Everything is very rough but we got some decent food at last — I got so tired of bread and jam and bully beef and water. I am so thankful that I'm out of it safe and sound — I can't say though whether we shall have to go back or not. The Battalion is practically wiped out. Just fancy — only 5 Officers left. I have 38 men left out of about 115. You see we've attacked 5 times in 7 days. On the night of the 24-25th we attacked all night, advancing about 4 kilometres and capturing several guns — prisoners and all kinds of things — But I can't tell you all about it dear. I've only got a confused idea of it all myself.

It's quite true Gordon Allen is killed — on the 26th — also Capt. Case — my word dearest but I had a narrow escape. It's rather shaken me up. That show on the 26th was Hell. Absolute murder I call it.

I'm awfully sorry, dear, but I couldn't write you often no chance of getting any letters away. You see for two days we got no food at all. it was during that fearfully hot weather too — we had hardly strength enough to do anything — However all that is over now — anyway for the time — But that last week has been like 10 years to me —

I am still O.C. 'A' Coy — a Lieutenant — but I rather think the wandering pip will shortly return.

One thing that's very cheering: the war news is splendid. What little I have heard of it. I haven't seen any papers for a long time.

That tophole week we had at Scarboro seems like a dream now — But never fear dearest we'll have many more good times together.

By the way Watt of Hessle was wounded on the 26th too.*

Capt. Ewing — the Adjutant — hit through the head — after being dressed by the M.O. walked out of the line — no stretcher being available. So far he's alright I believe, though he was hit clean through the forehead.

What a brute I am dear to tell you these gruesome details ain't I.

Well I must close now dearest. Will write again tomorrow.

Heaps and Heaps of Love. Yours Jack.

*[*With the exception of Jack and Lt Constant there was no officer remaining who had been with the Battalion longer than six weeks. Watt was shot through the arm and returned to England. Some time later when he took his uniform from the wardrobe to show the bullet-hole and bloodstain to a relative he was mortified to find that his mother had had it cleaned and invisibly mended. Ewing had been brought in by Raine, the Medical Officer. He died in hospital two weeks later.*]

29:8:18

My own darling Phyllis,

I am glad to say that we haven't moved forward again since I wrote to you yesterday. I only hope that we haven't got to. I think that we have done our share in this battle.

We haven't got our valises here — but I've got my trench coat lining sent up so I manage to keep fairly warm at night. But I am looking forward to getting back to civilisation again and having a bath etc.

W. Sutton of the 4th E.Y.R. joined us yesterday as signalling officer — I left him at the Base you know.

It appears that Jack Ferens has got the job of Educational Officer 31st Division. Some people seem to have all the luck don't they.

This rest here is doing me a lot of good — though I still feel a bit done. My nerves ain't anything like so good as they were. After all, I suppose the strain is bound to tell in the end.

The war news generally is splendid, isn't it. But I fear that we haven't finished yet — not by a long way.

I don't see how this Division can be kept here much longer without a relief. And I believe that when we go out it will be for a long time. This of course is only a rumour, but a very pleasant one.

Oh my dear but I do want to see you again so badly. Is it only a month since we were at Scarborough. I think that under the circumstances it's just as well that I didn't pack you up in my valise — though at the time I was sorely tempted to do so.

You must beware or I shall be running off with you one of these days.

Has the chest put in an appearance yet. I read an article in the paper on the furniture question to the effect that people were buying it to hoard it and sell after the war. Rather a bad look-out for us dear, isn't it? Looks like orange boxes, rather.

Looks as if I want to rush you into being Mrs. Jack as soon as possble, doesn't it? I'm afraid that you'll think me rather a wretch.

By the way there is a Lt Constant here who knows Vic Mason very well — was with him in the 12th E.Y.R.

Will write again tomorrow if possible.

Heaps and Heaps of Love. Yours, Jack.

30:8:18

My own darling Phyllis,

Since I wrote yesterday we have moved forward a little — as a matter of fact to the scene of our last scrap with the Hun [*Le Sars*]. But the line is far away — several miles I believe.

Last night we found Capt. Case — and Gordon Allen — and have buried them this morning. They were both shot through the stomach.

It seems so strangely quiet here now — you can walk about as you please whereas before, if you showed yourself for a second you were fired at.

I have been on this ground in former days — 1916. For miles it is nothing but a mass of crosses. However, we've taken it with less loss of life this time than before.

The padre came round this morning and cheered us up a bit with rumours of relief — but I'm beginning to be rather sceptical: have heard tales like that so often.

I'm sure that you must think that several of my letters of late have been very cold. I don't feel that way at all — very much the reverse (I'll prove it to you when I see you!!!) But somehow I think that all the fighting makes it rather difficult to express what you really feel inside.

Well, I don't think I've any more news. Will write again tomorrow if possible.

Heaps and Heaps of Love. Yours, Jack.

31:8:18

My own darling Phyllis,

I was very bucked indeed last night to receive your letter of the 23rd. It brightened things up a good bit. My Quarter Master Sergeant tells me that there is a lot of old mail waiting for me at our starting point. I must admit, dear, I didn't quite see why they should take my Captaincy away from me. In fact, to be candid, dear, I felt damn fed up about it — the army is a strange place.

However I'm glad to be able to tell you that in 7 days from now the wandering pip will have returned. The Adjutant told me so yesterday. You see, you've got to be in command of a Company for 15 days before you put can put it up. I took over this Coy on the 22nd — the day Capt. Watson was wounded, you know. But it was rotten coming down to a Lieut. again — in England it really doesn't make much difference but on active service it does.

Yesterday afternoon I saw G. Allen and Case buried — we had a little service. Their graves are practically the actual places where they fell. [*Much of this day was spent collecting the dead and burying them.*]

I was very glad indeed when it was done — I do hate that kind of thing, don't you? War is a rotten business.

Four of our wounded men who were captured by the Hun the other day were found ysterday. The Hun had dressed [*their wounds*] and left them behind. So we sent them straight on to the C.C.S. I think that they stand quite a good chance of recovery.

You know dearest, I'm very glad now that I took those 35 Huns prisoner the other day. The men asked me what they should do with them — spare them or do them in. But they had thrown down their arms — it would have been a dirty trick if I hadn't, wouldn't it? Not that I have any love for the devils, far from it.

205

By the way dear, I simply can't get cigarettes at all — reduced to smoking a few odd woodbines I can pick up. So if you could send me a few they would be *most acceptable*.

I'm sure dear that I don't think you're a horrid little cat or that you've changed either — in fact I think that you're more a dear than ever and I want to love you *so badly*. I suppose I might try and be patient but it's a hard life without you.

I feel very eager indeed to continue the treatment!!! Rather a s'nice one isn't it!!!

Remember me to the family, won't you.

Heaps and Heaps of Love. Yours, Jack.

3/9/18

My own darling Phyllis,

Just out of the line after being over the top again;* glad to say I'm quite safe. Feel rather done though.

Must buck up or I shall miss post.

Will write again later today and give full details.

Lots of s'nice letters from you — lovely.

Goodbye for the present dearest. Heaps and Heaps of Love. Yours Jack.

*[*The attack, on Lubda Copse, went fairly smoothly, with weak German resistance, and 70 prisoners taken*].

4:9:18

My own darling Phyllis,

I was simply delighted dear to receive your letters of the 26th and 27th last night — also the parcel. I just wanted something to read and was pining for some cigarettes — they are fearfully hard to get just at present.

I'm afraid dear that I've been causing you a lot of worry — and I must admit I've had a risky time. Pretty stiff going — six times over the top in 10 days, isn't it, though it's in open not Trench warfare.

I got 3 new officers attached to me last night — so makes things easier. [*Lt G. A. Lee, 2Lts G. A. Cotton, R. B. Bingham*].

I had a glorious sleep in my valise and pyjamas. It was simply great.

The C.O. was very affable (for him) this morning. I believe that the Staff are very bucked with us too.

I've put in quite a lot of recommendations — hope that they go through because some of the officers and men did so well.

As a matter of fact I still feel rather dazed and confused about all the recent fighting — done so much that I can hardly remember what.

I am sending a German dagger and automatic revolver home today by an Officer going on leave. They are the only souvenirs I've got — I never seem to have time to bother about them during the attack.

I feel awfully bucked with life now that I have come through it all safely. Of course, in the near future I expect we shall be going into it again. But I think that I shall be left out as nucleus.

By Jove but I would like to see you again *at once*!!! I'm simply aching to s'love you again — and I'm sure the treatment ought to be renewed. Don't you? However, we must wait unfortunately — too much waiting these days for me. Still, the war news is excellent just now — isn't it. A German officer I spoke to said it would end by Xmas and that we should win. Some of the Hun officers were very haughty, but the ordinary men weren't. One man said to me, I didn't make the war. I must say I rather felt with him. We took quite a lot of prisoners and as long as they were quiet and behaved themselves they weren't harmed at all. I won't have unarmed men shot — dirty trick, I think.

I rather think that I may very shortly have an attack of trench fever, but it may pass off. A week or so in Hospital would be very s'nice.

Well, I don't think I've any more news today dearest, so will close now.

Heaps and Heaps of Love. Yours, Jack.

6:9:18
My own darling Phyllis,

I was very pleased to receive your two s'nice letters of the 29th and 30th last night. They bucked me up a lot.

Yesterday was rather an unfortunate one for us. When we moved off our day's rations were left behind, and although I sent a man back for them he didn't get back here until 7 this morning. We had some of the men's stew for lunch but had to wait until 10 pm before any more food was forthcoming.

We got one of those waterproof sheets and formed a kind of tent in which we all slept. I had on the whole quite a good night — thanks to rum and the lining of my trench coat.

I'm doing my best dearest to get left out of this next action, whenever that may be. But although I have five officers besides myself none of them know the Coy at all.

However, I pointed out to the Adjutant this morning that it was time I had a bit of a rest and he said he would see the C.O. and do his best.

As soon as we get out — at rest — I am going to put in for my third pip. Of course, now that we are right forward here nothing of that kind can be done. But it's rather annoying having to do Captain's work on Lieutenant's pay.

Well, no more news today. Heaps and Heaps of Love. Yours, Jack.

7:9:18
My own darling Phyllis,

After I wrote to you yesterday we got the order to move forward again.

At our destination I was given a chalk quarry as the billets for my Coy. But I found some trenches to put them in so they were fairly comfortable. Myself and the other officers found a little shack made of railway sleepers into which we all got.*

We are now occupying some artillery dug-outs — they were vacated by the Hun early this morning — so we are very comfy now. They know how to do things, don't they?

Really, dearest, but isn't the war news topping — Lens fallen. I hear a rumour about Cambrai, though I don't know if it's true. You see, apart from what happens on our own particular bit of front we hear very little indeed and it's generally several days after it has actually happened.** We generally are given an open field for our quarters for the night. It's surprising how quickly little bivouacs of corrugated iron etc. are rigged up. Except for two nights I've slept out in the open with nothing else but my trench coat since August 19th.

By the way, dearest, I enclose a P.C. from a prisoner of ours in Germany asking for clothes. Could you ask your Mother what is the best way I can do something for him. Peel House deals with them I think, doesn't it?

Really I'm afraid that this letter dear is developing into a kind of diary. But I thought that you would like to know all that I'm doing.

I want you so badly this morning. Got one of those fits on you know. Still, we'll have to make up for lost time when we next see each other, won't we?

Heaps and Heaps of Love. Yours, Jack.

*[*The move was to Sorel le Grand, across the Canal du Nord. Jack, the Medical Officer Raine, and Lt Howard, who later wrote up much of this campaign for the* **Snapper***, were familiar with this country, having retreated through it in March. See Appendix 2.*
** The "news" of Lens and Cambrai was incorrect: Lens did not fall until 1 October; Cambrai was entered by the Canadians eight days later.]

8:9:18
My own darling Phyllis,

I was very bucked indeed to receive your two letters of 31st and 1st. I'm simply bursting to s'love you this morning — and I'm sure that I could do it very thoroughly!!!

Well, to continue my narrative of yesterday (sounds terrible that, doesn't it?) we moved again last night, forward a few kilometres.

All the O.C. Coys went on with the C.O. to reconnoitre the positions in advance of the Battalion — we had rather a job as the roads were in a rotten state: lots of wire about in which the horses got entangled. Our quarters, though nearer the line, were quite comfy — old huts we left when we retired in March. Bed for all the Officers and some of the men.

We were awakened at midnight by the Bosche shelling all around us — gas shells. We hadn't any cover but the corrugated iron of the huts, which wouldn't stop anything except rain. They fell all round, but none within 50 yds, so all was well.

This morning early I was up — 6 am — and found a topping easy chair and feather bed. My luck was in, wasn't it?

Behind us is a battery of 4.5 howitzers. Unfortunately the first shot they fired this morning burst about 1 yard from the muzzle of the gun. All the gun crew were knocked out and sad to relate one of our officers got a hit just above the eye. We thought at first that he had got it direct in the eye. As it is he's jolly lucky — on the way to the Base now for a certainty.

I feel almost fit again this morning — just had a wash and a shave and haircut —needed them too. Looked like Mr. Dawson of Hessle — sort of another musician.

Heaps and Heaps of Love. Yours, Jack.

9:9:18
My own darling Phyllis,

We haven't moved since I wrote to you yesterday, and would be quite comfy but for the Hun: at various times during the night he put over some heavy shells which were too near to be pleasant.

We have a lot of our horses and transport just behind our hut and this morning at 9 am the Hun began to shell us. The first fell about 100 yds away. I took the warning and left the hut tout de suite and took shelter in a neighbouring dug-out.

The next just missed our hut and landed right amongst the horses and mules. Several had to be shot after — bad wounds and broken legs. C'est la guerre, I suppose.

I think that when the Battalion goes forward [*to attack Chapel Hill*] I shall remain here.

Really darling you seem to be fading away — only just 7 stones. This won't do at all dear, will it?

I honestly think I've had more — shall we say adventures, escapes and attacks in the last fortnight than in the whole of the rest of my other active service put together. We always said we wanted a war of movement, and by Jove we've got it.

You know, dear, I've missed you a fearful lot ever since I left you, and I'm simply aching to s'love you again. I think that it's getting worse and worse. I'm afraid that you're in for a very very strong dose of the treatment when we next meet — so beware!!!!

I do hope that you won't fade away. Heaps and Heaps of Love. Yours, Jack.

11:9:18

My own darling Phyllis,

Very many thanks indeed for your letter of the 4th which arrived last night.

Last night we — the nucleus — moved from our Hut to a little hill about 200 yds along the same road. I took all my furniture with me — tables, benches, stove and mattresses, beside lots of wood and corrugated iron sheeting so that in a very short time I soon had a very decent place rigged up and the table laid.

I am glad to say that my Coy had no casualties at all, but the other had a rotten cutting up — 1 officer killed, 2 wounded, 4 missing and 300 prisoners. So my Coy was lucky, wasn't it? The officer who was killed was an old friend of mine, Lt Spragg. We served together in the 4th at Bertin, afterwards in '16 in France. He was hit first, a nice one in the right arm. As he was walking down to the dressing station though he was hit in the "tummy" by a Machine Gun bullet and as usual — poor chap — died in a few minutes. His first time over the top too. The names of the other officers I won't tell you — as you wouldn't know them at all.*

Two of the NCOs I recommended for the first stunt August 19th have received the M.M. One I regret to say has been killed since and the other is in England wounded. I hope that I'm as fortunate with all my recommendations as I was with those.

I am hoping that we shall get out for a rest now, though candidly I haven't seen or heard anything which might point to a relief in the near future. Still, men can't go on fighting forever, — and the new draft of men, though comparatively fresh, have no fight in them to start with.

If I could only see you!! I've been wanting you very very badly for days now and nights too — and am always wondering what you're doing. I do wish this beastly war would buck up and finish.

Heaps and Heaps of Love. Yours, Jack.

*[*Jack refers to the other Company's losses. The Diary speaks of no more than 20 casualties in a failed attack on Chapel Hill, overlooking Epehy, an assault conducted, against the advice of Du Moulin, in appalling wet weather.*]

209

13:9:18

My own darling Phyllis,

I was delighted to receive your letter of the 6th yesterday and also the cigarettes. I hadn't had one for 3 days.

My Captaincy hasn't come through yet, but I have reason to believe that it will do so shortly.

We haven't moved since I last wrote you. I have hopes that when we do it will be to a place farther back. But of course, you can't really tell.

But I am sick and fed up with all this business. I want to get away from the sound of the guns.

I'm really quite comfortable here, dear. I've got my valise again, you see. I had a fire to go to bed by last night — tea in bed at 8 am and then another fire lit before I got up. Living in the lap of luxury. But we've had some rotten cold nights —sleeping in a shell-hole in the open with only a trench coat to keep you warm. The issue of Rum is a great help though — keeps you nice and warm inside.

Well, I must close now darling. Please give my love to Doris and remember me to the rest of the family.

Heaps and Heaps of Love. Yours, Jack.

14:9:18

My own darling Phyllis,

I was very pleased indeed to receive your two letters of the 7th and 8th today, also dear very many thanks for the parcel. It is sweet of you, dearest, to bother so much about getting cigarettes for me. Honestly, I like any kind of Virginia cigarettes except "Greys" and woodbines. I like de Reszke very much — only they are fearfully expensive.

Really, you know, you are a darling — but I do wish I could see you right now. I feel as if I could give you lots and lots of the "treatment" tonight. I need some too very badly.

I have been put in for my Acting Captaincy again. It will soon be coming through in orders. The sooner the better, say I.

Well, darling, I've no further news today so will close now.

Cheerio. Heaps and Heaps of Love. Yours, Jack.

Field Post Card dated 14/9/18, post marked 16/9/18

I am quite well.

Letter follows at first opportunity.

B.E.F. 16:9:18

My own darling Phyllis,

I was very bucked to receive your letter of the 9th today.

Well, sweetheart, I've always been frank with you so I'll keep it up. I shall in a few days' time find it impossible to write you [*a renewed assault on Chapel Hill is being planned*]. So if you don't hear from me for a day or two you'll know the reason and won't think I've forgotten you or anything of that sort, will you? However, I've always been very lucky and I've still got your charm so all is well. I have no qualms at all much.

I don't think I've any more news today, dearest, so will close. Will write again tomorrow without fail.

Heaps and Heaps of Love. Yours, Jack.

16:9:18

My own darling Phyllis,

I was very pleased and cheered to receive yours of the 10th today.

I've had my Nucleus — sad to relate — so I shall have to take my turn up the line again. It was such a short one — only one night. Still, I missed a very nasty business.

Sorry though to hear that you're having such long hours — 8.30 am - 7.30 pm . Haven't any of the Nurses come back yet? Seems to me, dearest, you're the only one that sticks it.

Heaps and Heaps of Love. Yours, Jack.

Field Post Card dated 20/9/18, post-marked 22/9/18

I am quite well.

Letter follows at first opportunity.

B.E.F. 20:9:18

My own darling Phyllis,

I was delighted to receive your three letters of the 11th, 12th and 13th.

Well, dear, I've been over the top again — it came off on the morning of the 18th and I feel very bucked indeed to be out of it safe. It looked rather a hopeless job on paper, but turned out to be a great success. After being rained on and getting throughly wet through we attacked and there was hardly a shell. We advanced some two miles without much difficulty, taking several hundred prisoners [*about 450*]. We had an artillery barrage to follow.*

Our objective was a trench [*the Munier Trench*] but just before we got to it we ran into a Sunken Road — and would you believe it — we captured 6 guns and a complete Battalion transport — horses and wagons. Most extraordinary, wasn't it? The Huns rushed out crying Kamerade, Transport Transport, waving white flags etc.

We got into our trench and surprised Huns having breakfast. When they saw we were there they ran for miles. Later on, about 3 pm though, they tried a bombing attack on my right flank and my men got into rather a panic. But we stopped them and managed to push the Hun back again, after which we hadn't much trouble. I lost a lot of men though from Hun Machine Guns. The best always seem to get hit. I had 38 Casualties in all. Everyone is very bucked with us. I only hope that we are going to have a decent rest now. I'm sure that we've earned it long ago. The Battalion lost 3 officers killed [*Lts Webster, Butt and Barrett*] and 4 wounded. I was lucky though; I didn't lose any. That makes the 7th time over the top since I came back. Rather too much for me.

As a matter of fact, dear, I haven't written Mr. Allen yet, but I will do so. You see, I didn't know Gordon Allen very well, and I've really been so busy.

Heaps and Heaps of Love. Yours, Jack.

*[*This latest action was a part of the battle of Epehy, Chapel Hill being captured at last*].

21:9:18

My own darling Phyllis,

I was delighted to receive your letter of the 14th today. I'm afraid, dear, that my letter of yesterday must have seemed rather confused and dreadfully cold, but honestly, dear, I felt fearfully tired.

You know, the day after you get out from an attack a sort of reaction sets in —you generally feel rather rotten. However, I'm quite fit today. We've had a long march today, and Thank Heaven in the right direction — out of the battle [*to Lesboeufs*]. I really believe that we are out at last for a rest.

That last attack we did was a great success — we all know the country round there very well too — memories of last winter. The Hun really put up no fight at all. We captured a Colonel amongst a lot of others. He looked as if he'd like to kill us all.

I picked up another automatic and a tophole pair of prismatic field glasses —one of the best makes there are. Cost anything from £15-£20 in England.

We're in quite comfortable quarters now, considering at one time it was a Bosche Ammunition Dump.

I'm sorry to hear that you've had to go to the Hosp. on Sunday again. Seems to me it's rather a pity though when you've got to come from so far.

I wrote to Mr. Allen yesterday — rather a hard letter to write. I only hope I didn't put things too plainly. To be quite candid, dear, I've got fearfully callous of late. Seen so many fall that I'm quite accustomed to it.

I always try and write to the next of kin of the men that fall in action but I've had so many lately that up to the present I haven't been able to cope with it. Those War Office telegrams are so cold-blooded, I think.

Heaps and Heaps of Love. Yours, Jack.

22:9:18
My own darling Phyllis,

I was very bucked to receive yours of the 15th today. It was a very s'nice one too.

Do you know, dear, I could do with one of those Sunday afternoons at Hessle very well. I was just thinking how s'nice it would be when your letter arrived. I haven't kissed or s'loved you for such a long time and I'm simply aching for it. As you say it's no use grousing, but Oh I do want you so much — though I always do for that matter.

So you had to go to the Hospital on Sunday. I think it's a good thing that you're stopping at Ferriby for the night. Must be getting dark early now too, isn't it? Have you stopped fading away yet? Pity we can't give each other some of the TREATMENT, isn't it?

Heaps and Heaps of Love. Yours, Jack.

24:9:18
My own darling Phyllis,

We have been on the move again today [*to Manoncourt*] and I regret to say forward once more to the fighting zone. However, it's no use being depressed.

I've got a tophole billet for tonight. Must have been at one time a German Corp Head Quarters. Looks only an ordinary felt-covered hut from the outside, but inside it's all panelled, glass windows, fire-places in every room, beds and so on. So we are in the lap of luxury. The only thing that mars it is that we are going up and not down from the line. Still, I don't think that we've got anything nasty to do.

I spoke to a German Doctor we captured the other day and he said that the war would be over in 2 Months as they couldn't stand our Artillery fire. It certainly looks like it. I mean, of course, about the Artillery fire.

Heaps and Heaps of Love. Yours, Jack.

26:9:18

My own darling Phyllis,

I was delighted to receive your letter of the 29th today. There's been quite a bit in the paper about the 21st Division lately. I can imagine, dearest, how worried you must have been,

We are in trenches now, but a long way back. We arrived here at 10 pm last night. The Hun planes bombed us on the road but no-one was hurt. We've got a fairly decent dug-out but it was bitterly cold last night. We only had trench coats —left all out kit behind. However, I've collected a lot of wood so we'll have a good fire going tonight.

Well, I must close now, dearest. Heaps and Heaps of Love. Yours, Jack.

27:9:18

My own darling Phyllis,

I only sent you a F.P.C. today, but I've been really very busy and I didn't expect to remain here tonight at all. But at the last moment we received orders that we hadn't to move, so we shall have another night's respite — and a good sleep.

I really haven't any news at all; as I've done nothing at all except sleep and eat for the last 3 days. When you come to think of it we've had a pretty rough time in many ways since August 20th. Thank Heaven, dear, I've come through it safe and sound so far. I'm a firm believer in your charm now. I intended to send you that belt of mine as a souvenir, but I've lost it somewhere or other.

Well, I must close now, dearest. Heaps and Heaps of Love. Yours, Jack.

30:9:18

My own darling Phyllis,

Just a line, dear, to let you know that all is well. We've been very busy, but we aren't in the front line yet, Thank Heaven.

It's a week now since I had my clothes off [*The Bn has been on stand-by, ready to move at 15 minutes' notice*]. I'm afraid that I have some companions again — these dirty Bosche dug-outs. Disgusting, isn't it?

Well, darling, I must close now. Heaps and Heaps of Love. Yours, Jack.

3:10:18

My own darling Phyllis,

I was very pleased indeed to receive your two letters of the 25th and 26th yesterday.

I heard some more about my Captaincy today. Division sent it back — the recommendation, I mean — to the Battalion saying that they had never been notified that I had reverted to Lieutenant and wanted to know how it was. So I have written an explanation.

So you see, all the time I've been a Captain. They'll either have to revert me to Lieutenant and then promote me again or simply let things stand as they are. If they don't let it stand as it is though I shall have to pay the difference between Lieutenant and Captain.

We are still in the same old trenches, in spite of various alarms, orders and counter-orders. We aren't finished with this offensive yet. If only this war would end. Well, I don't think I've any more news today, dearest.

Heaps and Heaps of Love. Yours, Jack.

6:10:18

My own darling Phyllis,

We had to leave our billet this morning and move into another farther down the road [*to Banteux, where it was found that that section of the Hindenburg trench was deserted*]. It's been a chateau at one time but very knocked about. The Bosche have built some huts inside of what remains of the house and we've got a tool shed as a Mess, so we shall be very comfortable. I'm fixing up one place as a Bath Room. Doing my best to keep a clean boy, you see.

A year ago today I was up on the Passchendael Ridge. A Sergeant who was up there with me reminded me of it this morning. I hope that I'm not in this country next year at this time.

October is my lucky month though, isn't it, dear?

Just fancy, we've nearly been engaged a year, haven't we? The 16th October 1917 was the great day, wasn't it?

I've been awfully happy ever since in spite of the war, and I really love you more than ever. You know you're such a darling. I should so like to s'love you this afternoon. It's Sunday too!!

Many here have taken on bets that all serious fighting will be finished within 28 days.

Well dearest, no more news today. Heaps and Heaps of Love. Yours, Jack.

7:10:18

My own darling Phyllis,

I was delighted to receive your letter of the 22nd tonight.

I've not been in the front line for quite a long time. I hear that during the few days I've been in Nucleus the Batt. has been over the top twice. I'm very lucky to have missed it, ain't I? I've done too much of that lately.*

Oh, my dear, I do want to see you so much — worse than ever tonight. The days seem to pass so slowly. It's only just over two months since I left you — the longest time I've ever spent. Those fits of mine are very frequent in these days. I shall have just to lump it.

Cheerio dearest. Heaps and Heaps of Love. Yours, Jack.

*[*The Bn has been involved in the battle of Cambrai: they attacked Mont Ecouvez Farm on the 5th and Bonne Enfance Farm on the 6th, sustaining total casualties of around 150.*]

E.F.C., OFFICERS REST HOUSE AND MESS, 8:10:18

My own darling Phyllis,

This morning I set out to find a civilised place. I heard of an Officers Club at a certain place so I made tracks for it. Imagine my delight when I found it. The first sign of anything at all decent I've seen for 2 Months. Another Officer is with me, Cotton by name.

On route I saw hundreds of Hun prisoners, several Hun tanks with their big Iron Crosses painted all over them. They are awfully clumsy things compared to ours.

I hear that the Battalion has had about 100 casualties — 3 officers. One with his foot blown off. You know, dear, I feel so thankful that I'm out of it. I've never been quite the same since I got that hit in the "Tummy". Took the stuffing out of me rather. After all, one can't keep on attacking for ever.*

214

The Hun planes were over bombing last night, but fortunately none of their eggs fell near us.

One hears the usual rumours about ice cream land, but personally I don't think that there is much in it. Certainly it would be quite a nice place to spend the winter in, though a fearful long way off from you, dear.

Well, no more today, dearest. Heaps and Heaps of Love. Yours, Jack.

*[*In Jack's brief absence the Battalion – and the Nucleus Party – were now in action at Walincourt (not to be confused with the Butte de Warlincourt), attacking the Beauvoir Line.*]

10:10:18
My own darling Phyllis,

I was very pleased to receive your letter of the 3rd today.

Many — many — congratulations, dear, on passing your exam. You're some "nut" now!— It's simply great. I thought you would too — rather like saying I told you so, ain't it?

I'm back with the Batt. again — joined this morning. We are in a village lately captured from the Hun by this Batt. [*Walincourt, taken on the 9th. See Appendix 2*]. It's hardly damaged at all and — would you believe it — some 40 civilian inhabitants. They have been under the Hun for 3 years so you can imagine their delight now. They've had no meat, butter or anything like that since 1914. We are sending them up lots of rations.

I saw the old village priest today in his long black cassock and black cap. Every time my men saluted him he took his cap off and bowed.

The Hun left this place in such a hurry that all the furniture, crockery etc. of the houses are intact, so we are living in the lap of luxury. Nearly all the houses are empty so we can help ourselves. I only wish I could send you some of the things —any amount of furniture of all kinds, some the real old stuff, cut glass glasses, decanters and Heaven knows what. Many of them would be a great assistance to our furnishings, wouldn't they dear? But of course it's impossible to send anthing. In the house I'm in we've got 3 pianos and an American organ [*There were also, in the cellar, a number of mines – mostly shells with time-fuses attached*].

I don't know how long we shall be here — the line is miles off now. Things are going very swiftly. Seems to me we shall soon have the Hun out of France. I do wish I could tell you plainly all about it, but the censor stands in the way. Our Brigadier says in 3 weeks the war will be finished. I hope so.

There's a Frenchman waving the Tricolour in the street now — seems very excited.

I should like to hug you!! Rough old thing, aren't I? But I want some *s'love* so much!!

Heaps and Heaps of Love. Yours, Jack.

11:10:18
My own darling Phyllis,

We are still resting in the village I spoke of yesterday. It's very nice to have a real home again for a bit.

The Hun seems to have treated the inhabitants very badly from all accounts —especially the women — and if they wouldn't do as they wished right away they simply starved them until they did. What a rotten lot the Huns are. Makes me feel rather sorry I've taken so many prisoners. Still, when we capture so many what can we do, and I hate doing them in in cold blood.

One rather curious thing happened during the attack on the village — a baby was born in it. Rather a stormy entrance into the world, wasn't it?

During the 4 or 5 days that I've been away 2 Captains have arrived, one an N.F. posted to my Coy and another Oxford-Bucks [*Murray and Brown*]. So I am no longer in Command of a Coy. It's a strange life. My third pip may come through, but I'm too fed up to care much.

A great friend of mine [*Keech*] is now Adjutant — he was Lt and Quartermaster until a few months ago, so he may do me some good.

Heaps and Heaps of Love. Yours, Jack.

P.S. I returned to the village where I left the Nucleus [*after two days at the Rest House*] — and imagine my surprise when I found that they had all gone forward. Cotton and I pursued them and caught them up after a trip of 12 miles on a motor lorry. I am now at the transport lines. I expect I shall rejoin the Batt tomorrow. They are in a village, I hear, from which we have recently driven the Hun. The civilians are still living in the houses, which are in a very good condition. I mean the houses, not the people.

Goodnight, dearest. Heaps and Heaps of Love. Yours, Jack.

12:10:18

My own darling Phyllis,

Many thanks for your letter of the 4th and the parcel. The apples are in splendid condition. I was awfully glad to get the magazines and cigarettes — very expensive ones though, weren't they?

I had rather a pleasant surprise yesterday. I was told that I should be on Nucleus again when the Batt. goes forward once more. Great, dear, isn't it? My luck in that way seems to be in, and now we've got some real houses to live in I ought to have a comfortable time.

We are simply overflowing with officers now — that's why I've been so lucky. Still, I think I've done my share so far.

I've been looking round the village a bit more this morning. Some of the furniture in the houses is very good. Of course, a lot is the usual cheap stuff, but some of it must be really valuable. I wish I knew more about it. Principally oak —chairs, tables, sideboards, dressers, and in the chateau, tapestries and so on. The Hun has tried to carry a lot of it away, but he was hustled out too quickly. You find mantle clocks, mirrors, china, sofas lying in the street.

By the way, I have a safe but so far have been unable to open it. Nearly all the houses were mined but the engineers were up early and rendered nearly all of them useless. A few houses though went sky-high. No casualties though. The civilian inhabitants still seem unable to realise that they are free from the Hun. They've had a devil of a time from all accounts.

You are a darling, but I must keep myself in hand or I shall explode! And that would be sad. I don't see why you should have been worried about going to London, dear. I only wish that I was there with you!

Heaps and Heaps of Love. Yours, Jack.

13:10:18

My own darling Phyllis.

I was delighted to receive your letter of the 8th tonight. I'm very pleased indeed to hear that you are having such a good time. There's no place like London to have a good time in, I think.

I took a Church parade this morning. It was held in an old French Protestant Church. I hear that after the service one of the men was puttering around its altar when greatly to his surprise he found a mine. He rushed out and eventually got some REs to disconnect it and take it away. Dirty Dogs the Huns, aren't they?

We got some most extraordinary news through tonight on the wireless — that the Huns had agreed to President Wilson's Peace terms and would evacuate all occupied territory. But I don't believe it — though I hope it's true as it means the end of the war. No doubt we shall hear further details in the morning.

I have been warned as a member of the Field General Court Martial to assemble on Oct 16 at No. 6 Stationary Hospital. I have been trying to find out where this hospital is situated.

Two more Captains [*Bentley & Beckett*] have flown up to the Batt today, so the prospects for my getting my third pip back are now practically nil. I feel very fed up about it but I shall simply have to lump it. But after taking this Company through the hard fighting of the last two months to lose it just as things are easing off a bit seems to me to be rather hard luck, don't you think so?

All of us (the Officers of this Coy) — Captain Murray also — have rather run up against the Brigadier today on account of some dirty Lewis Guns. He threatens all kind of things — stoppage of leave for a brief period for all the officers of the Coy. He has only succeeded so far in getting our backs up. I assure you we're not going to sit quiet. I must confess I think it's damned annoying (excuse adjective, but it just fits in).

I heard that song "The First Love is the Best Love" tonight, and also that old friend "Destiny". My thoughts immediately wandered away to Scarborough and other places where we've had such topping times together. "Destiny" always brings back some very pleasant "memories". Makes me want to s'love you even worse than usual! By Jove dear but it's a long time since we've seen each other. I've got such a lot of love sort of tucked away until I see you that when I do I shall have to be careful or you'll have a "rending" time. I think that an old dress would be best, don't you? Perhaps I had better stop now, dear, or what shall I be saying next!!

Cheerio. Heaps and Heaps of Love. Yours, Jack.

P.S. This is Hun writing paper — not bad stuff, is it?

14:10:18

My own darling Phyllis,

I have just received orders to proceed to the Court Martial. I have to make my way to the nearest Railhead — and then I've got a tremendous journey before me. I must only write a short note now as I must be off. I expect to have quite a good time.

Heaps and Heaps of Love. Yours, Jack.

E.F.C. OFFICERS REST HOUSE AND MESS, 14:10:17 17:00 Hours

My own darling Phyllis,

I've come quite along way since I last wrote to you — some 70 miles. I've succeeded in getting lifts in cars and lorries all the way. I am now in the civilised parts again — I don't see why I shouldn't tell you the name: Doullens. I shall stop here tonight.

It's true then, after all, about the Hun accepting President Wilson's terms. I wonder what will happen now. Wouldn't it be simply great, darling, if we actually got Peace. Anyway, it shows that the Hun is pretty groggy — but he's such a deceitful devil.

Well, no more now, dearest. Heaps and Heaps of Love. Yours, Jack.

E.F.C. OFFICERS REST HOUSE AND MESS, 15:10:18
My own darling Phyllis,

Last night I put up at a little hotel here called "Les Quatre Fils" and managed to get quite a nice room.

I had the good luck to meet an RAF Private with a motor bicycle and sidecar, and after a little bribery he agreed to take me to my destination.

On arriving at the Hospital I reported to the Orderly Room and saw the Colonel. He said he didn't think there was a Court Martial being held there at all today. But in the meantime he told me to go to the Mess and get some breakfast.

After breakfast I returned to the Orderly Room and saw the C.O. again. He said that the Court Martial had been cancelled 2 days ago. I waited a bit on the road and caught a lorry back here, the same place as I wrote you from yesterday. Just fancy, dearest, all that journey for nothing at all. I'm at least 80 Miles away from the Batt. now, but I'm not going any farther today — spend the night at the Quatre Fils.

Heaps and Heaps of Love. Yours, Jack.

E.F.C. OFFICERS REST HOME AND MESS, 16:10:18
My own darling Phyllis,

I am going to leave here today and push on up the line again, though I have no intention of reaching there today.

I stayed at the Quatre Fils again last night and didn't get up until 10 this morning — just down in time to get some breakfast.

Well, dearest, I don't think I've any more news today. Hope you are feeling better and not so fagged.

Heaps and Heaps of Love. Yours, Jack.

E.F.C. REST HOUSE AND MESS, 17:10:18
My own darling Phyllis,

I have travelled a long way this morning — just stopped here for lunch. That car brought us up here splendidly. I quite enjoyed the run to _ _ _ _ 60 miles. This is the last civilised place until we get among the liberated villages — some 30 miles away.

I hear the train that came up here from the Base yesterday was practically blown up by a Hun mine — the engine and tender anyway. Lucky I didn't come by it, isn't it?

The rumour is very strong today that Turkey has made a separate peace. I wonder how much truth there is in it.*

Cheerio, dear. Heaps and Heaps of Love. Yours, Jack.

*[*The Turks had been on the retreat for some time, but did not begin formal negotiations for an armistice until late in October, an armistice which took effect on the last day of the month.*]

18:10:18

My own darling Phyllis,

I got back to the Battalion again last night and found them in the same place [*Walincourt*].

I'm afraid that my third pip has gone west. We have now 5 Pukka Captains, so I've no hope of getting mine back. There is nothing I can do so it's no use worrying. But it's completely fed me up.

Also I told you a few days ago about the row between the Brigadier and the dirty Lewis Guns. Well, would you believe it — he has stopped our leave for 2 months. That is, all the officers of 'A' Coy. The most unjust thing I ever heard of. We made out a statement to be sent to him but the C.O. wouldn't send it on — so there we are. In my case, for instance, as second in Command, I have nothing whatever to do with Lewis Guns. Personally I think it's the limit, don't you? But of course, we are simply powerless.

Heaps and Heaps of Love. Yours, Jack.

18:10:18   24.00 Hrs

My own darling Phyllis,

It seems to be becoming a habit of mine to write you twice a day now. But as a matter of fact, dear, I shall be very busy tomorrow and may not have a chance of writing. I'm in the Nucleus Party — so all is well in that direction.

Many many thanks dear for the pipe and tobacco. It's a beauty — just the best kind there is on the market too. I was just hoping for a pipe too.

We have just got it through that Ostend and Lille have been taken. If it's true it's simply great, isn't it?

These French inhabitants are a queer lot. In the villages nearer the line the inhabitants refuse to leave their homes in spite of shelling and gas. Very foolish of them I think, don't you? Saw quite a lot coming down today wounded.

I've got such a lot of tales to tell you about all these latest stunts. I must try to remember it as I'm sure you'd be interested. I sometimes wish that I'd kept a diary, but it's rather too late to start now.

I had a letter from Mr. Allen today in reply to mine. He says that he has not received Gordon Allen's glasses, compass and revolver and asks me to trace them and, if found, send them to him. I'll do my best of course — but you see dear after he was killed he was lying out in the open for four days before he was buried, so I expect someone pinched them. I'd like to catch anyone stealing things off our own dead, but it's done often enough, I know.

It's a beautiful evening tonight — bright moonlight. The Hun is taking every advantage of it too — and is dropping his bombs very freely — at least a mile away from here so there is no need for excitement.

There hasn't been a mail in today from England. I think that engine and tender being blown up on the line has affected it.

Heaps and Heaps of Love. Yours, Jack.

20:10:18

My own darling Phyllis,

I am now with the Nucleus Party — we have stayed in the same village — but have moved into the house vacated by Batt. Head Qtrs. I haven't been so comfortable

219

before — got a topping bedroom with fire place and everything, so I don't care how long we stay here.

I had rather a find yesterday — I was puttering about in one of the rooms and amongst a lot of straw etc I unearthed a pewter tankard. I've cleaned it up and it looks well. It's been a government measure for wine and beer. But stamped on the bottom in two places — on the rim round the top of the handle — is the crown and something else that I can't make out. This government stamp (the crown) was last used in France just before the French Revolution, I am told — so I think I've got hold of quite a good thing. I don't quite know how I can send it to you dear, but I'll manage it somehow.

The pipe is going strong — it's a beauty. I'm not smoking nearly so many cigarettes now.

Heaps and Heaps of Love. Yours, Jack.

A rather curious thing has just happened. A French soldier on 3 days' leave has just returned to his native village in search of his family. Our men are occupying his house as a billet. He says he has found his Father, but that the Hun have carried away his wife and Mother. He has just departed to see if he can trace them at all. Rather a rotten homecoming for him after 4 years, isn't it? No more now.

21:10:18
My own darling Phyllis,

I am having quite a peaceful quiet time here — rather a pleasant change to be able to slack about a bit.

I saw a lot of prisoners today — all of them were big tall men. One of their crack regiments, I believe. It's surprising how readily they give themselves up nowadays.

Do you know, dear, it's a month ago tonight since I was in action. We came out of the Sept. 18 stunt on the night of the 20th.

I'm really very lucky to have been put on Nucleus again this time. [*Meanwhile the rest of the battalion is involved in the Battle of the Selle.*] I feel confident that it's only a question of a few weeks and we shall see this war over as far as fighting is concerned.

What a thrilling letter this is — and it sounds fearfully cold! Not a bit like me —because I'm simply aching to s'love you, dear, though I can't really do that "properly" till I see you again.

Heaps and Heaps of Love. Yours, Jack.

22:10:18
My own darling Phyllis,

I was simply delighted to receive four letter from you last night — 12th, 13th, 14th and 15th.

I feel I'd like to run off with you at the present moment, but you know what I'm like when I feel like that, don't you? So perhaps it's better that you're not here. I feel I could give you some *excellent* treatment tonight and soon bring the roses back —and could do with a little (or a lot) of treatment myself. However, as you're not here it will have to be stored away for future use.

Well then, to change the subject — I'm still with the Nucleus, and I may be wrong but I think that it will be a good long one [*the Battalion has advanced to Montigny, and thence to Inchy and Neuvilly*]. Anyway, we are really very comfortable. I have a fire in my bedroom every night and often during the day too.

During the day — in the morning rather — we have a few men to train.*
Heaps and Heaps of Love. Yours, Jack.

*[Reinforcements continued to arrive and had to be prepared for action.]

23:10:18
My own darling Phyllis,

I haven't received a letter from you today, dear, though I had 4 yesterday so I can't complain.

I haven't changed my quarters — and everything is very quiet. The war is miles and miles away now, Thank Heaven. We can hardly hear the guns. [The Battalion is now in action at Ovillers]

This afternoon having nothing to do I went through a lot of the empty houses. My word but they are in a Mess — drawers all dragged out and their contents scattered all over the place. I had a long talk with some of the people who had just come back to one house. They were very depressed to see the wreck everything was in. The Huns have taken all the girls away with them. Some of the tales one hears make one's blood boil. Simply starved them into submission. Those that have been left have a very cowed sort of look. Thank Heaven the war is in France and not in England.

You know, I have been lucky to keep out of action so long. I only wish I could get a job to keep me permanently away from the battle line. That's frank, isn't it — but I've had just about my fill of it.

Heaps and Heaps of Love. Yours, Jack.

24:10:18
My own darling Phyllis,

I was ever so pleased to receive two letters today — and feel quite bucked with life again as I've been simply pining to hear from you. The first mail for 2 days.

By the way, dear, I sent you a Brass candlestick and a small brass trumpet today. I'll keep my eye open for anything else too, though I'm afraid I can't very well start sending you sideboards etc. can I?

All the French people here seem to be re-furnishing with the furniture of their absent neighbours. It's really rather amusing to watch them.

I am still with the Nucleus Party and miles and miles away from the line — I don't know where it is exactly. I went up towards it this afternoon to get some food, etc. for the Mess from our Divisional Canteen and had to go 20 kilometres. The nearer you get to the front the more civilians you see, and I must say their villages are practically undamaged.

We were burning some wood on the fire the other night and for a time had rather a funny feeling in our eyes as if the room was full of smoke — which it wasn't. I think that the wood must have had some Mustard Gas Liquid on it as my eyes have been "running" — weeping should I say — ever since slightly, and when I wake up in the morning my eyelids are stuck together rather. Two other officers besides myself have the same symptons, so we saw the M.O., today and he has given us an eye wash.

It's just a year since we got engaged dear, isn't it? The 16th, wasn't it? You did get a shock when your Father consented, didn't you dear, though you carried it through very well until we were alone, didn't you? But the news certainly took your breath away. It's very s'nice of you dear to say that you've never regretted it. That's a great compliment to me, you know. I'll do my best to see that you never do regret it, either. I'm sure that it's the happiest time that I've ever had, only I haven't been able to see half enough of you. I was a very lucky chap, but I feel more so now than ever. I love you more than ever — but I think you know that, don't you dear? The most wonderful thing is that you actually care for me. I'll never cease to marvel at it. There isn't such a tophole girl as you anywhere. That's what I think, anyway.

Heaps and Heaps of Love. Yours, Jack.

25:10:18
My own darling Phyllis,

I'm sorry to say that the Mail has failed to arrive again today. I've never known it so irregular as it is at present.

We've heard some bad rumours about the Batt. today — they've been in action again, you know. Fearfully heavy casualties, though whether it's true or not no-one can rightly say. The M.O. Capt. Raine has had his leg broken by a bullet. It's a pity as he's such a splendid chap in action. Still, it will get him across to England, won't it?*

On the whole I'm having a very uneventful time, but I feel very thankful to be here — might be having a rotten time up in the line. I'm perfectly safe here. I assure you, dear, I've lost all desire to fight the Hun. I was quite keen once upon a time too.

I do feel like some treatment now, dear!! What a long time ago it is since we had any s'love, isn't it dearest? I'm simply longing to see you again. The sooner the better! Well, dear, I think I'd better stop now — and I'm afraid I've no more news so Cheerio.

Heaps and Heaps of Love. Yours, Jack.

*[*In mopping up the villages of Ovillers on 23rd, and Poix Du Nord on the afternoon of the 24th, the Battalion suffered some 160 casualties.*

The loss of Raine left the Battalion without an M.O., but fortunately they captured a German doctor and some stretcher bearers and put them to work.]

26:10:18
My own darling Phyllis,

I was delighted to receive your two letters of the 17th and 19th tonight, dear, and feel quite bucked with life again.

Up to the present, dear, I've seen none of the inhabitants kissing the troops. All the girls (young) have been taken away by the Hun. Still, farther on it may be different!! Honestly though, they all seem to want a good wash. They seem to do it once a week here, I think.

I was very sorry indeed to see from the Newspaper cutting you sent me that Foster has been officially reported killed. It will be a great blow to Mrs. Foster as she was so sure he was a prisoner. He's an only son too, I believe.

I am rejoining the Battalion tomorrow but please don't worry dearest as they are out of the line — though for how long I cannot say.

It's very rotten about my leave being stopped for 2 Months, isn't it? I feel it especially as I had nothing whatever to do with the guns. I think it's the dirtiest trick I've ever heard of because it's just the one thing one lives for out here. I really feel too annoyed (that's mild) to be fed up.

By the way, dear, I think perhaps you'd better address my letters as Lieut —there doesn't seem to be any chance of my getting my wandering pip at present.

Heaps and Heaps of Love. Yours, Jack.

27:10:18

My own darling Phyllis,

I was more than delighted, dear, when I arrived back at the Battalion today [*at Inchy*] to receive your two letters of 20th and 21st.

The Batt. has had a very rough time indeed, but I'm glad to say very few killed [*total casualties by now amounted to 222*]. The Officers of 'A' Coy have had some wonderful escapes — only Tucker was hit, you know [*on the 23rd near Ovillers*], but the other three — their tunics and trench coats are full of bullet holes. I'm not exaggerating, honestly, dear. They must have had charmed lives.

We've got a splendid mess — the people of the house are, I believe, quite nuts in their way and are known to several of the Divisional Staff. The old lady — a great grandmother aged 85 — told me that the house was the Head Quarters of the German Prince Damstadt (?) during 1870.

Another woman in one of our mess billets showed me the place underneath the floor of her house where she had hidden her son aged 19 for 4 years so that the Germans shouldn't take him away. The Huns knew that her son was about though they couldn't find him so they sent her to prison for 5 days at a certain town which is now in our hands. But on the whole the inhabitants have had rather better treatment and say that the Hun officers were quite civil, though when they were forced to leave this place they took everything of value.

Bingham and I have a topping billet — sheets, etc. The people of the house will do anything for you. We seem quite popular at present. The lady of the house has three daughters! I thought you'd like to know the worst! Nothing exciting has happened up to the time of going to press though. My room was last occupied by a Hun Captain — fitted up with electric light, but sad to say it won't work.

I often think that it must be a very fascinating job getting people fit again after they've been so ill. Aren't our jobs different — yours to heal, mine to kill.

Well, dearest, I've no more news tonight so will close now. Hope you're keeping fit and well. I do feel like some s'love now too — such ages since we've had any, isn't it?

Heaps and Heaps of Love. Yours, Jack.

28:10:18

My own darling Phyllis,

I am sorry to say that no letter arrived for me from you in the mail today, dear.

I think, dear, that stoppage of leave for 2 Months for all the officers of 'A' Coy has been washed out as two of them, Murray and Cotton, are going shortly. The Adjutant told me that the C.O. has or is going to speak to the Brigadier about it.

If I see the Adjutant today I'll ask him. The Coy has done so well in the last show too, so that may help things a bit. A Sergeant I recommended the other week got a D.C.M. last night. They take a long time to come through. I've been very lucky really — all the people I recommend seem to get something.

By the way, dearest, I enclose some German medal ribbons — Iron Cross 2nd Class. I thought that you might like to have it.

Heaps and Heaps of Love. Yours, Jack.

29:10:18

My own darling Phyllis,

We set off this morning at 9 am and after a fairly long march have stopped at

223

another village [*Vendegies au Bois*]. There are civilian inhabitants — quite a lot of them in fact.

We have got quite a good billet and shall be fairly comfy, though of course no sheets or anything like that. The inhabitants all seem to spend the night in the cellars as the Hun puts over occasional shells. A few have come over tonight but so far nothing to get excited about. Anyway the entrance to the cellar is just outside the door of our room, so if they get too near I can soon pop down there and join the family.

We were all very excited to hear a rumour that Austria had made a separate Peace. We have an English paper where it is unofficially reported this is taking place. Seems almost too good to be true, dearest, doesn't it?

I am once again in charge of the Coy. It is nice to be your own boss again. I think you understand what I mean, don't you? Captain Murray has gone to the Nucleus Party.

Heaps and Heaps of Love. Yours, Jack.

30:10:18

My own darling Phyllis,

I was delighted to receive your letters of the 22nd and 23rd this morning. They always seem to arrive in couples now, don't they?

I spent quite a good night and slept like a top. All of the shells went well over the house.

We have had it through from the Wireless Press this morning that Austria has made Peace. Everyone is very excited about it. Everything points that way too, but I should like to know if it's true because it will bring the war to an end very quickly. With all these Peace Rumours floating about no-one feels like fighting. I'm sure that I don't for one.

Heaps and Heaps of Love. Yours, Jack.

31:X:18

My own darling Phyllis,

I was very pleased indeed dear to receive yours of the 24th today.

Isn't this news about the armistice with Turkey splendid? It only came through at 1500 hrs and everyone is very elated — also the 33,000 Austrian prisoners by the Italians.*

A lot of pamphlets were dropped from a German plane yesterday. On them was as follows: "We, the German people, intend to have Peace at any price."

We did a little training this morning but it was so cold we were all frozen to the marrow.

I'm delighted to hear, dearest, that you've got a lot more things for our bottom drawer. I am very interested in it too, as you know. We seem to be doing quite well in that direction, don't we dear? I should think that by now the pewter jug ought to have reached you. I do hope it gets through safely.

Hope you're keeping fit and well. Heaps and Heaps of Love. Yours, Jack.

*[*It is interesting to see the first use of the form "1500 hours". As of October 1st the order was that this new universal method of recording time should be used. Like Jack, the writer of the Bn Diary – Keech, the Adjutant – took a full month to start using it.*]

1:11:18

My own darling Phyllis,

I was very pleased to receive your letter of the 25th this morning.*

We only heard the news about the armistice with Austria this morning. It came through officially while we were on parade. We've all got our "tails up" now. Isn't it great, dearest? We've only got the Hun to deal with now — and I don't think it will be long before they throw in too. One of the Divisional Staff said this morning that he expected Peace within a week. Just fancy, dearest, Peace at last. The war finished with — no more going over the top. What a time we shall have, shan't we!!! It would be simply lovely. I've often imagined too what times we shall have together when this is all over. Oh, it will be s'nice. I'm simply pining to see you, dear. Almost on the point of exploding. I fear that you'll have your work cut out to keep me in hand!

I wish the Hun would stop throwing his shells about here though. However, I'll keep my head well down and won't do anything rash. Too near the end for that, isn't it?

Yes, dear, the pipe is going strong. I like the straight ones best too. It was a straight you used that time to cure your toothache, wasn't it? Just fancy — you smoking a pipe!

Heaps and Heaps of Love. Yours, Jack.

*[*The armistice with Austria came into effect on 4 November having been signed on 3 November, negotiations having been under way for several days.*]

Sunday 3:11:18

My own darling Phyllis,

I was delighted to receive your two letters of the 26th and 28th and also the parcel. I was simply pining for something to read too, and a decent cigarette. Thanks ever so much, dearest.

The war news is great just now, isn't it? If only the Hun would throw in too. However, dear, I'm sure that we shall have it over before Xmas, though I expect we shall have some pretty tough fighting first. However, I haven't any qualms. I shall come through alright, never fear.

I examined that cross bow I found. It looks to me quite old. If I can manage it I'll bring or sent it home. We shall soon be able to set up an antique shop, shan't we?

Cheerio, dearest. Heaps and Heaps of Love. Yours, Jack.

4:11:18

My own darling Phyllis,

I was delighted to receive your letter of the 29th today. I hope that the tankard has turned up by now. It must be safely in England as the letter I sent with it had turned up.

I am just snatching this chance of writing you a line, dear, as I shall not be able to do so for a day or so after this. I'm sat on a pail in an orchard writing this. We've left our village far behind now. However, dearest, when you receive this it will be all over, so please don't worry more than you can help, dear. I'll take care of myself as best as I can but I feel quite optimistic about it all.

Cheerio, dearest. Heaps and Heaps of Love. Yours, Jack.

5:11:18

My own darling Phyllis,

Things have gone quite well and I am in a billet safe and sound.

We've been marching ever since 8 am this morning in the rain and got simply wet to the skin. We were told that we should have to spend the night in a wood so we lit fires and tried to make the best of things, but it was a dreary prospect, so you can imagine how glad we were when we moved into this village.*

The inhabitants as we waited in the street rushed out with coffee and other refreshments which were most acceptable. They were very bucked with life. One old man marched along in the middle of my Coy singing some French song.

Last night I spent in a house entirely smashed by shell-fire except for 1 room and the cellar. Myself and 5 other officers occupied the room while down in the cellar were the French people in bed — an old man and his wife and 3 daughters. We didn't disturb them, so they were rather surprised to see us next morning. My servant Houston took them some tea in bed which seemed to please them very much.

I've had some strange experiences of late. I'm sleeping in a farm tonight amongst the Hay — I've got a good Mess but the floor is stone and I've no blankets so I think I shall be more comfy in the Hay.

I don't know how I shall get this letter away but the rations haven't come up yet so I'll try to get it away with them.

Goodnight, dearest. Heaps and Heaps of Love. Yours, Jack.

*[*They now appear to be in La Grand Carriere, which the Diary refers to as "Grand Carliers". The Battalion at this time were flushing Germans out of the Foret de Mormal.*]

6:11:18

My own darling Phyllis,

I wrote you a long letter last night, but I'm afraid that it's gone astray. After I'd written it I returned to my stable and put the letter in the pocket of my tunic and in a few minutes I was dead asleep. I have confused memories of speaking to various people during the night — the C.O. was one. This morning when I looked in my pocket for the letter it had gone so I must have given to someone to post. That sounds very bad, doesn't it dear. Looks as if I'd been having a drop too much —but I assure you I had nothing stronger than coffee. Simply very tired.

We expected to move early this morning but it was washed out, thank Goodness. It's simply pouring with rain again just as it did yesterday. Makes one feel very thankful for a good billet and a roof over one's head. The Hun too has been shelling us a little, but so far no damage has been done.

The French people are very cordial — give you everything they can and absolutely refuse any payment. In the street they frequently come and shake you by the hand and get so excited.

We passed a Hun Prisoner of War Camp last night — a lot of English had been there. It looked a dirty hole too. One little boy here is being made much of because as the Huns were marching out he killed one with a rifle. They chased him into the woods but couldn't catch him. He can only be 10 years old.

The houses here are absolutely unharmed — not a pane of glass broken in this house even. So we're well off for once. It's certainly a life of many changes. But you

226

have no time to get bored as you are always moving — what a difference to the old days of trench warfare. I don't think that we shall see that again anyway.

This censoring of letters, dear, is such a bother. I've got such a lot of things I should like to tell you — quite interesting too — but I'm not allowed to. I must try and remember them until I see you next. I want to see you so badly!! It's such ages since we've had any s'love, isn't it. By Jove but I do want some!!!!! And there's only one girl in the world for me — she's such a darling too!

Heaps and Heaps of Love. Yours, Jack.

8:11:18
My own darling Phyllis,

I was delighted to receive your letter of the 30th this morning. I am sorry, dear, but I couldn't manage to write to you yesterday because we were stunting and only came out this morning.

The C.O. du Moulin was killed — shot through the neck. Keech the Adjutant —shot through the chest — and I had an officer Cotton hit through the shoulder.

I knew the C.O. would get killed. I'm very sorry, but he certainly asked for it —there is such a thing as being too brave, I think. [*The Snapper: "brave to a fault".*]*

Well, dearest, we didn't take our objective until quite late last night. It was a village, of course, the worst thing about the whole show was the wet and cold. Sleeping out for two nights without cover and wet through to start is rather a poor do.

The march back to the town we're in through various villages was very interesting. You see, the people had seen us going into the scrap. I halted the Coy at one small place at 6 am this morning for a few minutes' rest. A house door opened and a French woman asked us to come in, Bingham and I. She took us down her cellar where we found her husband and two children — very comfy place too. She then produced coffee with sugar, etc. After finishing this and thanking her we started to make our way back to the men when we were stopped and the same thing occurred over again. I didn't really like to refuse. We both looked awful wrecks —haven't washed or shaved for 3 days, and covered with mud. I don't think you'd have recognised me if you'd seen me.

However, to continue, in rejoining the men we found that they all had had the same good fortune. Very decent of the people, isn't it?

Really dearest, what a fearful lot of shop I'm writing, but I thought you'd like to know. Oh, I've got heaps of things to tell — I must try and remember them if I can. You ought to have seen the excitement of French People here this aftenoon when the Highlanders with their kilts and bagpipes marched through. Never seen them before, of course.

When I arrived here at 8 am this morning my Quartermaster met me and showed me the billets. We got the men in and then went to our own — only Bingham and I left, you know. We've both got topping beds. Old Lady here about 90 yrs insisted on me wearing a pair of her bedroom slippers and also socks, for which I was very thankful having no kit of my own at hand.

Well, I must close now, dear. Heaps and Heaps of Love. Yours, Jack.

*[*After passing through Berlaimont on November 7 the Battalion had progressed over the river Sambre towards Limont Fontaine and Eclaibes. Total casualties 96; Keech, who survived his wounds, had been with the Batt. continuously since its arrival in France in September 1914.*]

9:11:18

My own darling Phyllis,

Many thanks for your letter of the 31st received this afternoon.

We are all very excited at the news — the prospect of the armistice. It does look hopeful, dear, don't you think so? Anyway, we shall know by 11 am Monday. Just fancy, Peace.

What I didn't like about that last stunt was that I felt we were so near the end of the war, and didn't feel a bit like a scrap. Perhaps we shan't have any more fighting to do. I hope not. I'm trying not to build too much on this Peace idea because if it didn't come off it would be such a blow.

The Batt. attended Lt Col. Du Moulin's funeral this morning. He was buried with full military honours — three volleys fired over his grave and the Last Post sounded. Sounds awfully weird that, I think.*

Quite a lot of French people were there too. I hate funerals, though: so depressing. Still, I'm cheerful enough now. Now that the C.O. has gone I'm the only Officer in the Batt. who has gone right through the fighting since the beginning of the advance in August. I think that the charm you gave me must have had something to do with it.

Well, dearest, I must close now — will write again tomorrow. Hope you're keeping well.

Heaps and Heaps of Love. Yours, Jack.

*[Du Moulin was interred at the Catholic cemetery at Berlaimont, and at the special request of an old French gentleman was placed in his family vault so that if at any future time his family wished to remove his remains they might do so.]

10:11:18

My own darling Phyllis,

I was very pleased indeed dear to receive your letters of the 1st and 2nd today.

I feel very bucked today with the good news. The Kaiser abdicated and the Crown Prince renounced his claims to the throne. We are all wondering if the Armistice will come off by tomorrow.

We haven't had any parades today as it's Sunday. This morning I went to the C of E Service. Halfway through a French woman fell into the river running just at the side and we had to go and pull her out, after which the service was continued.

You are having a rotten time at the Hospital — so busy, I mean. I don't wonder at all that you feel like passing away. Looking after 33 Patients all on your lonely own. I hope that some of the other nurses buck up and come back. Seems to me dearest that there are precious few that stick to it like you do. My word, I expect I shall get strafed for that, but it's quite true.

Please don't worry about those few souvenirs I've sent you, dear. They aren't of much value. The rightful owners, even if they are not dead, would never have got them if I'd left them.

Heaps and Heaps of Love. Yours, Jack.

11:11:18

My own darling Phyllis,

I was delighted to receive your letters of the 3rd and 4th tonight.

Well, dearest, isn't the news simply great? I couldn't sleep last night wondering if we should get the armistice. About 12 Midnight I heard cheering in the streets but we didn't get it through officially until about 9 am this morning. You ought to have heard the cheers. We marched away from that town I spoke of this morning and are now in the village we captured 4 days ago [*Eclaibes*]. The good news had arrived before us. I never saw such excitement.

Honestly, darling, I can hardly realise that to all intents and purposes the WAR is OVER. It's too much to grasp all at once. Just fancy — no more war or fighting, nothing to stop me coming back again to you. That has always been one of my greatest fears, that I might never see you again. I thank God that I've been allowed to come through it all safely, and the sooner I can get home the better I shall be pleased, because I simply long to see you again, dear. But isn't the prospect lovely, dearest. By Jove but it's good to be alive, to have come through it all and be engaged to the dearest and sweetest girl in the world.

All those clouds of uncertainty which were always hanging over us completely done away with. What a relief. In fact, dear, I can't find the words to express anything like what I feel. I can imagine what excitement there must be in England tonight, It must be tremendous. We are very quiet here, but very happy.

Of course Peace hasn't been declared, but I'm sure that we've finished all the fighting. I'm not far from the line now and there's not a sound — it really is weird. What a fall for the Kaiser, isn't it? I don't know what is going to happen to us —whether we shall march into Germany or not.

All I want now is to get home to you. I want you so badly and I've got such lots and lots of things to tell, and I do want some treatment!

I am sorry to hear, darling, that you've got a bad throat. I have myself, so I can sympathise with you. I'm afraid mine's through smoking too many cigarettes. I've stopped doing so for the time.

You must be having a fearful time at the Hospital with all this flu. I think that's topping of you to carry on as you do. For God's sake don't catch it yourself, though. Well, it's getting late so goodnight, darling.

Heaps and Heaps of Love. Yours, Jack.

12:11:18
My own darling Phyllis,

I'm just beginning to realise that this armistice is real and not merely a pleasant dream. It does seem so strange after all the fighting — everything perfectly quiet, no shelling, no night bombing, It's just like a new lease of life — honestly, dearest, can't grasp all that it means at once.

Just fancy, there's nothing now to stop me coming home to you safe and sound — because I'm sure the war won't start again. Simply a question of waiting a month or two.

You know, dear, I feel so happy. Thank God we're both alive and well. We'll have a lovely time as soon as we see each other. No more going back and leaving you after 14 days. I'm simply bursting to s'love you too. I can see, dear, that you're going to have a hard life in that direction!! though I never heard of anyone dying through being s'loved, have you? Anyway, I'll take care that you survive alright!

What a great time we shall have, shan't we? I must set to work and save as much as possible now!! I shall be able to get a move on shortly — once I get clear of the army.

I believe that we are stopping here for some time. I'm very comfy — got a nice bedroom, beautiful white sheets, and everything very clean.

Will write again tomorrow. Heaps and Heaps of Love. Yours, Jack.

14:11:18

My own darling Phyllis,

Last night we heard, as we thought, the guns firing again. But it turned out that it was our people blowing up old Hun Dumps. The French people though were very alarmed and thought that the war had started again. No fear of that. I haven't seen all the terms of the armistice but they seem very stiff for the Hun — and quite right too. What a fall it is for them. I expect that when we go into the Hun Towns we shan't be loved exactly.

We are having rather a busy time here at present getting all the men spick and span. It takes some doing too. Haig is going to inspect us at some future date, I hear.

Isn't it a tremendous relief, darling, to feel that we have got the war over — no more of those battles to go through and knowing that we may get done in any time.

I'm simply pining to see you again and I dream of the lovely times that we are going to have together. I do want some treatment too! What lots of things we shall have to talk about. I can never tell you half what I really want to in letters. That sounds bad, doesn't it? I do hope a letter arrives from you tomorrow, dear. Of course there was no mail in today.

I had a brief note from Norman today. I don't think that we are so near each other now, as it was written on the 5th. It's such a long time since I've seen him too. However, perhaps we'll meet in Berlin!

Goodnight dear. Heaps and Heaps of Love. Yours, Jack.

14:11:18

My own darling Phyllis,

I was so pleased to receive yours of the 5th today.

Yes, you were quite right: I was in the advance of 5th — the last one for me, I hope.

Hasn't the aspect of everything changed in the last few days. What a lovely time you and I have in front of us now — haven't we? It really seems too good to be true. The war practically over and done with, and no danger much of us not seeing each other again. I feel as if I'd been under a death sentence and then suddenly reprieved.

I want you so badly too. If I had my way I'd come right now at this very moment. I think I may tell you that we expect to go to Germany shortly and occupy some other town or other.

I hope dearest that the censoring regulations will soon be washed out — no reason why they shouldn't be after Peace has been fixed up. I've really got such a lot of interesting things to tell you — only at present I can't do so.

I went into a town near here today on the French-Belgian frontier [*Maubeuge*]. Quite a long ride on horseback — 8 miles each way. It was a quiet old place with Ramparts right round. The streets too are very narrow; the place is simply covered with the flags of the Allies, chinese lanterns and all kinds of decorations. It's full of civilians too. They were all dressed in their Sunday best too. So strange to see a girl again! They all had their escorts too and seemed very bucked with life.

By Jove, but I wish I could see you for myself. It's time I came home and took care of you. Well, dearest, I don't think I've any more news tonight — I'm simply longing to see you!!

Heaps and Heaps of Love. Yours, Jack.

15:11:18

My own darling Phyllis,

I regret to say dear that no mail has arrived today — at least, none from England.

We are having a very quiet time here practising Ceremonial Parades. Tomorrow morning we have a march Past in front of the Brigadier — and others. I can't say that I'm looking forward to it.

There have been some fearfully heavy explosions today — and the concussion has smashed some of the windows. The Hun blowing up his Ammunition Dumps, I believe.

Well, I must close now, dear. I do hope that you're not ill. Cheerio.

Heaps and Heaps of Love. Yours, Jack.

16:11:18

My own darling Phyllis,

I was ever so pleased, dear, to receive your letters of the 6th and 7th this afternoon. Very many thanks too for the parcel. Those magazines especially are a great blessing.

Yes, Thank God, the armistice is real— it almost seems too good to be true. On the 7th — when you heard the first rumour that it had been signed — we went over the top. I must confess, dear, it didn't look much like Peace then. The night of then 7th and 8th I spent holding a sunken road. I had a little niche cut out of the bank to sleep in — the coldest night that I've ever spent, and yet we slept.

But really, dearest, I must cease talking shop.

We had the Brigade Ceremonial Parade this morning and we all feel greatly relieved at having got it over. We are getting very busy with Football, games, boxing, etc., though I expect we shall move on towards Germany very soon now.

I'm going to bed so early nowadays — 9.30 pm nearly every night, and sleep until 8 am. See if you can beat that.

Heaps and Heaps of Love. Yours, Jack,

17:11:18

My own darling Phyllis,

The mail has failed to arrive again today, dear, but as I received two letters from you yesterday I can't complain.

I see that immediately demobilisation starts one may apply for leave providing that you have a job to go back to. I should like to have a talk to Norman about things. Having got the war over at last — Thank Heaven — I'm wondering what I can do when I do get back. One thing is certain — no more Bank for me. I'm sure that you'll agree with me there, dear. I'm not stopping in the army either.

We ought to get quite a nice little sum as "Blood Money" and then there's the exra pay for every year of Commission service after the declaration of war, which in my case is just about £200. It's a case of all contributions thankfully received, isn't it? I hope, darling, I haven't bored you with all this, but I've been thinking a good deal of the future prospects the last day or so.

Heaps and Heaps of Love. Yours, Jack.

18:11:18

My own darling Phyllis,

The English Mail has failed to turn up again today.

This morning at 10 o'clock High Mass was held in the church here by the village curé for the officers and men of this Brigade who fell in action on the 7th. Our Brigade took this village, you see. 10 Officers and 50 other Ranks were present from each of the 3 Battalions. The General was there too, and a lot of civilians.

They had a coffin covered with robes near the altar. When we had all got settled down the 3 curés and the choir — about 100 strong — came down the aisle and took up positions near the altar. At the head they carried the Union Jack and then a tremendous wreath about 10 ft high which they put on the coffin. After that they sung a lot of stuff in Latin, after which one of the curés gave the sermon in French and praised the British Army up to the skies, though I couldn't understand half of it. Took him half an hour too.

The KOYLI had their band there, so after the sermon had finished they gave the Dead March followed by the "Last Post", the French and our national anthems. It was really a most impressive show — the church shattered by shell fire made it all the more so. It's the first R.C. service I've ever been to. But it was so cold — I was frozen to the bone. Snowing a bit too.

Heaps and Heaps of Love. Yours, Jack.

19:11:18

My own darling Phyllis, I was ever so pleased dear to receive your 3 letters of the 9th, 10th and 11th today.

I'm so sorry dear that you've been so worried about me. Thank Heaven those days are all over and done with — and what a lovely time we have in front of us, don't we?

I was very glad to hear that you've got a couple of days off from the Hospital. You seem to need it, dear. It's an awfully rotten feeling when you're wobbly on your "pins" I agree.

I think that it's high time we had another fortnight (or longer) at Scarboro (or elsewhere) together, don't you? I often think of that Scarboro trip last August. I've never had such a s'nice time before ever.

There seems to have been great excitement in Hull about the Armistice — far more than out here. We had no celebrations of any kind. The men just mentioned it casually in their letters too. You know, dear, we got used to the idea of it before it actually came — and then on the morning of the 11th we were on the move. We're right in the heart of the country here too. You could hear the guns pounding away as hard as they could until 10.59 — when they suddenly stopped. It was very weird —many of the men thought that we were pulling their legs.

You and I must have a Peace celebration all on our own as soon as I can get home. We'll have some time!! I'm simply aching to see and s'love you once more —not just for 14 days either this time. I'm sure you must need some treatment — I do *very very* badly!

They are trying to form classes here to instruct all ranks in their former civilian occupations. Rather a big job to tackle. I've had to send a return in about everybody — what they were before the war and so on. All the officers here have to fill in a form saying what job they intend taking up on being demobilised. That has rather "stumped" me.

However, the first thing is to get home again, isn't it dear?

Heaps and Heaps of Love. Yours, Jack.

21:11:18

My own darling Phyllis,

The mail failed to arrive again today. I've never known the letter service be so bad as this before.

The Sergeants held a smoking Concert last night and all the Officers were invited. They had rigged up a bit of a stage and altogether it was quite a good show.

You must have had some exciting times in Hull with the prisoners-of-war from Germany landing there. Did you see anything of them yourself? Have Slack and Major Jackson got back yet? The Hun put all the 4th EYR Officer prisoners together and seem to have given them quite a decent time, allowing them to fish, play golf and tennis — very different treatment to what some have had.

I can't understand how that pewter tankard has gone astray. The Regimental Sgt. Major assures me he posted it alright.

Heaps and Heaps of Love. Yours, Jack.

22:11:18

My own darling Phyllis,

I'm sorry to say dearest that the mail failed us again today. Isn't it disgusting?

This afternoon Capt. Trollope and myself, feeling energetic, set out for a walk. After we had gone a kilometre or so I saw an Artillery Wagon with Norman's Divisional sign on. I stopped him and asked where the D.A.C. were. He said they were about 5 kilometres away. While we were considering whether to go on or not a lorry came along so we both jumped on and he landed us right at the D.A.C.

I soon found the Mess and trekked in. Norman was out on some job or other, but turned up before tea-time. He looked very well indeed. I hadn't much chance to talk to him properly as there were several other officers there. However, tomorrow I'm going over by myself with a horse early in the afternoon so we shall be able to talk over things.

We're having another Brigade March Past tomorrow. I do loathe these Ceremonial Parades. One Battalion in this Brigade has already sent some 100 of its men — miners — home.

Heaps and Heaps of Love. Yours, Jack.

24:11:18

My own darling Phyllis,

I was delighted to receive your 3 letters yesterday of the 13th, 14th and 15th.

I hope by now you'll have got my letter of the 11th and know that I'm safe and sound. I expect to be away on leave very soon. I'll try and find out today when exactly I shall be going.

We will have a time, dear, won't we? I've still got the explosive feeling, so be warned and prepared for the worst. I'm afraid you'll find me rather a handful to manage, but we'll have a very very s'nice time, you may be sure!! I'm simply pining to s'love you once more.

I was very sorry indeed to hear that Bernard's and Ethel's baby had died from the flu. It's terrible. This flu does seem to have been awful in England. I hope to goodness that you don't catch it, dearest. I must write Bernard today. Those kind of letters though are so hard to write.

I hope that you manage to see some of the returned prisoners-of-war. I expect that they will have had a tremendous reception.

So far, dearest, I haven't been kissed by any little French girls. Sad, isn't it? But, candidly speaking, there don't seem to be any young girls at all. The Hun must have taken them all with him, I think. The Huns have treated them shamefully. There are some tales which I think will not bear repeating.

I've ceased worrying as to what I'm going to do when I come home for good. Things have altered so, and really nothing can be done until I am home and can have a look round. Don't you agree, dear? There must be a lot of good jobs about, and after all of these years of fighting out here I feel that I have a right to one. There are many people in England who I think don't realise how war has changed the men out here. The men for instance feel that they've risked their lives out here for years — and now that the Hun is beaten and the war over they expect some return from the country — and, dearest, they are right to expect it.

Heaps and Heaps of Love. Yours, Jack.

29:11:18
My own darling Phyllis,

I was very bucked indeed to receive your letter of the 20th this afternoon. I'm glad to hear that you did eventually see the boat with the returned prisoners.

It's extraordinary how the Huns have kept the news from their troops. We captured a Bosche Sgt. Major a bit back and he didn't even know that Ostend had fallen. Wouldn't believe us either, until we showed him a paper with it in.

It's hard to believe out here that Peace has actually come at last. I've often said what a time I intended to have the day Peace or the armistice was declared. But as a matter of fact the news simply took our breath away — and we had quite a quiet time. Strange how things turn out, isn't it?

Heaps and Heaps of Love. Yours, Jack.

30:11:18
My own darling Phyllis,

Norman sent over his servant this afternoon with a note asking me to go to dinner tonight, so I got a horse and rode over, arriving just in time for tea. He was alone, so we had quite a good talk about many matters! The first we've had yet. In fact we both had quite a good evening. I have just got back and though it's 11.45 pm I felt that I couldn't retire without dropping you a line.

I had quite a nice ride back. It was rather dark, especially coming through the woods, but the horse knew the way so all was well.

Norman was very cheery. He tells me that the King is going to inspect them on the 3rd. I'm glad to see tonight dearest, from our Battalion orders, that the censoring regulations have relaxed somewhat, so I can tell you where I am — I'm at a place called ECLAIBES midway between BERLAIMONT and MAUBERGE. I'm only 7 kilometres from the latter. This place Eclaibes and the next village Limont Fontaine are the two villages we captured from the Hun on the 7th. Norman is at a place called St. REMY about 8 kilometres from me. Isn't it great to be able to let you now know where we are without the fear of being strafed for doing so?

I've got millions and millions of kisses stored away for you. Hard life, isn't it? I'll do my best to bring the roses back to your cheeks. I think s'love agrees with you —it certainly does with me anyway. I'm starving for it at present!

Goodnight, my darling. Heaps and Heaps of Love. Yours, Jack.

1:12:18
My own darling Phyllis,

I'm very sorry to say dearest that no mail has turned up today.

The King was only a kilometre away from here today, so I hear. He stopped and took a photo of a big mine crater which the Huns had blown up at a crossroads near a place called Beaufort on the main Mauberge road.

I rode into Maubeuge a few days ago. First you pass the forts about 2 kilometres outside the town. The town itself is just like a big fortress — walls of concrete all round, gates, drawbridge and so on. In fact, it's really quite a quaint place. I'd like you to see it. The French people were very bucked — streets covered with flags and other emblems. Of course, the place wasn't defended at all by the Hun. Our men simply walked into it.

My great fear is that I shall catch something or other and get sent to Hospital. This village is very unhealthy — we've had Measles, Scarlet Fever etc. amongst the troops. I think that it must be the water.

Heaps and Heaps of Love. Yours, Jack.

2:12:18
My own darling Phyllis,

I was delighted to receive three letters from you today, dear — the 22nd, 23rd and 24th.

This election does seem to be a mix-up. We have all got very confused ideas about it out here. I hope that your father gets in again without much difficulty.

By the way, we have to send an Officer to England soon to get the Battalion colours from Withernsea — and as Senior Subaltern of the Battalion at present it's my job to go and get them. But whether I shall be sent or not of course remains to be seen.

Yes, we shall have to talk over prospects, etc — I'm really very keen to get on with a job. but I can't take any steps towards it until I get home. Strictly between ourselves, I don't think much of the idea of joining Norman and Harrison. However, I've no intention of going back to the Bank again.

Heaps and Heaps of Love. Yours, Jack.

4:12:18
My own darling Phyllis,

I received a lot of election papers today — from both Fenby and F. S. Jackson. I wasn't aware that I had a vote until now. As far as I can see both of them say precisely the same thing. We've had some tremendous arguments in the Mess about it, though of course no-one knows anything about politics.

The C.O. tells us that we must get ready and prepare for the next war! Nothing like looking on the optimistic side of things, is there? He seemed quite surprised to hear that all we wanted to do was to get out of the Army and home once more.

Goodnight, darling. Heaps and Heaps of Love. Yours, Jack.

4:12:18

My own darling Phyllis,

I've had a very quiet time today, dear, as I haven't been out at all. The M.O., a Colonel this time, came round at about 11 o'clock and found me in bed —disgraceful, wasn't it? But really there was no object in getting up before. He gave me some yellowish looking medicine to take for my throat, which is a lot better now —only I still feel a bit rotten.

I don't think I ever told you what a fine thing a French woman did at Bertry, did I? During the Mons retreat [*of 1914*] she gave shelter to one of our cavalry men who had just come from the scrap at Le Cateau — quite nearby, you know. She hid him in a big cupboard or Press for 4 years until a Division on our right took the place and released him. All the time she had 6 Huns billeted in her house in a top room. He spent all day in the cupboard except to come out and skip to keep himself fit. She showed me the rope too.

At night he slept underneath her bed, returning to his cupboard at 6 am when the Huns started moving about. She begged scraps of food from her neighbours to feed him. She's about 55 or 60 years old too. I think it's simply marvellous how she managed to do it. She showed me the letter and £5 note he had sent her from England. Everyone who goes to see the place gives her 10 fr at least, so she's reaping the benefit she deserves now. Just fancy too, the whole population of the village keeping a secret like that for 4 years and never letting it out to the Hun.

Really, darling, I seem to have written at some length about it, don't I? I think I've got quite a lot of bits of news of this kind to tell if I can only remember it till I see you. I rather regret that I haven't kept a diary now that it's all over — but to all the people I've seen who've kept one it's been an ill omen, so I never did. Foolish of me, wasn't it?

Well, darling, I don't think I've any more news tonight except that I do want some s'love very badly!

Heaps and Heaps of Love. Yours, Jack.

6:12:18

My own darling Phyllis,

It's sad to hear that you don't think you'll be able to stand the strain of having me home for good. Sounds as if I led you an awful life, doesn't it dear? But really I think a continued and unbroken spell of my special treatment would be just the thing for us both! Don't you agree, dear?

By the way, dear, Mother tells me that I've been put forward as a prospective manager of the Bank. I was really rather surprised to hear it. We shall have to see what comes of it, shan't we? Still, I don't feel very keen about it, although of course it's a job. It would no doubt pay me better at first, but not in the long run. Much more scope outside. We must talk all these things over when I get on leave.

Heaps and Heaps of Love. Yours, Jack.

7:12:18

My own darling Phyllis,

I didn't receive a letter from you today, dear, but really I could hardly expect one as I was lucky enough to get 3 yesterday. It is getting near to Xmas time now, isn't it — just a bit over a fortnight. The Adjutant was in today and I asked him if he thought I should get away before Xmas. He said I stood quite a good chance.

236

But I shall be very fed up if I have to spend Xmas in this country. Anyway, it will certainly be a much better one than last — which was spent in the front line near Villers Guislain. Thank God there's no fear of my having to do that again.

But you know I'm simply fading away through wanting to see you, dear. I never seem to be able to say half of what I really feel in letters either, though I try to do my best! Oh, but you are a darling. I do so want to s'love you too! Honestly, I think I'm getting much worse in that way! What an awful prospect for you dear, isn't it? I'm sure I'm very thankful indeed — engaged to the best and dearest girl in the world, and then to come through this awful war safe and sound. My word, but I am a lucky chap.

Heaps and Heaps of Love. Yours, Jack.

11:12:18
My own darling Phyllis,

I was delighted to receive your letter of the 3rd today, dear.

So you're getting impatient and want me to come on leave now, do you dear? Do you know, that's exactly how I feel too! I can see that when we do meet we're going to have a great time! I've had that explosive feeling for days now, and it's steadily getting worse and worse. Sounds bad, doesn't it? But I want you so much!

I heard today — only a rumour — that attached Officers are going back to their own units. If this turns out to be true, where shall I go? The 4th in France is no more — perhaps it might be to Hornsea. That would be topping, wouldn't it, dear? I had a look at the Army list today — October's. I see that I'm still an acting Captain. I'm still getting the pay too. I'm 3 off my Captaincy in the 4th now — so it shouldn't be long.

This morning I rode into Berlaimont to draw some money from the Field Cashier. Unfortunately he failed to show up, so I had my 18 kilometres ride for nothing. My word but I am stiff and sore now! Haven't ridden so far for ages.

Talking about politics, I don't think that any of the men are taking the slightest interest in the election. Rather wondering as a matter of fact why there's an election at all at this time. It's the way I feel myself, I must confess.

Heaps and Heaps of Love. Yours, Jack.

12:12:18
My own darling Phyllis,

I am now at Berlaimont and in the same old billets that I had before. The people were quite surprised to see us turn up again. Quite a lot of the civilians have returned, making it much harder of course for us to get billets. Unfortunately it's been raining hard all day so we all got somewhat damp to say the least. Hope it's fine tomorrow.

I was talking to an M.O., a Major Starling, yesterday. He was with me in that C.C.S. near Poperinghe [*see letter of 23.4.18*] last April, gassed. He stayed there a day after me and he says before he left the Huns were shelling the place.

Heaps and Heaps of Love. Yours, Jack.

13:12:18
My own darling Phyllis,

I was ever so pleased, dear, to receive your two letters of the 4th and 5th today. I am now at Vendegies au Bois. We left Berlaimont at 8. 30 am this morning and got

237

here at 2 pm. It was some march — 16 miles with a full pack; rained in torrents too. We came right through the Foret de Mormal — had some 12 kilometres of it. Seemed never ending. However, the worst part of the journey is over, and after a little searching I secured a fairly good billet. The people are fairly affable as it was this Batt. which took the place from the Hun on 23rd October, so they were quite pleased to see us. Madame made me a hot bath in a big tub, which put new life in me. I must confess, dear, before that I felt simply done to the world — feet fearfully sore, especially the right one. We only have 7 miles to go tomorrow Thank Goodness.

We passed close to the village today where we slept in a tiny room and the family slept in the cellar — you remember me telling you about it — Futoy it's called.

We received a heap of *Daily Mirrors* today. Nothing else in them except Lloyd George. It's certainly been done thoroughly. I suppose his party will get in. I don't think he's very popular with the troops out here. They seem to favour Labour more than anything.

Of course, you'll be at Gainsborough now, won't you? The Poll is on the 14th. I hope your Father hasn't a Labour Candidate against him as well as a Tory —would make it a much harder job, I should say.

I wonder if Godfrey Vick will get in. Seems rather funny to me to think of him standing for Parliament.

Heaps and Heaps of Love. Yours, Jack.

17:12:18
My own darling Phyllis,

I'm sorry to say dear that no mail arrived today.

I've been very busy with these ballot papers today — the post yesterday brought in hundreds of them. Many were addressed to men who have been killed or wounded months and months ago. I have to go through all the rolls and find what has happened to them. Out of the lot today I only found 12 ballot papers for men at present in the Coy. It seems to me that not half of the men will get their papers at all.

From the point of view of the men voting out here it's a wash-out, this election. However, dear, to change the subject — I'm going to visit Amiens tomorrow —that is, of course, if the C.O. gives me permission. There's a light railway running past here — so we will get a lift in on that.

I'm getting very impatient, dear — want you now!

Heaps and Heaps of Love. Yours, Jack.

18:12:18
My own darling Phyllis,

I went into Amiens today — had to walk 3 kilometres to catch the train at 8 am. Hadn't time to get any breakfast here so had it at the Hotel de la Paix in Amiens. My word, but the place has changed. Nearly half the shops are closed or blown down by the Hun bombs. The place seems to have suffered more from bombs than shells.

The cathedral has come off very well — as far as I can see it doesn't seem to have been hit at all. Of course, all the stained glass had been removed by the French before-hand. I left Amiens at 6 pm — got back to Revelles at 7 pm.

Heaps and Heaps of Love. Yours, Jack.

19:12:18

My own darling Phyllis,

I was delighted to receive yours of the 8th and 10th this morning. The mail arrived very late last night so wasn't distributed until this morning.

You'll be feeling rather relieved at having got the election over. Hope it's been a successful one for your Father.*

All the papers seem to crack up L. George but, as you say, the papers are owned by the Coalition. We've received hundreds of them out here. By the way, I voted for Mr. Fenby. Rather surprised to find I had a vote as a matter of fact.

You villain!! So you'd rather I didn't come home for Xmas. But of course, darling, I quite understand. When I do come I want to see as much of you as possible and if you couldn't get off from the Hospital it would be sad.

However, dear, it doesn't look now as if I shall get away on leave by Xmas. Very near now, isn't it? But you may be sure I'll come as soon as ever I can as I'm just pining to see you. We'll have a great time together as soon as we get a chance, won't we dearest? I do feel like some treatment!

Heaps and Heaps of Love. Yours, Jack.

[Mr. Bentham was defeated at Gainsborough. When the Liberal party split he had joined with the Asquith faction in opposition to the Lloyd George supporters.]

20:12:18

My own darling Phyllis,

I was very pleased indeed dear to receive your p.p.c. of 13th and your letter of the 11th last night. So you've been nearly exploding have you dear? Strange to say I feel the same myself. I can see that we are going to have a great time when we do meet!!!

By the way, I'm top of the Brigade Roll now — so ought to be off any day. I think it may come off this time. Probably on Boxing Day — if so I shall be with you before this letter arrives — I hope so, anyway!

We are making preparations for the Mess Xmas dinner. Turkeys are too expensive at 80fr apiece. We should want about 80 at least, so we've bought a couple of pigs for a start, but things are fearfully expensive.

Heaps and Heaps of Love. Yours, Jack.

Revilles 21:12:18

My own darling Phyllis,

I was delighted to receive your s'nice long letter of the 12th last night.

You will be pleased to hear that I have quite recovered, at least as far as I can until I receive some special treatment. I hope soon to be home for that though!

I hear that 4 extra days' leave are to be given to anyone who wishes to have his decoration presented by the King — so I think when I come on leave I'll go and get it. Worth while, isn't it dear?

I do hope it won't be long before I'm home myself as I do want some s'love so badly — lots and lots of it too. However, dear, I think the 26th will see me away —only 5 days more to wait. The sooner it comes the better. We're having a very quiet time here — in fact we are all rather bored with life.

I'm afraid that it will take ages for me to be demobolised. The men are slowly going — Iron and Steel workers — and By Jove they are glad to go.

Well, darling, I don't think I've any more news today. Hope you're keeping fit, dear. Perhaps I may be with you before this letter and then — oh, for some s'love. I have still got the explosive feeling, dearest! It gets worse every day! So beware.

Cheerio. Heaps and Heaps of Love. Yours, Jack.

Post Office Telegraph, Folkstone Pier 1135 am 23.12.18

Just landed Folkestone Love Jack.

Post Office Telegraphs, King's Cross, 2.53 pm 23.12.18

Leaving King's Cross 5.40 Love Jack.

POSTSCRIPT

Jack and Phyllis married in October 1919. They had one child, Peter, born in 1921. Jack had made it plain in his letters that a return to the bank was out. Not surprisingly, he — and Norman — entered the Benthams' family business, William Jackson & Son. In 1942 Jack became Managing Director, to be succeeded in time by his son Peter, who presided in tandem with Norman's son Brian.

Jack died in 1958, his deteriorating health attributed in part to the gas poisoning he suffered in 1918. Throughout the rest of her life Phyllis wore the good luck charm which had seen him through the hell of the trenches. She was buried with it in 1981.

Phyllis was to know again the dreadful uncertainties of 1914-18 when, in 1939, Peter walked out of school to join up in his father's regiment. Fortunately, while he had inherited his father's appetite for action, he had also inherited his instinct for survival: he too came back in one piece when the war was over.

APPENDIX 1

Extract from War Diary, 1st Battalion East Yorkshire Regiment:

"Report on Operations 3rd to 7th October 1917"

[Battle of Broodseinde]

The 1st Battalion The East Yorkshire Regiment left camp at SCOTTISH WOOD at 11 pm 3rd inst. and marched by XXIst Divisional track with orders to form up WEST of GLENCORSE WOOD, the Lewis Guns being sent by road to CLAPHAM JUNCTION, to be there at 2 pm.

On reaching Bde H.Q. I received orders that, instead of being in reserve, the Battalion was to form up 800 yards more to the EAST, attaching 1 Coy to the 10th Bn K.O.Y.L.I., performing the role originally allotted to that Battalion.

The Battalion was very much spread out at the time, but owing to the Lewis Guns having been delayed by shelling on their way to CLAPHAM JUNCTION, the Battalion had halted close to that place.

There was a very heavy enemy barrage there at the time, under which all ranks displayed great steadiness, and I was able to find each Company and give its Commander orders personally.

Having done this, I pushed on with the Adjutant and a runner to reconnoitre the forming-up place and to get in touch with O.C. 10th Bn K.O.Y.L.I.

Thanks to a party of Brigade Signallers I was able with some difficulty to find my way and get in touch, and by the time the leading Company arrived to show them where to go.

In this way all my companies were formed up soon after 5 am with the exception of the Reserve Company, which had adopted "snake" formation to pass through the barrage, with the result that its two right platoons lost direction to their right, became bogged in the POLYGON BEEKE and eventually went over with the left of the 5th Division. Captain GREEN himself with about a dozen men joined the Battalion just before ZERO hour — This Company sustained more casualties from the barrage than either of the other three.

Bn H.Q. were the only people with whom I was unable to obtain touch in the vicinity of CLAPHAM JUNCTION, and they proceeded according to previous orders to GLENCORSE WOOD, where they were informed of the change of programme, and eventually arrived at the new forming-up place just before ZERO hour.

At ZERO hour the three Coys of the Battalion advanced — I had in the meantime established Bn H.Q. in a "Pill Box" shared with H.Q. 10th K.O.Y.L.I., about 200 yards WEST of JERK HOUSE and 100 yards S.E. of BLACK WATCH CORNER.

The leading line of 9th K.O.Y.L.I. being apparently held up owing to the presence of wire or some other obstacle B Coy of the Battalion under Lieut. Oughtred advanced and assisted in the capture of the 1st objective.

At ZERO + hour 40 mins. the three Coys advanced according to programme, "A" Coy on the right and "C" Coy on the left in support of and in rear of 10th K.O.Y.L.I.

All three Companies assisted in the capture of the 2nd objective, were ably re-organised by Capt. Case, and dug in on the line [*map reference*].

During the afternoon of the 4th inst. two or more German counter-attacks were observed in process of forming up and were dispersed by Artillery Fire, and during the evening of 4th inst. the S.O.S. was twice sent up by troops in our front line, each time producing a barrage which nullified enemy attempts to counter-attack.

Our own Artillery fired some short rounds causing casualties on each occasion.

Captain Case was wounded during 5th inst. and after carrying on for six hours was compelled to proceed to the Dressing station.

During the night 4th-5th October Captain Green did splendid work collecting stragglers from other Battalions and digging in about 100 yards EAST of Battn. H.Q. in position to cover the gaps about the REUTEL BEEK which then existed between our right and the left of the 5th Division.

About 2.20 am, 5th inst. I received a message numbered M.13 giving orders from the Division as to the line to be taken up if we were compelled to withdraw from REUTEL RIDGE. I conferred with O.C. 10th K.O.Y.L.I. and as neither of us had any available reserves, took the responsibility of ordering O.C. 15th D.L.I. to dig in one Company about JOIST FARM and one Company about the end of JOIST FARM — REUTEL ROAD in S.E. corner of [*map ref.*] informing Brigade of this action I learned about mid-day 6th inst. that as O.C. 15th D.L.I. had not received a copy of M.13., and was in touch with 5th Division he had moved more to his right, S.W. of JOIST FARM. This I reported and was informed by Brigade that one Company Leicestershire Regiment had been sent to fill the gap.

Captain Case being wounded, I sent up Captain Green to take over the front line, in the afternoon of 5th inst. He very ably re-organised the front into a system of posts and supports about [*map refs*].

This position was held until the Battalion was relieved by 7th Leicestershire Regiment on the night of 6th/7th inst.

On the afternoon of 5th inst. the Germans counter-attacked against the left of 5th Division: Captain Green led the line forward and changed front ½ right in order to bring rifle and Lewis Gun fire on this attack, with great success.

[*Signed*] R. Waitham, Lieut. Col. Commanding 1st Bn. The East Yorkshire Regiment.   11.10.17

APPENDIX 2

Extract from 1st Battalion East Yorkshire Regiment War Diary:
"Mentions of the 21st Division in the Commander-in-Chief's Dispatches from January to October 1918".

April 24th 1918:
During the first two days of the enemy's offensive S. of Arras, the 21st Division maintained its positions at EPEHY against all assaults and only withdrew from the village under orders when the progress made by the enemy to the S. rendered such a course necessary. Before this Division withdrew it inflicted a great loss on the enemy and the German Official reports acknowledge the bitterness of the fighting.

April 30th 1919:
8.34 pm. Following a bombardment of great intensity the French and British positions from the neighbourhood of METEREN to ZILLEBEKE LAKE were

violently attacked this morning by large hostile forces. attacks were made also upon the Belgian positions N. of YPRES.

Fighting of great severity developed rapidly on the whole Allied front.

The 25th, 49th and 21st British Divisions completely repulsed every attempt made by the enemy to enter their positions and despite the constant succession of determined attacks in great strength, maintained their line intact.

May 2nd 1918:

Please inform the G.O.C. and Officers and men of the 21st Division that the share taken by them in the recent fighting N. of the LYS, following so closely upon their gallant action on the battle front S. of ARRAS, reflects credit alike on their Division and upon the British Army. I thank them for the great courage and devotion they have already displayed and am confident that any further test which the future may bring will be met with the same unflinching resolution.

May 29th 1918:

On our right the 21st Division in touch with our Allies held their battle positions throughout the day and successfully withstood the enemy's attempts to advance.

September 4th 1918:

The 21st Division which on March 21st distinguished itself in the defence of EPEHY, was in line opposite BEAUCOURT on August 21st, capturing BEAUCOURT. During the following days it advanced with great gallantry over the SOMME Battlefield, overcoming stiff resistance in the neighbourhood of LE SARS and BEAUCOURT L'ABBAYE.

September 9th 1918:

North of PEIZIERE, the 21st Division attacked over the Northern position of the Sector defended by it with so much gallantry on March 21st and 22nd. Having captured its old front trenches, together with the strong point known as VAUCELETTE FARM and beaten off a hostile counter-attack, it pushed forward more than a mile beyond this line, capturing several hundred prisoners and German Battery complete with teams in the course of its advance.

October 9th 1918:

In the centre, Welsh and English troops of the 38th and 21st Division broke through the German defence system known as the BEAUREVOIR-MASNIERES Line and captured WALINCOURT and the trench line West of WALINCOURT. Abstinent resistance was met with from strong bodies of the enemy with M.Gs. in VILLERS OUTREAUX. After a period of hard fighting, Welsh troops gained possession of the Village.

October 24th 1918:

English troops of the 25th Division had hard fighting in BISHOP'S WOOD (E. of LE CATEAU) and made good progress through it. East County troops of the 18th Division advancing to a depth of 9½ miles captured BOUSIES. English and Scottish Battalions of the 21st and 33rd Divisions secured the crossings of the HARPIES at VENDEGIES WOOD and captured VENDEGIES Village.

Headquarters   General Staff
30th October 1918   21st Division.

APPENDIX 3

Jack Oughtred's notes on the operations of the 1st Battalion E.Y.R. during August 1918, written after the War.

It is from these notes that his contribution to *The Snapper* was taken. Some of this material also appears to have been used in Wyrall's history of the East Yorkshire Regiment. The text as it appears here is largely faithful to his original manuscript — hence the rather disjointed style; where it enhances the sense of the account, however, the punctuation has been corrected.

"I rejoined the 1st Batt. after having been invalided home in May after Kemmel, on August the 10th or thereabouts — while it was in the line at Auchenvillers at 11 pm, and took over command of 'A' Coy — which I had commanded for some six months or so previously.

The Coy Commanders at this time were Capt. Case, M.C. 'C' Coy who had rejoined the Batt. after recovering from his wounds received on Oct. 4th 1917 at Reutel in 3rd Battle of Ypres; Lt. Atkin 'D' Coy — just out, late 5th E.Y.R.; Capt. G. Lambert of 11th E.Y.R., and myself 'A' Coy. Lt. Col. du Moulin, M.C., was C.O.

The news had apparently come through re the German retirement. 2Lt Nichols had been sent forward with his Platoon to form an Advance post earlier in the evening — for which work he later received the M.C.

At about 12 Midnight the Batt. advanced over our old front line and over the late German front line — It was rather a weird business, but there was not a sound of any kind. Order of Companies: 'B' on the left, 'A' on the right, supported by 'C' and 'D'.

Towards the dawn we came to a valley with a road down the centre (Beaumont Hamel) with steep banks on either side onto a Plateau. 'B' and 'A' Coy advanced some 200 yds when we met heavy Machine Gun fire, also trench Mortars. We advanced by rush from shell hole to shell hole but it was slow and costly work without any artillery support.

The Germans having ascertained our positions we were shelled with heavy stuff from Miramont direction — particularly the valley and road before mentioned. Head Quarters suffered some casualties.

'B' Coy now unable to proceed further frontally, they worked away to the left flank and 'A' Coy split up — half to left and half to the right. We mopped up the Machine Gunners who fought to the last at their guns. Then 'A' Coy covered the rear of 'B' who continued advancing. 'C' and 'D' now came up and 'A' carried on the advance some 600 yds into line with 'B' on the left. It was a fearfully hot day and very clear and we had very little water. I personally drank large quantities from the shell holes and suffered no ill effect.

Our casualties continued to grow as we came up against a stronger nest of M.Gs. Eventually we were stopped and remained in the shell holes all night and were relieved in the morning by the D.L.I., and although we had to go out over the top did not lose too many men, and returned independently to Auchonvillers.

The Batt. moved off on the 15 August to a village some few miles back, where we rested for some 3-4 days. On the 18th August we marched up overnight via the Auchonvillers-Beaumont Hamel road, which had been heavily shelled with Gas shells, and climbed the banks and continued to advance in the direction of Miramont and Pys[?]. We encountered M.G. fire and shelling but not of much importance and night finds us in a valley with some German huts in it, nearer Miramont and fording the ANCRE. The 1st Lincolns now passed through us and formed an outpost line some 600 yds to our front. We received an order to go forward and hold the Bridge heads of the Ancre in readiness for a further advance on the morrow.

The Batt. set out about Midnight 19th August, passed the Lincolns over the main road and then down the banks to the Ancre.

All was very quiet — not a sound. 'C' and 'D' Coys held the river bank and 'A' and 'B' protected their flank and rear and joined up with the Lincolns. Our presence was soon discovered and some shelling with 8″ also sharp rifle fire from German posts across the river which was not very wide. Lambert, O.C. 'B' was wounded and Lt Hutchinson killed and many others. Here we remained all day —the heat in the Marsh was intense. Several of our wounded were shot at and wounded while being carried away. As I have said the Batt. was in the form of a triangle, the left Base on the road joining with the Lincolns & its right Base on the river with perhaps 300 yds between the two flank Companies. At dusk the Germans attacked the Lincolns and our left flank and drove it in, placing those of us at the apex of the triangle in a very difficult position as we were nearly surrounded, and all the time an intense M.G. barrage was in progress. Case and I who were on the road decided to withdraw the Batt — which came out in some haste as they only had some 100 yds gap to get out by. The Batt. however was gathered together on the other side of the road and formed a line.

The situation being serious Case left to consult with Lt Col Du Moulin who was 10 minutes further back, leaving the line in my charge.

Nothing untoward happened and Du Moulin and Case returned and shortly afterward we were relieved across the valley before mentioned to some old trench and shell holes where we were glad to lay down in the sun and go to sleep. The Batt. remained there until about 21st August and moved off for a Brigade night attack on Miramont.

The Batt. crossed the Ancre and formed up on the other side — C.O. leading 'B' in support and 'A' in Brigade reserve with a Coy of Durham and KOYLI under the command of Major Constantine, 5 Yks Gd with whom I was acquainted having served in the same Brigade 50th Northumbrian Division throughout 1916.

We attacked and had few casualties at first and these were due I fancy to our own guns. Some 500 yds we came into touch with enemy and crossed a sunken valley full of Dug-Outs and 2 Light pieces of Artillery. These were dealt with.

Having obtained the 1st objective the Brigadier halted on the farther bank. The Brigadier went out to investigate with my own orderly but did not give notice of doing so. Everyone was naturally jumpy as we were being fired on from all four sides. The Brigadier on returning was bayoneted in error by a Private of the D.L.I. who mistook him for a Boche. Lt Col Du Moulin took command.

The remainder of the Brigade continued to advance, less the Brigade reserve, without very much resistance, some 1600 yds until dawn, the Brigade reserve covering their right flank, the left being covered by the Ancre.

As the leading Coys approached the heights of Miramont they had a very bad time both from M.G. and shelling and suffered very heavy casualties, but obtained their objective having advanced over a mile and a half that night and not lost direction., Lt Nichols and several other officers were killed.

At about 12 noon the enemy retired from our flank and the Brigade Reserve formed up with the front Companies in front of whom the Bosche had also gone. Here we remained and were relieved by the Lincolns that night and moved back to a valley in rear in which we dug holes in the banks and rested for two days, though the nights in the open were becoming rather chilly.

On the 24th August we moved back to our late objective in the heights of Miramont. We could see from this vantage point for many miles over the Somme country which was lit up in various places with burning oil dumps of the Germans who were firing them as they retired. The Butte de Warlincourt was most distinct and well I knew it having attacked it once unsuccessfully in 1916.

The Batt. left that night the 24th August and marched via Pys to a valley just in rear of Le Sars. The Coys Commanders were these: 'A' myself, Constant 'B', Case 'C' and Allen 'D'.

The weather now changed and all night it poured with rain, which was most depressing and chilly as we had no cover at all.

We went to a conference with the C.O. at Midnight in a hut which was a relief but only a very brief one.

Before dawn on the 25th August we moved off through Le Sars, 'A' and 'B' in front turned slightly to the right and passed the Butte de Warlincourt on our left.

As we ascended the slope we encountered heavy M.G. fire together with T.Mr shells. We had no artillery support. The Batts which were to support us on the right and left did not appear so we got the undivided attention of the enemy.

Eventually we reached the old trenches held by a few Lincolns and endeavoured to push on but with no avail. The losses were too great. There was not the usual roar of battle but except for the crackling of the M.G. and the whine of bullets and the occasional burst of a shell all was still.

Webster of 'C' and myself got a few men and proceeded down the C[ommunication] Trench which led to the enemy and managed very well though the German Field guns close to saw our object and tried to hit us but failed to do so. We eventually ran into two German M. Gun teams who surrendered with their guns. The Batt. strength was now very weak and the Germans attacked and drove us down the C.T. some 150 yds forcing us to leave the 2 M.Gs captured and also a Stokes Gun from the Trench Mortar Battery, who had got up with us splendidly, with which gun the Boche fired at us until all the shells were exhausted.

A bullet at this time hit the buckle of the belt of my Web equipment and went through that hitting my trench coat belt buckle underneath that — which, though it knocked me down, did not penetrate.

The Batt. now held on. It was a most disastrous day without much point, as we could have come up to that position in the dark the night previously without any loss, and though I have since been in many attacks I think that this was the most senseless waste of life and energy I have ever seen, and total lack of any co-operation whatsoever.

As this day closed the only officers remaining out of the whole Batt. were Du Moulin the C.O., Constant, O.C. 'B', Myself 'A' Coy and 2 junior subalterns whose names I forget.

Capt Case, M.C., who had been with the Batt. some time when I joined it in April 1917, was killed, Capt Ewing the Adjutant, who had served even longer —M.C and bar — died of his wounds. Lt Allen also was killed of 'D' Coy. Capt. Raine, M.C., our M.O., on hearing that Capt Ewing was wounded down the bank from which we had retired went back in spite of the enemy and, picking him up, bore him away — and though Ewing was able to walk away he died two days later: he was shot through the head. The losses in the other Ranks were equally heavy. That night, August 25th, we were relieved and a small body of men that had that morning been at Batt. moved to some old dug-outs some 400 yds from the Butte de Warlincourt on the Bapaume side.

We were relieved after two days and had a little shelling to contend with. The Leicesters also tried during our sojourn there to carry out the same attack but had to retire.

On the 28 August we moved back to some Huts a few miles in rear, past Le Sars and here we rested for 2 days and then moved to our old objective beyond the Butte de Warlincourt which as the Boche had retired was perfectly quiet. We looked after the fallen.

On the 31st August we march[ed] across the country to the front line in front of Beaulincourt [?] and took over from the 1st Wiltshires. I here met Capt. Tonkin, D.S.O. M.C. who was with the [indecipherable] EYR. He was an old friend of mine as he and I were Platoon Commanders in 'B' under Capt. Armitage in 1917.

Beaulincourt was heavily shelled, though we did not suffer much loss.

Sept. 1st arrangements for an attack towards Lubda Copse and Villers au Flos.

The Coys Commander were Myself 'A', Constant 'B' — 'C' and 'D' someone fresh temporarily — all the old ones had gone. We moved off about Midnight Sept 1st and passed through Beaulincourt, which was heavily shelled, and formed up in a shallow ditch, just across the road in front of us being a lot of Nissen Huts — the ground had formerly been a bayonet training ground for our troops before retirement.

Our guns, the heavy stuff first, commenced to fire on the huts and some of them went up in the air a whole hut at once. Some Germans had been there, because they were putting up Very Lights, but these soon ceased — even the coloured ones.

At 3.30 am on Sept 2nd we left our shallow ditch and 'A' and 'B' followed by 'C' and 'D'. It was an excellent barrage and the leading Coys walked within 20 yds of the advancing curtain of fire.

After some 600 yards we came upon the Boche in a sunken road apart from the M.G. in Lubda Copse they put up no fight. We here captured 60 prisoners, 2 Field Guns, 2 Light Minenwerfers and 8 Machine Guns and large quantity of signalling material, our casualties being about 70 [10?] in number."

APPENDIX 4

Further account by Jack Oughtred and Lt C. A. H. Sutton of events 17 September to 11 November 1918. Jack composed the opening section, which deals with the period to 1 October, and the concluding part, from 26 October to the coming of the Armistice.

On September 17th/18th midnight we left Sorel le Grand for the jumping off place to attack Munier Trench and Munier Support lines (on the right of Chapel Hill and on the outskirts of Villers Guislain).

We proceeded across country, avoiding the roads, passing Heudecourt on our right and Revelton on our left and came again to the Road at Railton Cross Roads.

We marched some 1500 yards up the Road and halted in the open, 500 yards short of railway embankment and in front of the strong point known as Vaucellette Farm. We here suffered some casualties from shell fire as there was no cover of any kind. It is perhaps interesting to note that the Battalion had held the railway embankment and dug the trenches in November 1917, and when the 21st Division was rushed there from Oppy owing to the German counter attack on the Cambrai Battle. The Leicesters of our Division held Vaucellette Farm for 3 days, though entirely cut off, during the March 1918 push of the Germans.

At 5 a.m. we attacked; owing to fog keeping directions was difficult. However, we were able to collect ourselves under the Railway embankment & took Vaucellette Farm without loss and continued down Leith Walk. Here we encountered a German strong post some 150 strong with 4 Machine Guns; these we surrounded and they speedily surrendered. Our barrage was excellent.

The road here branched: the Battalion less one Platoon took the left turn, and one Platoon to the right; the latter, by the way, was never seen again.

Heavy firing was heard from Pozieres on our right flank, which we learnt afterwards did not fall until night.

Some 500 yards further on, in a sunken road, we came into a Germany Battery & Transport which was all limbered up to go, though our barrage had played havoc with some of them. All the Germans there surrendered instantly. Now the wire round Munier Trench was extremely thick, so much so that nothing short of a Somme bombardment could move it.

There was however a break in it on the road and through this small gap some 5 yards wide the Battalion passed — 'A' & 'B' Coys in front and 'D' & 'C' Coys behind. 'A' & 'B' Coys passed the Munier Trench and went on to the support and down it to the right and 'C' and 'D' did likewise in Munier Trench.

Our barrage followed us down the Trench while we bombed our way. 'A' & 'B' were successful in getting further down than 'C' & 'D', but ran out of bombs and could not continue; 'C' and 'D' did not get so far down the trench and Lieut Webster and Lieut Butt were both killed shortly after the objective had been obtained, leaving the writer and Lts Cotton, Manley and Hutton in the front lines. We were successful in keeping off several counter attacks and bombing attacks on our right flank and also rear, but our numbers were sadly thinned and it was with relief when a Company of D.L.I. reported that they had come to join us, and in a very sporty manner took over the right flank of our trench where we had all these bombing attacks. We had after this no more attacks from the enemy and we could see them from our position moving back in all directions. Probably the fall of Poziere had caused them to do this, and as that place was full of shell proof cellars and strong points it was able to hold out until nightfall on 18th Sept.

They did well to take it then, as having occupied it in the winter of 1917 to 1918 those of us who still remained knew its strength well.

In this attack we were assisted by something like twenty aeroplanes, I believe Bristol Fighters. The enemy also had a fair number of their own aircraft out who constantly swooped down and fired with Machine guns into our trenches, but these were driven off by our machines. Our position was in front of Villers Guislain. One of our patrols entered the village, but had to withdraw owing to re-occupation by the enemy. Battalion headquarters here were on the road side in a most exposed position and subjected to much enemy artillery fire; it was so intense that the telephone wires between the Bn headquarters and Brigade had over sixty breaks during the time we held this position, and our signallers did splendid service in keeping the line intact.

A rather amusing incident happened later in the day: a young German officer walked alone into our trenches and was taken prisoner. He stated that he had just returned from leave and was looking for his regiment.

In this show we took over 400 prisoners including a number of German Officers. A German Divisional Commander and his Adjutant, the former wearing the Iron Cross, were among the killed. The Battalion captured two Hows, two 5.9 guns, 1 Whizzbang, and a large quantity of signalling stores, Ammunition waggons, also 12 wounded and 24 sound horses. The Field Gun & Limber we captured complete had to be left with the horses yoked to it owing to its exposed position until dusk when, fortunately, we were able to release the animals but in a wretched condition.

Tanks brought up supplies to the Brigade in this attack.

On the following day, the 19th, we were constantly shelled by German long distance guns, and also a field gun carefully concealed near Villers Guislain, which latter was shelling our headquarters. With the assistance of two forward observation Officers from the Gunners the position of the gun was located and a few rounds from our batteries soon put it out of action. At midnight 19th/20th we were relieved by the 2nd Argyle & Sutherland Highlanders and went back to rest at Equancourt.

On the 24th we marched to Les Boeufs to re-organise and during that time we received new drafts to the Battalion and did a certain amount of training. September 27th the Battalion left Les Boeufs and marched to Manoncourt and spent the night there. On the following night we marched through Fins, which was being shelled with big stuff, and occupied some old trenches near Dessart Wood. Every day we received orders to move but these were cancelled. On the morning of Sept. 30th however we moved off and went through the centre of Dessart Wood and down to the main Gouzeaucourt-Fins road up which we marched until nearing Gouzeaucourt. Here we occupied some old trenches known as African Support trenches in which the Dug-outs and shelters were fairly good for all Ranks, which after the four nights in the open at Dessart Wood were a great blessing.

Shortly after arrival the writer with a party went into Gouzeaucourt and found the place littered with equipment of all kinds and piles of dead. The Germans had just been pushed out of it earlier in the day.

[*Here Lt Sutton takes up the narrative*] On October 1st we left African Trench and went through Gouzeaucourt, crossed the Railway in the Valley and occupied

Quentin Redoubt on the Hill, here we made excursions to Gonnelieu and beyond to view the ground for our next attack.

On October 5th we marched to Banteux and found no enemy in the Hindenburg Trench as supposed. Proceeding, we encountered heavy machine gun fire from the Beauvoir Line; we attacked Marconing Farm under heavy shell fire & obtained our objectives. In this encounter our casualties were three Officers and fifty other ranks.

The following day, the 6th, we attacked Bonne Enfance Farm and had great difficulty in obtaining our objectives owing to large numbers of enemy machine guns, which in places were on our flanks. Our casualties here were about 57 killed and over 37 missing.

On October 7th we went into support with a strength of 17 Officers and 383 other ranks.

On October 8th we attacked Mamiens, Beauvoir Line and took all our objectives after being heavily shelled.

On October 9th we attacked Walincourt. This part of the country was in a filthy condition, mud everywhere, we came in for more heavy shelling and machine gun fire from the North of the village (our line of attack). The village was taken and occupied by the Brigade. We found, after being in it a few hours that mines had been left concealed by the enemy everywhere. In our headquarters, a very nice house previously occupied by German Officers, we found mines in the cellars. Obtaining the assistance of the R.E. Mining Company, we had these removed together with others in the village. The inhabitants (elderly French peasants) were able to give us valuable information regarding the position of these mines (chiefly shells with time fuses).

The Civilians in this village were in a pitiable state chiefly through lack of food and clothing. The whole of the Division stayed in this area to reorganise and receive drafts. Col F. L. Du Moulin, our Commanding Officer, being a fluent French scholar, was of great assistance here as an interpreter.

On October 21st we received orders to move forward again. We arrived at Montigny, stayed the night there, and the following day marched to Inchy. Here we rested for a few hours until dark in an orchard and then moved on to our position, namely a Railway cutting at Neuvilly. The Brigade having its headquarters in the cellar of a ruined house near at hand.

This position had recently been held by the enemy. I believe the Manchesters took this cutting, honeycombed with small dug-outs and full of German corpses, and we were very pleased when the time came to leave it.

I remember quite well Lieut Quartermaster Billinghurst and the Transport Officer Lieut Knight bringing the Battalion up dixies of tea on mules through heavy shelling, and whilst we were enjoying this the Germans put up a barrage of gas shells which quite spoilt the flavour of the tea!

At 2 a.m. on the 23rd we advanced from this cutting through a heavy German barrage and machine gun fire to a position overlooking Ovillers. During this attack our most respected Medical Officer Capt Raine M.C. was wounded in the thigh while attending to a wounded man. Capt Raine was a great favourite and would go anywhere to assist the wounded.

We were now without a Medical Officer, with lots of casualties. Luckily we had just captured a German Doctor with some stretcher bearers and were now able to make good use of them, and I believe they did all they possibly could to help. We had four Officers in this attack wounded, and the casualties among other ranks about 116.

Another unit having gone forward we received instructions at 6 p.m. to advance in support to Vendegies. On arrival we received further instructions to attack Poix Du Nord. The Colonel called a hurried Officers conference in order to make the necessary arrangements. This took place in a ditch at the side of a road which was being constantly shelled.

We moved forward again at 3 a.m. the 24th, encountering thick enemy wire and at various intervals small gaps, the latter being covered by German machine guns which inflicted heavy casualties.

The village of Poix du Nord was entered and a number of prisoners taken. We released something like 500 French civilians who were delighted to see British troops and offered us black bread, the only things they had. Great difficulty was experienced in taking our objective, a line on the far side of the village, owing to enemy machine guns. This was however accomplished by 1 p.m. It was here that Colonel Greenwood of the 9th KOYLI obtained his V.C. for attacking a troublesome machine gun post. As the German gunners were doing considerable damage to the village through shelling and gas we were asked by Brigade to attack again at 4 p.m. for a position about 500 yards in advance of our present line in order to give better protection to the village behind. The new position was taken and consolidated by 5 p.m. with Battalion headquarters in a quarry immediately behind. Our casualties in this attack were about 141.

On October 25th we remained holding this position till the following day when we were relieved by the 2nd Lincolns. We went into reserve. I now left the Battalion to go on leave and Capt. J. A. Oughtred will carry on with the story.

Attack on the Foret de Mormal. On October the 26th the Battalion was relieved by the Lincolns and returned to Vendegies and next morning moved off to Neuvilly for a short rest.

Lt Col Du Moulin, Commanding: Major Brown 2nd in Command; Capt. Keech Adjutant; and the Company Commanders, 'A' Coy Capt Oughtred, 'B' an officer from the Somerset Light Infantry, 'C' an officer from the Border Regiment and 'D' Capt Trollope.

On the 4th November the Battalion left Neuvilly and marched to Vendegies and rested there in an orchard. Towards dusk we moved off towards the Foret de Mormal and halted about midnight just on its fringe and in the vicinity of a broken down farm, the small back kitchen being the only part standing. The inhabitants of the farm were all in bed in the cellars. The Battalion was mostly composed of fresh recruits from England and the idea of spending the night in an open field was rather a shock to them.

We moved off again at 4 a.m. on the 5th November and entered the forest. The Lincolns were ahead so we experienced no resistance — perfect quiet but much rain. The forest is a very large one and towards mid-day we reached a village in the centre. After this, wounded were met occasionally coming back. We could hear shell bursts in the distance. Very shortly we passed a Prisoners of War Camp (used by the Germans for allied prisoners). The prisoners were used to cut the trees etc; there were however no occupants. Towards night we got clear of the Forest and came to a little village some 5 or 6 kilometres on the forest side of Berlaimont. All the houses here were intact and the inhabitants greeted us with great enthusiasm and all ranks were glad to be in a billet with a rain proof roof overhead as all day it had rained. The Germans were shelling the road near Berlaimont with great regularity but only a few kept falling near the village.

The troops were very weary after their long march through the wet and several of them — mere boys, in reality — collapsed while we were halted in the street and were taken in by the women. An old man joined in our ranks and sang the Marseillaise. We remained here for some two days, and at 2 a.m. on the morning of the 7th November moved off to Berlaimont, a market town. This the Germans had evacuated. The noise of our passage awakened the inhabitants and shuttered windows and cellar doors were thrown open and people of every age and in every attire welcomed us.

We did not stop but pushed on over the river Sambre by means of an R.A. pontoon bridge and went first by road then across country in the direction of Limont Fontaine and Eclaibes. At 7 a.m. we caught up and passed the Lincolns who were in a sunken road and continued up it in a column of route. On going another 400 yards we came under heavy Machine Gun fire and we broke into Artillery formation, 'B' and 'C' Coys in front, 'D' in support, 'A' in reserve. The ground gradually rose to a crest over which the three leading Companies went but could make no progress and suffered considerable casualties.

The Germans now brought their T.Ms into play and 'A' Coy which had been in the open moved to a sunken road on right flank and dug itself in. Without Artillery support, of which we had none, no further progress could be made. The fall of ground seemed to coincide with the trajectory of the machine Gun bullets. Lt Col Du Moulin, who had been walking about almost heedless of risk, was later in the day hit in several places and died instantly. Capt Keech who was Adjutant at the same time was with Battalion Headquarters some 150 yards further down the same road as 'A' Coy and was also hit. He had been continually with the Battalion since its arrival in France in 1914. A Captain of the Border Regiment who was in command of 'C' Company took command and Lieut. Wild Adjutant.

As night fell the Germans gave us a lot of extra T.M. Bombs causing us some nasty casualties in the road.

As soon as it was dusk we all moved off down the road and crossing the ford at the bottom turned to the right. 'D' and 'B' Companies pushed on to Eclaibes and 'A' Company guarded their right flank with the aid of machine guns and teams.

On the early morning of the 9th November we were relieved by the Border Regiment and made our way back to Berlaimont. The inhabitants in one of the villages entertained us to coffee, the only thing they had to offer. Lt Colonel Du Moulin was buried at the Catholic Cemetery at Berlaimont and at the special request of an old French gentleman was placed in this family vault so that if at any time his relatives wished to move him they could do so. On the morning of the 11th November we were formed up to march into Eclaibes and as we were moving off were informed of the Armistice. We were billeted in Eclaibes and remained there some time.

The Command was taken over by Major Wailes who had left the Battalion, I recollect, in April 1917 at Bailleulval near Arras for Staff work.

After remaining here for some time the Battalion early in December marched back to Inchy and from there was taken by lorries and buses via Cambrai, Bapaume and Albert to a village called Letoile on the farther side of Amiens, where it remained.

ACRONYMS, INITIALS & OTHER ABBREVIATIONS
USED IN THE TEXT

APO	Army Post Office	NCO	Non-Commissioned
ASC	Army Service Corps		Officer
BEF	British Expeditionary Force	NF	Northumberland Fusiliers
Bn	Battalion	OC	Officer Commanding
CCS	Casualty Clearing Station	OR	Other Ranks
CO	Commanding Officer	PBI	Poor Bloody Infantry
Coy	Company	RAMC	Royal Army Medical
DLI	Durham Light Infantry		Corps
EFA	Emergency Field Ambulance	RFA	Royal Field Artillery
FA	Field Ambulance	RFC	Royal Flying Corps
FPC/FSPC	Field (Service) Post Card	TBD	Torpedo Boat Destroyers
GS	(Fit for) General Service	TMB	Trench Mortar Brigade
IBD	Infantry Brigade Depot		(or Battery)
KOYLI	King's Own Yorkshire Light	VAD	Voluntary Aid
	Infantry		Detachment
MC	Military Cross	WAAC	Women's Auxiliary Army
MG	Machine Gun		Corps
MO	Medical Officer		

'NEAR MISSES'

As well as commenting frequently upon his general good fortune, and his belief in fate, Jack mentions these specific instances when he came close to death:

Date of letter	Nature of Incident
17. 1.16	Bullet passes between himself and Slack, 2 feet away.
20. 2.16	Shrapnel hits buckle of web equipment.
16. 6.16	Large piece of shrapnel hits back.
27. 6.16	Officer replacing him blown to pieces.
19. 7.16	Hit on hand by shell fragment.
29. 7.16	5.9″ shell explodes less than 10 yards away.
19. 9.16	Buried by shell.
19. 5.17	Should have been in tent in which Shackles was killed.
19. 7.17	Shell lands two feet away, killing Capt. Cemery.
9.10.17	"A number of narrow escapes".
23. 4.18	One bullet through scarf, another through trench coat.
23. 8.18	"Some narrow escapes".
27. 8.18	Machine-gun bullet goes through buckle of web equipment and smashes buckle of trench coat, knocking him down.

BRIEF SYNOPSIS OF JACK OUGHTRED'S MOVEMENTS
May 1915 — Nov 1918
1915

May 11	Takes commission in 4th Battalion East Yorks	
May 20	Commences training. Benton Camp, Northumberland	

1916

Jan 9	Arrives Le Havre	
Jan 15	Arrives at front	YPRES SECTOR
	[*May 18-29 HOME LEAVE*]	
May 31	Transferred 150/1 Trench Mortar Brigade	"
Aug 10	Marches south to	SOMME BATTLEFIELD
Aug 12	Becomes full lieutenant	"
Sept	In action at Shelter Wood	"
Sept-Dec	Mostly in reserve positions	"
	[*Dec 20 HOME LEAVE*]	

1917

Jan-Apr	[*SICK LEAVE*]	ENGLAND
	[*SCOTTON CAMP*]	"
April 16	Returns to France	
May 7	Transferred 1st East Yorks	SOMME AREA
July 7	Takes command of Company	"
Aug	Hospitalised with trench fever	"
Sept	Returns to Battalion	YPRES SECTOR
Oct	Battle of Broodeseinde	"
	(3rd Ypres, or Passchendaele)	"
	[*Oct 13 HOME LEAVE*]	
Oct 16	Engaged to Phyllis Bentham	"
Oct 27	Takes command of 'A' Coy	YPRES SECTOR
Oct 30	Awarded Military Cross	"
Nov 3	Gains Captaincy	"
Nov 18	Moves to	SOMME AREA

1918

Jan 23	Lewis Gun course	"
	[*Mar 20 HOME LEAVE*]	
	(Misses Battle of Saulcourt)	
Apr 13	Rejoins Battalion at Wytschaete	YPRES SECTOR
Apr 16	Gassed at Kemmel	"
Apr-Aug	[*Sick; convalescent*]	BROCTON CAMP
Aug 6	Returns to France	
	Joins 1st EYR on R. Ancre, near Albert	SOMME AREA
	Battle of Albert	
Sept	Battle of Bapaume	PERIOD OF RAPID
	Assault on Hindenburg Line	ADVANCE
Sept 16	Battle of Epehy	"
Nov 7	Battle of Sambre	"
Nov 11	Armistice	"
Dec 23	Arrives home	

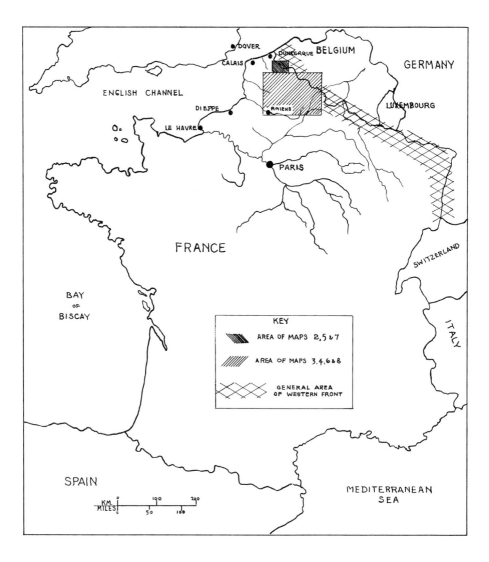

France, showing general area of western front and areas covered by maps that follow.
(*Maps kindly reproduced by Patrick Burton of Hornsea*).

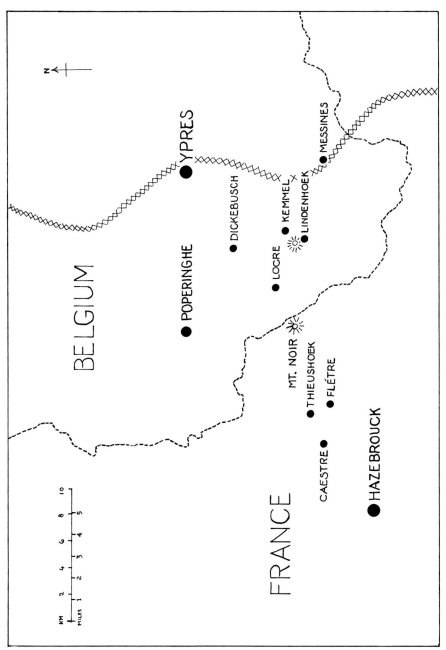

Locations mentioned, Ypres sector, January – August 1916 showing general course of front line.

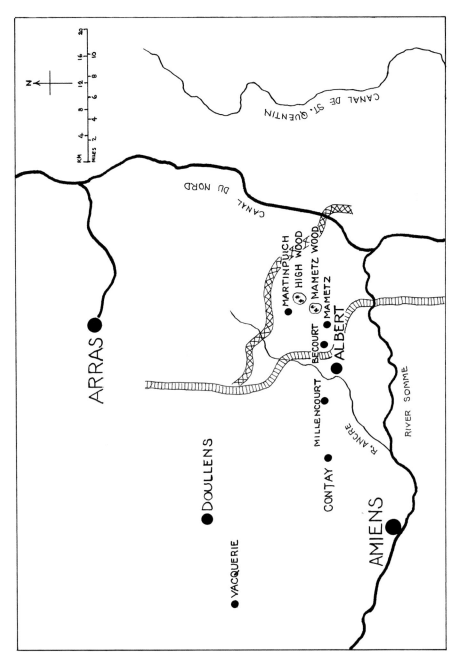

Locations mentioned, Somme area, August – December 1916 showing front at July 1916 and gains to north and east after Battle of the Somme.

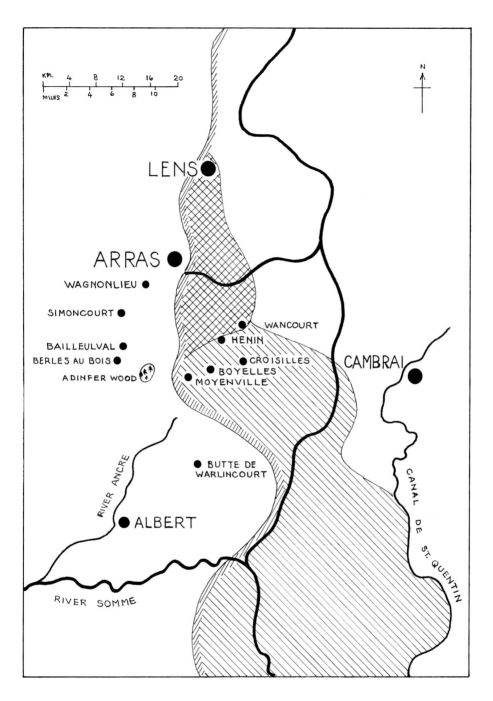

Locations mentioned May – August 1917 showing German withdrawal Feb – April 1917 (large hatched area) and British gains April – May 1917 (cross-hatched area).

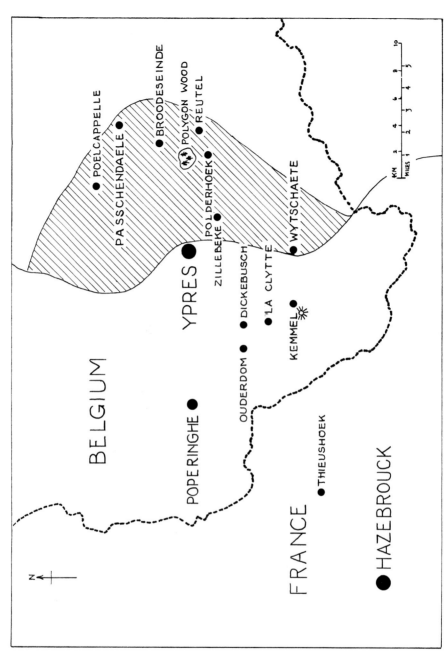

Locations mentioned, Sept – Nov 1917 showing British gains at Third Battle of Ypres, Autumn 1917 (hatched area).

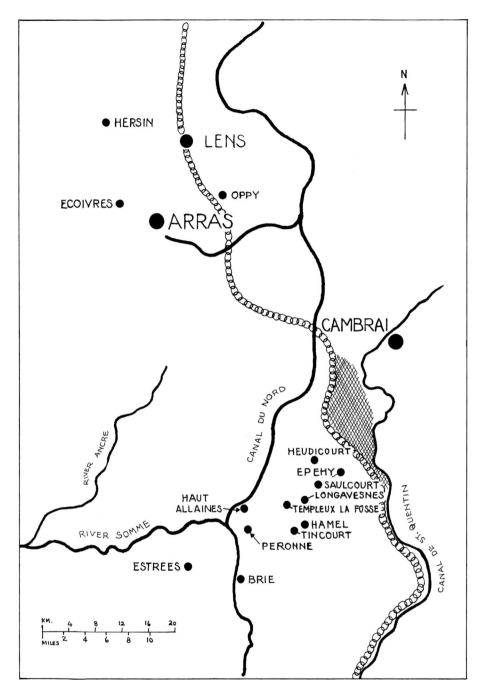

Locations mentioned Nov 1917 – April 1918 showing front line at November 1917, and British gains at Battle of Cambrai (cross-hatched area).

261

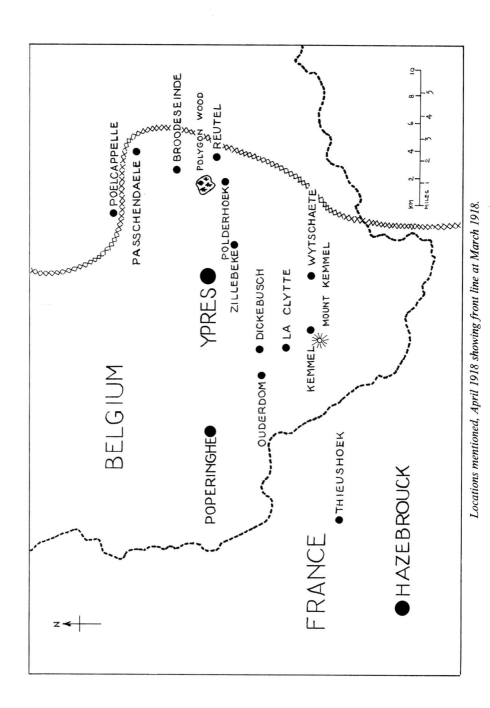

Locations mentioned, April 1918 showing front line at March 1918.

262

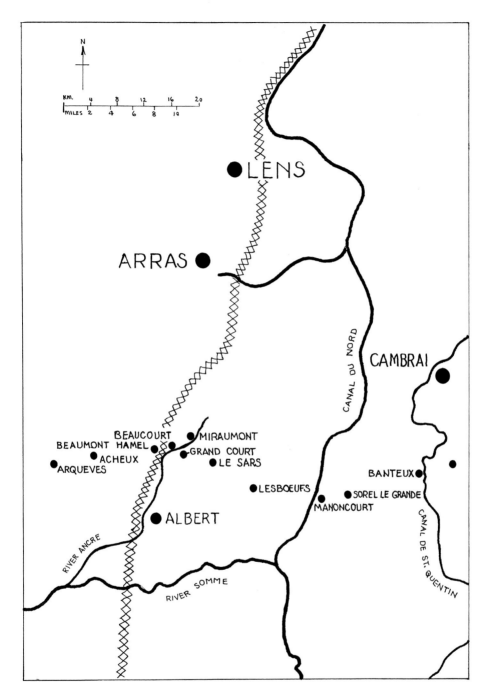

Locations mentioned August – November 1918 during period of rapid advance eastwards from line of furthest German advance, June 1918.

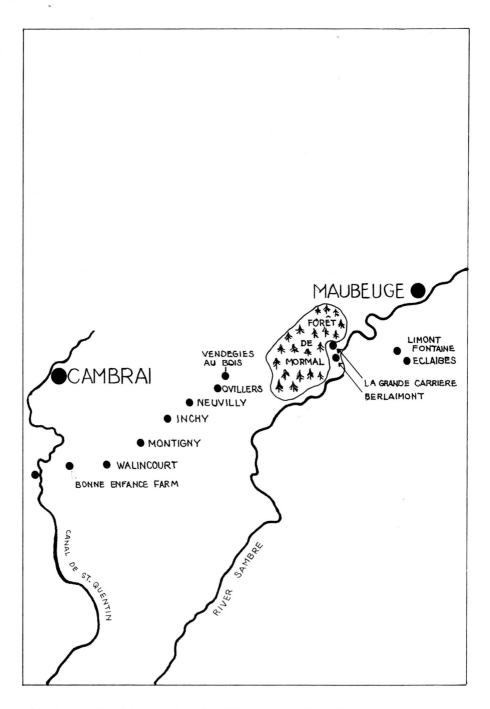

Locations mentioned August – November 1918 during period of rapid advance eastwards from line of furthest German advance, June 1918.